RECONSTRUCTION

AFTER THE

CIVIL WAR

THIRD EDITION

John Hope Franklin

WITH A NEW FOREWORD BY
ERIC FONER

THE UNIVERSITY OF CHICAGO PRESS
Chicago and London

JOHN HOPE FRANKLIN (1915–2009) was the James B. Duke Professor of History Emeritus at Duke University. He is the author of many books, including *Mirror to America: The Autobiography of John Hope Franklin* and *Racial Inequality in America*.

The University of Chicago Press, Chicago 60637
The University of Chicago Press, Ltd., London
© 1961, 1994, 2013 by The University of Chicago
All rights reserved. Published 2013.
Printed in the United States of America

22 21 20 19 18 17 16 15 14 13   1 2 3 4 5

ISBN-13: 978-0-226-92337-6 (paper)
ISBN-13: 978-0-226-92339-0 (e-book)
ISBN-10: 0-226-92337-1 (paper)
ISBN-10: 0-226-92339-8 (e-book)

LIBRARY OF CONGRESS CATALOGING-IN-PUBLICATION DATA
Franklin, John Hope, 1915–2009, author.
    Reconstruction after the Civil War / John Hope Franklin ; with a new foreword by Eric Foner. — Third edition.
        pages cm. — (Chicago history of Amerian civilization)
    Includes bibliographical references and index.
    ISBN-13: 978-0-226-92337-6 (paperback : alkaline paper)
    ISBN-10: 0-226-92337-1 (paperback : alkaline paper)
    ISBN-13: 978-0-226-92339-0 (e-book)
    ISBN-10: 0-226-92339-8 (e-book) 1. Reconstruction (U.S. history, 1865–1877)
I. Foner, Eric. II. Title. III. Series: Chicago history of American civilization.
    E668.F7 2013
    973.8—dc23

                                                        2012010482

⊗ This paper meets the requirements of ANSI/NISO Z39.48-1992 (Permanence of Paper).

For

THEODORE S. CURRIER

Great Teacher and Friend

Contents

Illustrations

Foreword to the Third Edition

By Eric Foner

Over half a century after its publication, John Hope Franklin's *Reconstruction* remains a brief, readable account of one of the most significant and most misunderstood eras in our nation's history, and a landmark of American historical writing. To appreciate its contribution it is worth recalling the state of Reconstruction historiography in 1961, when the book appeared. (The text that follows is the revised edition, published in 1994, but Franklin made only a few minor changes for this version, primarily adding recent scholarship to the bibliography.)

For most of the twentieth century, the Dunning school, named after William A. Dunning of Columbia University, dominated historical writing and popular thinking about Reconstruction. In a nutshell, it portrayed the period after the Civil War as the lowest point in the whole saga of American democracy. According to Dunning and his disciples, President Abraham Lincoln at the end of the war hoped to bring the defeated South back into the Union in a quick and lenient manner. After his assassination his policy was continued by his successor, Andrew Johnson. Johnson was opposed and eventually thwarted by the villains of the piece, the Radical Republicans in Congress, motivated, depending on which historian one chose, by a vindictive hatred toward the South, the desire to fasten the grip of northern capitalism on the region, or simply the aim of keeping the Republican Party in power.

In the Dunning school account, Johnson established governments in the South headed by loyal whites who were willing to treat the former slaves fairly. But the Radicals overthrew Johnson's lenient plan and imposed black male suffrage on the defeated South. Since blacks, according to this view, are innately incapable of exercising the rights of political democracy, an orgy of corruption and misgovernment followed, presided over by African Americans, carpetbaggers, unscrupulous northerners who came to the South to reap the spoils of office; and scalawags, white southerners who turned their backs on their race and cooperated with blacks in this misgovernment. Eventually, patriotic groups like the Ku Klux Klan restored what was politely called "home rule" or, to put it more accurately, white supremacy.

This interpretation, which shaped the writings of three generations of historians and reached a broad popular audience through films like *Birth of a Nation* and *Gone with the Wind*, had an amazing longevity. For it was congruent with the racial system of the United States from 1900 until the civil rights era of the 1960s. The political lessons of the traditional view of Reconstruction were very clear. First, it was a mistake to give black people the right to vote during Reconstruction; therefore the white South was justified in depriving them of suffrage around the turn of the century. Any effort to restore political rights to African Americans would simply lead to a repeat of the "horrors" of Reconstruction. Second, Reconstruction was imposed upon the South by outsiders. The outcome proved that the only ones who understood southern race relations were southern whites, and they should resist northern calls for change in the region's racial system. Finally, Reconstruction was created by the Republican Party and therefore the white South should remain solidly Democratic (which it was until the late 1960s).

A few writers challenged this dominant account of Reconstruction. Early in the twentieth century John R. Lynch, an African American who had represented Mississippi in Congress during the 1870s, published

The Facts of Reconstruction, a far more accurate and positive render-
ing of the events of that era. In the 1930s, the great black scholar and
activist W. E. B. DuBois wrote *Black Reconstruction in America*, a full-
fledged assault on the Dunning school, which viewed Reconstruction
as a noble struggle for political and economic democracy. The tragedy
of Reconstruction was not that it was attempted but that it failed, leaving to subsequent generations the difficult problem of racial justice in
American society. But outside the historically black colleges, these works
were largely ignored by the academy. (DuBois's volume, a classic of
American historical writing, was never even reviewed by the *American
Historical Review*). Not until the 1960s, when the civil rights revolution
altered historians' views of race and destroyed the assumption of black
incapacity—the intellectual underpinning of the Dunning school—did
a revisionist wave sweep over the field. Franklin's book made an important contribution to this development.

By the time he wrote *Reconstruction*, Franklin was already one of the
country's leading historians, and certainly the most prominent African
American historian.

His first book, *The Free Negro in North Carolina*, appeared in 1943,
yet it remains not only the standard work on its subject, but a key reference point for those investigating the status of free African Americans
before the Civil War. At the time he wrote, historians were devoting
little or no attention to what was then called Negro history. Almost
no scholarly work existed on antebellum free blacks. Franklin utilized a
wide range of primary materials, demonstrating that mainstream historians' neglect of African American history arose from a conscious decision, and could not be explained or excused by a paucity of available
sources.

Franklin next published his path-breaking survey of black history,
From Slavery to Freedom. This appeared in 1947 and has gone through
many editions since. The book has introduced hundreds of thousands

of students, as well as countless readers outside the academy, to the African American past. It ranges incredibly widely, from Africa to modern America, and from politics to culture, economics, and social life. Franklin did not mince words in describing the injustices and disabilities under which generations of black Americans have suffered. But as the title itself suggests, the book has an optimistic tone. It is a story of progress against heavy odds, not simply a condemnation of American racism.

But African American history is too limited a description of Franklin as a historian. In 1956, he published *The Militant South*, a searching investigation of white southern culture before the Civil War. Franklin was interested in the roots of southern radicalism and the ways a martial spirit came to pervade southern society. Of course, the institution of slavery and the violence associated with it played a central part in the analysis. But what interested Franklin was the white southern mind, and how its "militant" spirit helped to explain the coming of the Civil War. The book remains essential reading for those seeking to understand the antebellum South.

Although Franklin had not written about the post–Civil War era (except in his textbook, *From Freedom to Slavery*) before embarking on *Reconstruction*, in 1948 he had published a devastating review of *The South During Reconstruction*, a volume in the prestigious History of the South series. Written by E. Merton Coulter, this book exhibited all the flaws of the Dunning school, which Franklin carefully exposed: undisguised racism; the misquotation of some sources and ignoring of many others, especially those emanating from blacks; sweeping generalizations, unsupported by evidence, about alleged black malfeasance and the horrors endured by the white South. Because the critique appeared in the *Journal of Negro Education*, few white scholars took notice. But in the late 1950s, as the modern civil rights movement gathered force, writing on Reconstruction began to change. In 1959, the *Journal of Southern History* published Bernard Weisberger's influential essay, "The

Dark and Bloody Ground of Reconstruction Historiography," which pointed out that despite the enormous changes in southern and national life since World War II, writing on Reconstruction was still locked in an antiquated racist framework. Local studies had chipped away at the foundations of the Dunning school but textbooks still repeated the old mythologies, and no one had attempted to write a new narrative account of the era. This was the task Franklin set himself.

Reading *Reconstruction* today, it is striking how Franklin advanced interpretations that now form the pillars of scholarly understanding—Andrew Johnson was not the heroic defender of the Constitution but an inept, inflexible leader unfit for the presidency; the idea that the South suffered under the heel of military despotism is a myth; the Radical Republicans were motivated by genuine concern for racial justice, not vindictiveness toward the defeated South; carpetbaggers were mostly newcomers to the South interested in economic development and scalawags were wartime southern Unionists; Reconstruction was a time of genuine accomplishment, not merely corruption; and the Ku Klux Klan, stripped of the romanticism and extenuation advanced by earlier historians, was a terrorist organization that used violence to restore white supremacy. Since the publication of this work, numerous scholars (including myself) have built on and expanded Franklin's insights.

In some ways, inevitably, the book today seems dated. Franklin focuses on black political leaders (whom he rescues from charges of incompetence), but not grassroots black politics. He says little about issues that concern current scholars—the rise of the independent black church during Reconstruction, the transition from slave to free labor, how gender shaped the experiences of emancipation for black men and women. (Reflecting the state of historical writing before the advent of modern women's history, the name of only one woman appears in Franklin's index—Mary Baker Eddy, founder of the Christian Science religion.)

The book is a product of its time in other ways. It contains remnants of the long-popular Beardian approach to the Civil War era, such as Franklin's comment that the Civil War spawned an "industrial plutocracy" that exercised a "stranglehold on government." Given the vast task of revision he was undertaking, it is not surprising that on occasion Franklin adopted a somewhat defensive tone. Most blacks, he wrote, "were without the qualifications to participate effectively in a democracy," an unnecessary concession to the Dunning school. Countering charges that Reconstruction turned politics and society upside down, he seemed apologetic in insisting that in fact "blacks attempted no revolution in the social relations of the races" or any kind of "economic revolution."

Nonetheless, the book remains today a valuable introduction to the Reconstruction period, and a stinging critique of how generations of earlier historians sacrificed historical objectivity on the altar of racism. Generally, Franklin does not directly address the old view of Reconstruction, but simply replaces it with a new account. By the end of the book, however, his anger is palpable. American historians, he writes, produced "near-fictional accounts," replete with "misconceptions and distortions," that fundamentally misconstrued one of the most important eras of the nation's past. Franklin concludes with a scathing portrait of the post-Reconstruction South, a society dominated by "a small ruling clique" that ignored the needs of blacks and poorer whites and allowed northern investors to turn the region into a colonial economy.

Franklin's *Reconstruction* was soon followed by a flood of studies charting new directions in understanding the era, an outpouring that continues to this day (and which Michael Fitzgerald discusses at the conclusion of this volume). As for Franklin, he continued his prolific output. Two years later, in *The Emancipation Proclamation*, he explained for students and a nonacademic audience alike the origins and significance of this pivotal document at its centennial. Subsequently, among other works, he wrote a biography of the pioneering African American historian George Washington Williams, and edited, with August Meier, *Black Leaders of the Twentieth Century* (1982), a highly influential collection of essays. While well into his eighties, he published *Runaway Slaves* (1999, with Loren Schweninger), the first full-scale study of this important piece of antebellum history.

In 2005, Franklin's *Mirror to America* (2005), an account of his life's trajectory, appeared. The book is not simply a personal journey but a chronicle of American race relations during the course of the twentieth century, offering a candid assessment of how much changed during Franklin's lifetime and how far the country still has to go to achieve the reality of racial equality. It also presents a remarkable account of how the historical profession itself has changed and, while Franklin modestly does not make this point explicitly, how powerfully his own career affected how we teach and study history, not only because of his own scholarship, but through the large number of students he trained who went on to make their own substantial contributions to American and African American history.

John Hope Franklin died in 2009 at the age of 94. But his impact on American historical writing endures. Long before the "agency" of ordinary Americans became a touchstone of historical writing, Franklin demonstrated that blacks were active agents in shaping their own and the nation's history. Apart from their coverage of numerous long-neglected parts of our past (no small accomplishment in itself), his writings, taken together, make the indispensable point that no account of American history can be complete that does not afford a central place to the conditions and struggles of black Americans. This fundamental transformation in how we think about American history and society will undoubtedly survive him and his generation. It stands as John Hope Franklin's lasting intellectual legacy.

ERIC FONER

1

The Aftermath of War

The roads from Appomattox led in many different directions. Along the way each of the roads held strange sights for the weary, homeward-bound warrior in 1865. If his home was in the North he saw few evidences of destruction, unless he traveled through the region around Gettysburg in southern Pennsylvania. But there were other evidences of change, some of them as fascinating as they were subtle; and they were as much the product of the war as the crumpled bridges or the battered buildings that now lay far behind. Traveling through the North, one could feel a new sense of satisfaction. Everywhere wartime industrialization had brought signs of growth. There was also the clear determination to fulfill the destiny of power and prosperity implicit in the forces that had culminated in the smashing Northern victory. What Union soldier could not quicken his pace as he moved not only nearer his loved ones but also closer to what would surely be a glorious future!

As the Confederate warrior made his way homeward he was reminded in countless ways of the extent of the holocaust that had engulfed his beloved land. At the end of the war scores of visitors from the North and other parts of the world swarmed over the South, and their descriptions of the prostrate South dwell upon

1

the widespread devastation suffered by the Confederacy. Fields were laid waste, cities burned, bridges and roads destroyed. Even most of the woefully inadequate factories were leveled, as if to underscore the unchallenged industrial superiority of the North. And if the Union forces did not loot quite as many smokehouses and pantries as they were blamed for, what they did do emphasized the helplessness of the once proud Confederates.

Carl Schurz, with little sympathy for the South, was touched by the utter ruin that seemed to be everywhere. Traveling through the South on a mission for the President in 1865 he said that the countryside "looked for many miles like a broad black streak of ruin and desolation—the fences all gone; lonesome smoke stacks, surrounded by dark heaps of ashes and cinders, marking the spots where human habitations had stood; the fields along the road wildly overgrown by weeds, with here and there a sickly patch of cotton or corn cultivated by Negro squatters." To another, Columbia was "a wilderness of crumbling walls, naked chimneys and trees killed by flames." And for years to come many an hour would be spent in argument over who burned the proud Carolina town. But there was little room for debating the fact that a good deal of South Carolina had become a "howling waste," as Captain Daniel Oakey described it.

It mattered little to the returning soldier in gray whether Sherman and Grant had wrought the havoc or whether a defensive "scorched earth policy" of the Confederates had brought it about. The damage was done—doubtless by both sides. What really mattered was the staggering magnitude of the task now challenging the responsible white Southerner. As he looked upon the broken and scattered pieces of the way of life he knew and loved, he hardly knew where or how to begin. Somehow, though, he must begin the heart-rending task of trying to put the pieces together again.

Eleven states were out of the Union, awaiting readmission at the pleasure and the mercy of the North. The economy of the South had been smashed, and local resources for rebuilding were meager indeed. Thousands of white refugees wandered over the land, not certain that they had a home and even less certain of the treatment they would receive if they returned. Numberless blacks, free at last, had run either *with* their masters ahead of the Union invasion or *from* their masters toward the Union lines. Others of the four million were merely moving about to "test" their freedom and, inadvertently, to cause grave apprehensions among their former masters.

Even before the war white Southerners had frequently entertained a wild, nightmarish fear that the slaves would rise up, slay them, and overthrow the institution of slavery. It had happened in Haiti. Perhaps it would happen here. In 1865 Southern whites "knew" that there was nothing to hold back the tide. Wild rumors flashed through the South that the freedmen would strike in vengeance. Some whites were even certain of the date. It would be New Year's Day, 1866, they said. How could they keep their minds on rebuilding when their former slaves were poised to complete the destruction? That this was pure fantasy, born of a sense of guilt and despair, only the passage of time and the remarkable reserve of the freedmen could prove.

The vanquished people were not entirely without resources for rebuilding, however. Their recognition of defeat did not carry with it any acknowledgment of deficiency in leadership, self-respect, or the validity of their position. If anything, the crushing defeat on the field of battle had solidified the whites in their determination to preserve the integrity of their way of life. Four years of war, Wilbur Cash in *The Mind of the South* has said, "had left these Southerners . . . far more aware of their differences and of the line which divided what was Southern from what was not. And upon that line all their intensified patriotism and love, all their high pride in the knowledge that they had fought a good fight and had yielded only to irresistible force, was concentrated, to issue in a determination . . . to hold fast to their own, to maintain their divergences, to remain what they had been and were." The young white Southerner who described the South in 1865 as conquered but not subdued was, perhaps, more accurate than he realized. And the sense of unity created by the war did much to perpetuate and strengthen the view that the Southern cause was not entirely lost.

The heart of the white Southerner *had* gone out of the war. His confidence in his leaders *had* been shaken. The Confederacy *had* collapsed, and the vast majority of the Confederates *did* accept military defeat. It did not follow, however, that they accepted the politics of Lincoln, the economics of Chase, or the moral principles of Garrison. It was a naïve Northerner, indeed, who expressed the belief in 1865 that Virginia would be "regenerated by Northern ideas and free institutions." There would be regeneration of the entire section, white Southerners confidently believed, but only on the basis of *Southern* ideas and *Southern* institutions. Nothing had happened at Appomattox to change this fundamental conviction. The attachment of white Southerners to their way of life was as strong as ever, and they were determined to preserve it. To be sure, some were bitter that their lives had been spared in the glorious cause. Others, however, were determined to work and, if necessary, fight to preserve what was left. A Georgia editor spoke for many when he said, "to the hundreds of thousands of those descendant of high but broken-down families that are now bewailing their hard lot, we say, go to work!" The spirit and determination to survive were indeed powerful.

The economic resources of the South were its land and its labor.

Land has always been immensely important in the economy, and the Southerners still had plenty of it. Although a small fraction had been confiscated by Union officials, much of this was shortly to be restored to the rightful owners or to other former Confederates. And despite the trail of destruction left in the wake of the armies, a good deal of the land had not been touched by the war. The Civil War years antedated "saturated destruction"—a concept born in the waging of total war in the twentieth century. No one spoke much of the areas bypassed by the Union and Confederate armies; newspaper reporters and inspection teams found nothing exciting to report about such places. They existed, nevertheless. Portions of Texas and Arkansas and even Mississippi, Georgia, Florida, and the other Confederate states heard no roaring of Union cannon. And once the fighting had ceased, even the burned-over land could be cultivated again, if labor was available.

But what if the freedman could not or would not work? Some ex-Confederates, believing that the former slaves would not work, entertained thoughts of luring white workers into the South. Ignoring the untold suffering that cut across racial lines, some saw in the destitution and disease among blacks a portent of their complete extinction. The editor of the Natchez *Democrat* declared, "The child is already born who will behold the last Negro in the State of Mississippi." With almost equal prescience *and* precision the eminent Dr. C. K. Marshall expressed his views on this subject: "In all probability New Year's Day, on the morning of the 1st of January, 1920, the colored population in the South will scarcely be counted."

Most Southern whites seemed less pessimistic. Blacks would survive, with the benevolent assistance of whites. And their labors would be utilized for the rebuilding of the ravaged South. If there were any doubts about the ability or willingness of freedmen to work, these could be overcome with "adequate supervision." Fixing a weather eye on the Southern economy, the editor of *De Bow's Review* said that freedmen were working well on the plantations even during the first year of freedom. The great hope almost everywhere was that they would settle down to work as they had before the firing on Sumter. In the late summer of 1865 there was a strong chance that the great majority of them would do precisely that. The whites, anxious and confused, were quick to generalize. If they saw blacks idling away their time, they were inclined to conclude that they would not work. The plain fact was that some would work and some would not work. Some began immediately to look for jobs. Others delayed this unpleasant search as long as possible. Before the end of the year, it became clear to any who cared to look that in the black population the South still had a labor force and, for the most part, the South could employ this force on its own terms. But, as Leon Litwack has observed, "Even as they toiled in the same fields, performed the familiar tasks, and returned at dusk to the same cabins, scores of freedmen refused to resign themselves to the permanent status of a landless agricultural working class. Like most Americans, they aspired to something better and yearned for economic independence and self-employment.

To get off dead center, however, the South needed more than land and labor. It desperately needed capital. In earlier years capital outlay in the South, except for slaves, had always been quite limited. Farm machinery, for example, had been understandably scarce in an economy that placed such great reliance on slave labor. The war had demonstrated how pitifully inadequate the investments in industrial operations had been. Despite the desperate and surprisingly successful efforts of the Confederates to produce the goods they needed to carry on the war, the South remained no match for the North in this regard. There was more talk than action, more promotion than production. The Confederates were defeated in the Northern factories as decisively as they were defeated on the battlefields; and the first defeat made inevitable the second one. At the end of the war the ex-Confederates wanted not only to rehabilitate their old agricultural system but to strengthen their whole economic structure by moving toward greater industrialization. One of the most significant lessons of the war for them had been the importance of a vigorous, versatile economic order.

It was the North's economy, of course, that served as an example for the South. The war had performed wonders on the Northern "home front." Everywhere agricultural production had increased, while the industrial order had been practically revolutionized to meet the enormous demands. Labor-saving devices, such as the mechanical reaper and the sewing machine, released men for other pursuits while stepping up production tremendously. Meanwhile the use of steel and petroleum in countless ways merely suggested the direction the economic order would take in future years.

While the exigencies of war greatly stimulated economic growth in the North, government policies also did much to facilitate it. Liberal tariff and land policies, new banking and currency laws, and general laxity in the government's dealings with businessmen helped usher in a period of unprecedented economic activity and prosperity. In the first two years of the war one railroad doubled its earnings. Savings-bank deposits rose during the war from $149,278,000 to $242,619,000. And if the laboring and white-collar classes were pinched by the inflationary spiral, the accumulation of great wealth in some hands produced the country's first millionaire class. Patriotism and public morality were subordinated to greed. Unscrupulous businessmen and manufacturers seemed more interested in accumulating wealth than in achieving a Union victory. But widespread graft and corruption did not prevent the growth of the industrial order. In the wake of the new order emerged an incredibly large and powerful wealthy class. The wealthy had surplus capital, and they were looking for opportunities to invest it.

As preoccupation with material gain increased, zeal for reform declined. The garish display of wealth in gold, diamonds, and furs indicated the emergence from the war of new tastes and changed values. When the Secretary of the Treasury visited New York in the spring of 1864, he found that many businessmen gave more attention to the stock market than to the news of casualties from the battle front. "No one can fail to perceive," declared one observer in 1864, "the danger that a real or even a professed patriotism may be made the cover for a multitude of sins and gallantry on the field of battle be regarded as a substitute for all the duties of the decalogue." It would be difficult to focus the attention of such venal groups on some of the more basic needs of the majority of the people at the war's end. They had had greater concern for new and larger profits than for new and constructive approaches to the problem of intersectional relations. They were more interested in using the government to further their selfish ends than in developing a public policy that would create new bases for human and race relations.

The climate that produced frauds approximating $17,000,000 out of $50,000,000 worth of government contracts could hardly be expected to encourage public or private morality. There was little room for the social reformers of the prewar period; and, weary from the long struggle or burdened with the cares of age, most of them passed from the stage. William Lloyd Garrison had begun to feel that his work of "Negro-uplift" was about over; and if

Thaddeus Stevens still had considerable determination to carry the crusade to its logical conclusion, his energy was beginning to fade rapidly with age. Moving to the center of the stage were those deeply involved in the exciting alliance between government and business. New leaders like James G. Blaine of Maine and Roscoe Conkling of New York had less solicitude for humanitarian reform and the difficult problems of political reconstruction than for taking advantage of the peculiar postwar conditions to further the interests of themselves and their friends in the industrial and financial community. They would have much to do with shaping the course of history in the ensuing years.

The Yankee businessman, his pockets bulging with war profits, saw in the vanquished section a new and highly promising frontier. He continued to invest in western lands, mines, and railroads, as he had during the war. He was still working the mines in the region of the fabulous Comstock Lode and, with the generous help of the federal government, was building the first transcontinental railroad, the Union Pacific. The whole vast trans-Mississippi West became the scene of enormous activity, with investments running into hundreds of millions of dollars. The western frontier was rapidly disappearing under the systematic attack of the Yankee investor. But he still had some capital in reserve for the South.

Whitelaw Reid, Sidney Andrews, and other Northern visitors to the South encouraged the Yankee capitalist to do his part in "Northernizing" the Southern frontier. Even in the first few months after the war important representatives of the Northern business community were investing in Southern ventures ranging from plantations to railroads. In 1865 a syndicate of Northern men purchased extensive coal fields on the James River near Richmond. About the same time, several were investing capital in the turpentine and lumber business of North Carolina. These were among the first Yankees to set about the exciting—and profitable—task of "Northernizing" the postwar South.

The Northern businessman was as determined as the former Confederate to keep a firm hand on the future. He was anxious, of course, that the South resume normal relations with the rest of the country as soon as possible. But he was more than slightly skeptical about the possible effect of an unreconstructed Southern economic and social philosophy on his own position. Having come to regard the federal government as an indispensable ally in his business ventures, he shuddered at the thought that the relationship might be undermined by a renascent, uncontrollable South. He listened uneasily to rumors regarding Southern hostility toward the Yankee. If he was to invest in the South, he wanted to be certain that it would not spell defeat for him with the dissipation of his dearly earned capital.

During the first year of peace Thomas Conway, sometime agent for the Freedmen's Bureau, made a survey for the chamber of commerce of the state of New York to determine what the possibilities were for investing capital in the South. He concluded that while there were many Northerners who wanted to advance loans on crops, to purchase lands, and to assist the South's economic rehabilitation in other ways, there were serious impediments to such investments. The South's "temper of hatred for the Northern people had not abated sufficiently," nor was there "sufficient restoration of peace and order within her borders to justify men in the belief that they could live and safely transact business in any section of the South." Conway and his associates hoped that peace and law would soon prevail so that the Northern investor could without hindrance facilitate the South's economic recovery and transformation. Here, then, was one important reason for the strong interest manifested by the new Northern leadership in the South's social and political problems.

In order to bring the postwar inflation under control, many Northern businessmen, in the role of creditors, favored some contraction of the currency. They were already having great difficulty carrying the day because of the opposition of labor and debtor groups in the North and West. Would not the Southern states, back in the Union, side with the debtor elements and oppose deflation? The new national banks had helped the business community in numerous ways during the war and were continuing to do so. Would the Southern states, which since Jackson's day had hated any semblance of central banking, join the western state banking interests and the eastern debtors in their war on the national banks? A governmental policy of high tariffs was an important bulwark of the new industrial order. Would the South, traditionally opposed to tariffs, join the fight for reduction?

These major doubts and fears entertained by the Northern businessman regarding the future role of the South in determining governmental policy were joined by other questions. He wondered if the South, predominantly Democratic, would oppose a continuation of land grants to railroads. Many Northern Democrats were opposed. And where would the South stand in the frightening drive, under way by early 1865, to regulate railroads and other monopolies? What would the South do about the freedmen, and what would be the effect of this large new labor force on the already vexatious problem of workers in factories and business establishments of the North?

These fears loomed even larger when the Northern businessman thought of the possibility of the South's increased political strength. Before the war only three-fifths of the slaves were counted in determining congressional representation. By the war's end blacks were free not only by Lincoln's Emancipation Proclamation but also by a proposed amendment to the Constitution, the ratification of which now seemed a foregone conclusion. Ratification was to come before the end of the year. Would *all* the freedmen be counted, thereby giving the South greater representation than it had in 1860? As the Yankee businessman-politician pondered these problems he realized how important it was for him to take a hand in the course of reconstructing the way of life of his southern neighbors.

But the Northerners who sought to play a decisive role in the South had no uniform policy or program to follow. They seemed to know, in a general way, what they wanted, but they were far from united on any specific set of aims. Indeed, there were sharp divisions that sometimes cut across industrial and even sectional lines. They did not share a common view regarding the tariff. New England cotton manufacturers wanted lower tariffs, while the iron and steel interests in the Middle States sought a higher tariff. Similarly, there was division on the currency question. As Eric McKitrick has pointed out, Pennsylvania ironmasters and Pennsylvania bankers might agree on a high tariff and be worlds apart on currency. And even if they knew what they wanted, they experienced real difficulty in coming to some agreement on how to attain it. Such lack of common objectives and strategies could only serve to diminish their effectiveness.

The position of the North was not without a touch of irony. Its reforming zeal had had a good deal to do with the extension of social democracy through the abolition of slavery. But the bitter struggle that ended in emancipation had spawned in the North an industrial plutocracy that was seeking to keep a stranglehold on government in order to maintain its intrenched position. The Yankee wanted to extend his interests into the South, but the potential influence of the former Confederate in national as well as local councils frightened him. In exploring ways to combat this influence some Northern men of affairs even considered enfranchising blacks, a step toward political democracy that had never made much headway in the North. By the very threat of elevating the black man the new economic forces in the North might have brought about in a short time what a generation of prewar reforming zeal had been unable to achieve. But as a subordinate feature, a mere tactic in a larger struggle, the move for greater democracy for blacks was most uncertain and indefinite. When the move had served its purposes, the position of blacks was to be only slightly better than it had ever been.

These considerations were to affect the course of history in the decade following the war as surely as were the questions of "home rule" and "black Reconstruction." The returning soldier, North and South, could hardly be expected to see or understand them in 1865. Nevertheless, before the Southern states returned to the Union and even after they had been "redeemed"—rescued from Radical Reconstruction—these problems and others growing out of them were to remain. For they reflected the fundamental issues confronting the country as it emerged from civil war a mature, modern nation.

2

Presidential Peacemaking

The news reaching Washington from New Orleans at the end of April, 1862, was good. The city was in Union hands, and occupation by the colorful and controversial General Benjamin Butler had begun—and with it Reconstruction. Since the firing on Sumter, President Lincoln had been giving some thought to the problem of resuming normal relations with the Confederate states. He had never recognized the right or the fact of secession. From the outset he had argued that merely a state of rebellion existed, which should be put down under the leadership of the President. Likewise, Lincoln believed that the President should lay down the conditions under which the federal government would resume normal relations with the so-called seceded states. The surrender of New Orleans increased the urgency for formulating a general policy of reconstruction.

But the war had not yet reached the stage where President Lincoln felt it desirable to set forth a general policy. Thus, he dealt with Louisiana on an *ad hoc* basis. It may be surprising to learn that General Butler, excoriated by proud Confederates as a "cross-eyed beast," urged amnesty for all Louisianians who would take a simple oath of allegiance. Lincoln considered this proposal along with others but seemed neither to accept nor to reject any of them.

Butler inferred from the President's silence and from the clemency provisions of the Confiscation Act of July, 1862, that he could proceed. The Act authorized the President to seize all property and effects of those engaged in the rebellion and "to apply the same and use the proceeds . . . for the support of the army and navy of the United States." It also contained a feature that suggested clemency under certain conditions: "The President is hereby authorized at any time hereafter, by proclamation to extend to any persons who may have participated in the existing rebellion in any state or part thereof, pardon and amnesty, with such exceptions and at such time and on such conditions as he may deem expedient for the public welfare."

It was within the meaning of this provision that Butler began to administer the oath, and by early August more than 11,000 ex-Confederates had taken it. These oath-takers were the electorate that sent Michael Hahn and B. F. Flanders from the First and Second Louisiana Districts to the Thirty-seventh Congress. They were seated on February 9, 1863, and served until the end of the session in March.

With representatives in Congress even for a few months during the war, Louisiana's position was unique. In general, Confederate states had no congressmen in Washington. Tennessee had some representation in Congress during the first two years of the war, but these lawmakers from the Volunteer State were strong Unionists who had refused to resign their seats when their state seceded. Virginia's Pierpont government, which remained loyal to the Union even after the state seceded, enjoyed sporadic representation; but this was because it was regarded as the "restored" government of Virginia in contrast to the one in Richmond that had seceded. Thus, before Lincoln could formulate a policy and before Congress could develop a policy of its own, Louisiana had acted.

15

All her representatives had left Congress in 1861. But in 1863 Louisiana sent Hahn and Flanders to Washington as representatives. No other Confederate state was to enjoy this distinction until the Confederacy had collapsed and Congress had dictated the conditions of reconstruction.

By the end of 1863 Lincoln believed the war to be far enough along to set forth his plan of reconstruction. Regarding the task as essentially a presidential one, he hoped to encourage loyal groups in the several states to resume normal relations with the federal government through the establishment of provisional governments under executive control. On December 8 he issued his Proclamation of Amnesty and Reconstruction. In it he offered pardon to any former Confederates who would take the oath to support "the Constitution of the United States and the Union of the States thereunder." Exceptions were officers in the Confederate army and navy above the rank of colonel and lieutenant, respectively, those who had resigned commissions in the United States and aided in the rebellion, civil and diplomatic officers of the Confederacy, those who left judicial and congressional posts in the United States to aid in the rebellion, and all who engaged "in treating colored persons, or white persons in charge of such, otherwise than lawfully as prisoners of war, and which persons may have been found in the United States service as soldiers, seamen, or in any other capacity." He further stipulated that when persons equal in number to one-tenth of the votes cast in the presidential election of 1860 had taken the oath and established a government, he would recognize that government. Lincoln's plan excluded all blacks from participation either in oath-taking, voting, or holding office. Governments under presidential reconstruction were to be governments by white men.

The proclamation clearly set forth Lincoln's conception of how the President should function in an emergency involving the establishment and maintenance of peace. It went beyond this in indicating how the President should take the initiative in creating and operating the machinery of political reconciliation. It was clear, moreover, that Lincoln hoped to bring the plan gradually into operation as Union military success brought more and more territory under Union control. Perhaps through this means the machinery of political reconstruction would be operating efficiently by the time the war ended.

It was one thing for the President to set forth his program and philosophy of reconstruction. It was quite another for Congress to feel called upon to accept it. No pressure of circumstances similar to those that existed at the outbreak of the war imposed on Congress a course of action dictated by the President. If the President possessed extraordinary powers in time of war, there certainly was—or should be—a considerable contraction of those powers at the war's end. Even so, was the President too lenient? What actually was the status of the seceded states, and how should they be brought back into practical relations with the rest of the country? The President's answers to these and other questions were by no means satisfactory to any element suspicious of the President's use of power or fearful of the South's hasty recovery of political influence. Small wonder that the proclamation set off a full-scale debate in Congress that lasted, intermittently, for several months.

During the winter of 1864 members of Congress, upon receiving the Proclamation of Amnesty, not for action but merely as information, discussed questions that had little to do with the logistics of war or the problem of slavery and freedom. They talked a great deal about the nature of the government, the legality of secession, the function of the President, and the role of Congress. To Thaddeus Stevens, the Lincoln plan seemed preposterous. "If ten men fit to save Sodom can elect a Governor," he told the House, "and other State officers for and against the eleven hundred thousand Sodomites in Virginia, then the democratic doctrine that the majority shall rule is discarded and dangerously ignored. When the doctrine that the *quality* and not the *number* of voters is to decide the right to govern, then we no longer have a republic, but the worst form of despotism." "Where does sovereignty rest?" asked Representative W. H. Wadsworth of Kentucky. He answered his own question by saying, "In Congress and not in the President and his army. Conquests made by this country, foreign or domestic . . . are to be appropriated and settled and enjoyed and governed according to the laws of Congress, and by Congress admitted to the equal fellowship of states."

Out of the welter of debate came the first detailed congressional plan of reconstruction. Sponsored jointly by Senator Benjamin Wade of Ohio and Representative Henry Winter Davis of Maryland, the bill that passed both houses of Congress in July, 1864, went beyond the President's plan in several important respects. It required a *majority* of the enrolled white male citizens to take the oath to support the Constitution before a convention could be called to reconstitute the state government. In order to be a delegate to the convention or vote for a delegate, one had to take the "ironclad oath," the test oath contained in the Act of July 2, 1862, that he had never voluntarily borne arms against the United States or given aid to persons in rebellion or exercised the functions of any office under the Confederacy. Any person who in the future held any office, civil or military, except merely ministerial offices and military offices below the grade of colonel "in the rebel service" was declared not to be a citizen of the United States.

Speaking for a growing number of citizens skeptical of unlimited presidential authority, Davis declared that his bill deserved the support of all who thought that the rebellion "has placed citizens of rebel states beyond the protection of the Constitution, and that Congress has supreme power over them as conquered enemies." He left no doubt about his conviction that the former Confederate states should be governed by Congress until they formed governments of their own under the supervision of Congress. The sponsors of the bill were joined by many others in both houses who believed that the President not only had been too lenient in his program of reconstruction but had usurped power that rightly belonged to Congress.

By Lincoln's pocket veto the Wade-Davis bill failed to become law. The President wrote Stanton, his Secretary of War, that he disliked an oath requiring a man to swear he had not done wrong. "It rejects the Christian principle of forgiveness on terms of repentance. I think it is enough if the man does no wrong hereafter." The President then issued a proclamation in which he said that while he was unwilling by formal approval of the bill to commit the country to a single plan of restoration, he regarded the system set forth in the bill "as one very proper plan for the loyal people of any State choosing to adopt it." He did not want his "reconstructed" governments in Arkansas and Louisiana "set aside and held for naught." It was clear to anyone, however, that no state would prefer the Wade-Davis plan to that of the President.

"What an infamous proclamation," commented Thaddeus Stevens, who had not supported the Wade-Davis bill because it did not go far enough. "How little of the rights of war and the law of nations our President knows," he lamented.

The bill's sponsors were particularly irked by the President's treatment of their proposal. They saw in it political conniving, dictatorial usurpation, and defiance of congressional authority. They published in the New York *Tribune* and other papers across the country a Manifesto which was something of a landmark for its use of vigorous language in criticizing a President. In defeating the bill in order to prevent any limitation on his powers, the President had "greatly presumed on the forbearance which the supporters of his Administration have so long practiced," the Manifesto declared. "But he must understand that our support is of a cause and not of a man; that the authority of Congress is paramount and must be respected . . . and if he wishes our support, he must confine himself to his executive duties—to obey and execute, not make the laws—to suppress by arms armed rebellion, and leave political reorganization to Congress."

This was a shocking indictment by members of his own party of a President whose success as a war leader was more than considerable and who had already been nominated for re-election. Lincoln, hearing of the tone and content of the Manifesto, was deeply hurt and refused to read it. "To be wounded in the house of one's friends is perhaps the most grievous affliction that can befall a man," he said to a friend. Actually, he was too busy with the war, the campaign for re-election, and his own plan for reconstruction to give much thought to snipers. He would not be diverted from the principal tasks before him.

Already, Lincoln was deeply involved in trying to facilitate the establishment of state governments under provisions laid down in his Proclamation of Amnesty and Reconstruction. Virginia was the only Confederate state not included in his proclamation, for he had already recognized the government at Alexandria as the true government of the state. Still, the government that had been set up by the Unionist leader, Francis H. Pierpont, was little more than a puppet government; and he wanted it and the others not yet organized to be more than "mere shadows of governments," as his enemies were to claim. But the task was immensely difficult, and the problems were complex.

In Louisiana, Lincoln was happy to see that arrangements were being made to comply with the conditions of the proclamation. In February, 1864, Michael Hahn was elected governor by qualified white males, a procedure approved by Lincoln's military governor, General Nathaniel P. Banks. But the question of black suffrage, already raised by blacks themselves, was indeed not just rhetorical. The more than 18,000 free blacks who were living in New Orleans when the war came owned property valued at fifteen million dollars. They had a long and distinguished record of responsible and loyal service, dating back to their military exploits under Andrew Jackson in the battle of New Orleans in 1815. Most of them could read and write, and many could be described as educated and refined. Among the thousands of quadroons and octoroons were acknowledged kinsmen of some of the "best white families" in the state.

As early as November, 1863, the free men of color of New Orleans had addressed an appeal to Governor Shepley "asking to be allowed to register and vote." They reviewed their services to the city and state and reminded him that they had never ceased to be peaceable citizens, paying their taxes on assessments running into millions. Receiving no satisfaction there, they appealed to General Banks, who likewise rejected their plea. Then they made an appeal directly to President Lincoln, who, although promising nothing, must have been impressed. On March 13, 1864, he sent a congratulatory message to Hahn, "first Free State Governor of Louisiana." In discussing the franchise in Louisiana, the President took the liberty to "barely suggest, for your private consideration, whether some of the colored people may not be let in, as, for instance, the

BY THE PRESIDENT OF THE UNITED STATES OF AMERICA:
A PROCLAMATION.

WHEREAS, the President of the United States, on the 8th day of December, A. D., eighteen hundred and sixty-three, and on the 26th day of March, A. D., eighteen hundred and sixty-four, did, with the object to suppress the existing rebellion, to induce all persons to return to their loyalty, and to restore the authority of the United States, issue proclamations offering amnesty and pardon to certain persons who had directly or by implication participated in the said rebellion; and whereas many persons who had so engaged in said rebellion, have, since the issuance of said proclamations, failed or neglected to take the benefits offered thereby; and whereas many persons who have been justly deprived of all claim to amnesty and pardon thereunder, by reason of their participation directly or by implication in said rebellion, and continued hostility to the Government of the United States since the date of said proclamations, now desire to apply for and obtain amnesty and pardon:

To THE END, THEREFORE, that the authority of the government of the United States may be restored, and that peace, order, and freedom may be established, I, ANDREW JOHNSON, PRESIDENT OF THE UNITED STATES, do proclaim and declare that I hereby grant to all persons who have, directly or indirectly, participated in the existing rebellion, except as hereinafter excepted, amnesty and pardon, with restoration of all rights of property, except as to slaves, and except in cases where legal proceedings, under the laws of the United States providing for the confiscation of property of persons engaged in rebellion, have been instituted; but upon the condition, nevertheless, that every such person shall take and subscribe the following oath, (or affirmation,) and thenceforward keep and maintain said oath inviolate; and which oath shall be registered for permanent preservation, and shall be of the tenor and effect following, to wit:—

"I, —— ——, do solemnly swear, (or affirm,) in presence of Almighty God, that I will henceforth faithfully support, protect, and defend the Constitution of the United States, and the union of the States thereunder; and that I will, in like manner, abide by, and faithfully support all laws and proclamations which have been made during the existing rebellion with reference to the emancipation of slaves. So help me God."

(Courtesy of the National Archives.)

A portion of President Johnson's Proclamation of Amnesty and
Reconstruction, May 29, 1865.

(Courtesy of the National Archives.)

Test oath, signed by former Confederate Wade Hampton
in August, 1865.

very intelligent, and especially those who have fought gallantly in our ranks." The President's thinking had gone even beyond this proposal. To one of his intimates, he said that after much study he had decided what course he would pursue regarding the blacks, "who have so heroically vindicated their manhood on the battlefield, where, in assisting to save the life of the Republic, they have demonstrated in blood their right to the ballot." Then he concluded, "The restoration of the Rebel States to the Union must rest upon the principle of civil and political equality of both races."

The suggestion to Hahn was as far as the President would go in public in making a concrete proposal. This was enough, however, to indicate to the white leaders of Louisiana the importance of recognizing the significant implications of the changed status of blacks. After all, they were enlisting in the Union army by the scores of thousands, and the total number from the slave states would reach 134,000 before the war's end. What if they returned to their homes with no means of protecting themselves against their understandably outraged former masters? At least they should have whatever security the exercise of the franchise could give them. Louisiana, with its very advanced African-American population, could take the first steps if any state could.

The Louisiana constitutional convention abolished slavery and appealed to Congress for compensation for slaves. The delegates also adopted a resolution declaring that the legislature should never enact a law permitting blacks to vote. The hands of General Banks and Governor Hahn could be seen when this resolution was replaced by one authorizing the legislature to extend the right of suffrage to such persons, "citizens of the United States, as by military service, by taxation to support the government, or by intellectual fitness, may be deemed entitled thereto." When this was denounced by some members as a "nigger resolution," it was laid on the table by a vote of 48 to 32. In the fall of 1864 some five thousand blacks asked the legislature to permit them to vote, but no action was taken. Louisiana blacks were not any closer to the franchise than they had ever been. Likewise, Louisiana's elected representatives to Congress under the Lincoln plan were far from being accepted, for by late 1864 the sentiment was strong against seating any persons from the "Lincoln states."

Concerning representation in Congress or suffrage for blacks the situation was no better in the other states Lincoln sought to reconstruct. In Arkansas a new constitution was ratified in the spring of 1864, and a "free state government" was launched. In June, however, Congress decided that the new Arkansas government was not satisfactory and therefore not entitled to representation. Tennessee had enjoyed a measure of civil government since Andrew Johnson was appointed military governor in 1862. In September, 1864, and January, 1865, conventions to form a free government met in Nashville. Many citizens refused to co-operate on the grounds that the conventions were not truly representative. Nevertheless, the Tennessee constitution was amended, abolishing slavery and repudiating secession. In February, 1865, the colorful, volatile Unionist "Parson" W. G. Brownlow was elected governor. But in the fall of 1865 Tennessee's representatives were denied seats in Congress.

Lincoln worked hard to gain acceptance of his plan of restoration. He wrote letters to military leaders and civil authorities, making suggestions but no demands. He received representatives from Confederate areas and sent investigators into various parts of the South. He discussed the problem with members of the cabinet and with sympathetic members of Congress. He made concessions, such as his partial recognition of the Wade-Davis plan and his signing, under protest, the joint resolution excluding from the electoral count of 1865 all Confederate states, even those that had met the conditions set forth in his plan.

Lincoln hoped, moreover, to give the restored states a stronger position by removing the legal and political disabilities of the Confederate leaders as rapidly as possible. Shortly after his proclamation of December 8, 1863, he began to pardon persons in the "excepted" categories. Some Southern legislatures condemned his offer of amnesty as an insult, while some Northerners criticized it as much too lenient. As early as December 15, however, Lincoln pardoned Colonel E. W. Gantt of Arkansas, who, after taking the oath of allegiance, received a commission in the Union army. Meanwhile, in every portion of the South where Union armies had moved, Lincoln's men were authorized to administer the oath to all who would come forward. In Jacksonville, Florida, sixty persons presented themselves the first day. At Norfolk General Butler said that the oath was daily becoming more popular. In Nashville more than two thousand Confederate deserters took the oath during the last four months of 1864.

All to no avail. The harder Lincoln worked, the more adamant Congress became, persistently refusing to seat representatives from the "Lincoln states." Lincoln was distressed, but he never gave up hope. Kenneth Stampp, a leading authority on the period, says that Lincoln never gave up his hope "that the great mass of blacks could be persuaded to leave the country." It must be said, however, that by 1865 Lincoln had moved beyond the position he took when he attempted to negotiate with countries in Africa and the Caribbean to accept black Americans. In the months and weeks before his assassination he moved closer to the view that blacks could remain in the country and become an integral part of American life.

In his last public address on April 11, 1865, he vigorously defended his policies and commended them to Congress and the country. He conceded that as it had worked out it contained imperfections. He admitted, for example, that he would have been pleased to see the suffrage extended to some blacks in Louisiana. "Still, the question is not whether the Louisiana government . . . is quite all that is desirable. The question is, will it be wiser to take it as it is and help to improve it, or to reject and disperse." To Lincoln the answer was obvious. To those who were still dissatisfied he pledged his continued attention to the problem and indicated that he would at some future time have "some new announcement."

Within a few days Lincoln was dead, and any new announcement would have to come from the new President, Andrew Johnson. As far as the restoration of the Confederate states was concerned, Lincoln's policies had failed. But his policies had succeeded in establishing local civil government in four former Confederate states. Perhaps he was not fully pleased with what was happening, but local government in which ex-Confederates had a hand was an accomplished fact in Louisiana, Arkansas, Tennessee, and Virginia.

Andrew Johnson was sworn into office as the seventeenth President of the United States a few hours after Lincoln's death, April 15, 1865. Fiercely devoted to the Union, he was committed no less than Lincoln to bringing about a prompt restoration of the Southern states to the Union. Some had inferred from his scrupulous honesty, his utter devotion to duty, and his vehement strictures against the Confederates that he was as radical as any Unionist. Speaking of the defeated Confederates a week after he took office, he told an Indiana delegation, "They must not only be punished, but their social power must be destroyed." To Senator Benjamin Wade he exclaimed, "Treason is a crime and crime must be punished. Treason must be made infamous and traitors must be impoverished." Small wonder that some Northerners believed the country would benefit by a change from a "lenient" Lincoln to a "firm" Johnson.

Johnson's position was misunderstood, even in those early days. As a Unionist he was not anti-Southern. He subscribed to the honored Southern dogma of states' rights, but he hated the planter class whose reckless policies he believed to be responsible for secession and war. Before the war he had not been anti-slavery. He owned eight slaves and held no racial views that could be regarded as unorthodox in the South. Although a Democrat, he was more devoted to Lincoln and to what he believed were Lincoln's policies than many staunch Republicans. It was his hypersensitivity and obstinacy that caused him to miss entirely the great lessons of Lincoln's statesmanship—flexibility, adjustment, compassion.

The pressures on Johnson during his first weeks in office were enormous. A constant procession of members of Congress sought to win him to their views. Senator Charles Sumner, lacking no confidence in the soundness of his position, told him that the right of black people to vote was "the essence—the great essential." Johnson is reported to have said, "On this question there is no difference between us; you and I are alike." Among the many delegations of citizens was one from Pennsylvania, accompanied by Senator Simon Cameron, Lincoln's first Secretary of War, and Thaddeus Stevens, the great power in the House of Representatives. "To those who have deceived," the President told them, "to the conscious, influential traitor, who attempted to destroy the life of the nation—I would say, on you be inflicted the severest penalties of your crime." Stevens was pleased with much that he heard, but he was apparently disturbed by the President's assertion that it was nonsense to claim that the seceded states had gone out of the Union or had committed suicide. Two weeks later Stevens sought to apply some quiet pressure on Johnson. "While I think we shall agree with you almost unanimously as to the main objects you have in view," he wrote, "I fear we may differ as to the manner of effecting them. How the executive can remodel the *states in the Union* is past my comprehension. . . . My one object now is to suggest the propriety of suspending further reconstruction until the meeting of Congress." Johnson did not heed this suggestion from one who was regarded by some as the most powerful man in Congress.

But there were other pressures. Seward, convalescing from the April 14 attempt on his life, when the president was assassinated urged a continuation of Lincoln's policies, somewhat modified perhaps. In April and May, numerous Southerners, including women, visited the President. They pleaded with him for clemency for the "conscious, influential traitors." Some were Whig loyalists who had opposed secession and dragged their feet in supporting the Confederacy. As responsible men of standing in their communities they offered full co-operation with the administration. It is not possible to estimate the "flattering and seductive influence" of the pleas of those who had not previously even recognized Johnson as a social equal. On a person who had more than his share of vanity and egotism it could have been considerable.

There were still other influences and pressures on the new President. Democrats openly courted him and expressed the hope that he would return to the fold. During the summer and fall of 1865 many Northern newspapers expressed great confidence in him and asserted that the country was secure in his firm hands. The bipartisan nature of the support given him was especially heartening. As Northern individuals and delegations received a respectful hearing of their views, they mistook his polite silence for agreement. The impression he thus conveyed had the effect of enlisting greater support for him in his early months in office.

Johnson's retention of the Lincoln cabinet was one of the earliest indications that he would not strike out on an entirely new course. Another was his recognition, on May 9, 1865, of the Pierpont government as the legally constituted government of Virginia. Twenty days later he issued his first proclamation of amnesty. It was not unlike the amnesty provisions of Lincoln's proclamation of December 8, 1863. It required an oath of allegiance of all who sought pardon and a "restoration of all rights of property, except as to slaves." The most important addition to the classes "excepted" from pardon in Lincoln's proclamation was "all persons . . . the estimated value of whose taxable property is over twenty thousand dollars." He was determined to punish the wealthy who, he was convinced, had dragooned the South into secession and war. Significantly, he added that a special application to the President could be made by any person belonging to the excepted classes. He promised that such clemency would be as "liberally extended as may be consistent with the facts of the case and the peace and dignity of the United States."

On the same day the President issued a proclamation setting forth his plan for the restoration of North Carolina and appointing William W. Holden provisional governor. The President empowered his appointee to prescribe rules for calling a convention, composed of delegates chosen by the loyal people of the state, to amend the state constitution. The governor was also to exercise, within the limits of the state, all powers necessary and proper to enable such loyal people to restore the state to its constitutional relations with the federal government. No person was to serve as an elector or delegate to the convention unless he had been a qualified voter before secession and had taken the oath of allegiance. The convention, however, was to prescribe the qualifications of electors and the eligibility of persons to hold office, "a power the people of the several states . . . have rightfully exercised from the origin of the Government to the present time."

In "excepting" the $20,000 group from amnesty, Johnson was displaying a peculiar animus toward the wealthy; but that did not make their situation entirely hopeless. Indeed, he was remarkably generous in granting pardons to members of this and other "excepted" groups when they made special application to him. In requiring this special application, the President seems to have been motivated more by a determination to humiliate the leaders of the Confederacy by having them "kneel before him" in their plea for mercy than by a desire for efficiency or security.

In his plan for restoring North Carolina Johnson adhered neither to the "ten per cent" plan of Lincoln nor to the more stringent requirements of the Wade-Davis bill. He was willing to admit a state into constitutional relations with the federal government when "that portion of the people . . . who are loyal" had written a constitution and established a government under it. For leniency in this crucial requirement Johnson had far outstripped his predecessor.

Within six weeks after the issuance of the North Carolina proclamation, identical proclamations, including the appointment of provisional governors, had been issued for the six remaining "unrestored" states—Mississippi, Georgia, Texas, Alabama, South Carolina, and Florida. In the following months, before the Thirty-ninth Congress met in December, the ex-Confederate states were desperately busy establishing civil governments and reordering their social and economic system. President Johnson watched the proceedings with interest and anxiety. This was their great opportunity, greater than most had dared expect, to restore their governments with a minimum of interference from Washington. They were determined to make the most of it.

31

3

Reconstruction: Confederate Style

As spring gave way to summer in 1865, despair gave way to optimism in the South. The opportunity of Southerners, including former Confederates, to govern themselves was at hand; and a glow of confidence in themselves and in the Washington government came over them. "Every generous heart will feel . . . that the Government of the United States seeks not, and never has sought, to humiliate the people of the South," the provisional governor of Texas declared. With the kind of help and encouragement they were getting from Washington, former Confederates could soon be in control at home and, perhaps, even make themselves felt in higher quarters. This attitude was a far cry from the despair suffered by so many white Southerners in the closing months of the war. Lincoln's Second Inaugural Address, with its appealing phrase, "with malice toward none, with charity for all," was not altogether reassuring to the South; but his death a few weeks later left a vast uncertainty. Not until Johnson, through his actions, began to indicate that his strong Unionism had not completely destroyed his Southernism did the people of the former Confederacy experience some easing of their anxiety over future relations with the Washington government. Johnson seemed in a forgiving mood, and they would do whatever they could to keep him in that mood.

As clerk of pardons, to process the increasing volume of requests for clemency, the President chose M. F. Pleasants, a former Confederate colonel. The news of this unexpected gesture of good will spread rapidly through the South. Even the most prominent Confederate leaders saw in this action some real hope for their early amnesty. During the summer and fall of 1865 the President was literally besieged with callers, many of them Confederate generals, civilian officials, and charming women seeking amnesty for themselves or for others. Robert E. Lee encouraged his fellows to request pardons at the earliest opportunity; and on June 13, 1865, he submitted to the President, through General Grant, a request for his own pardon. Grant was pleased to submit the request with his "earnest recommendation" and also to beseech the President to have Lee's indictment for treason quashed. Lee did not inclose the statement, required of all suppliants, declaring that he had subscribed to the oath. This was at least one reason why he was not pardoned until the President's Third General Amnesty on Christmas Day, 1868.

Other prominent leaders fared better than Lee. Admiral Raphael Semmes was pardoned in November, 1865. The following month William A. Graham, former governor of North Carolina and Confederate senator, was pardoned by Johnson soon after his election to the United States Senate. Indeed, more than six hundred prominent North Carolinians were pardoned just before the election of 1865. Among others who sought early pardons were Confederate Vice-President Alexander H. Stephens and two members of Jefferson Davis' cabinet, Postmaster General John H. Reagan and Secretary of the Treasury Christopher G. Memminger.

Within a year most of them had obtained their pardons, and many of them were holding positions of trust in their state and local governments.

Important economic considerations impelled some former Confederates to seek presidential clemency. They could not reclaim their property until they had been pardoned and had taken the oath. This astounded Mrs. William Smith Mason of South Carolina, but as she saw no alternative she too sought pardon through Governor Benjamin F. Perry. Pardoning became a big business, with lawyers and brokers promising clients pardons for fees ranging from $150 to $500. This was an ideal climate for corruption, and the enormous pressures applied by those who wanted pardons in order to participate in political activities or to regain their property made graft inevitable. The denials of corruption by the office of the Attorney General rang hollow while agents and brokers were calculating their fees on the basis of how much money would be needed to obtain the "co-operation" of public officials. As pressure increased, pardons likewise increased. By September, 1865, they were being granted at the rate of more than one hundred per day. Within nine months after Johnson's proclamation approximately fourteen thousand in the "excepted" classes had received their pardons. By May 4, 1866, some seven thousand persons in the over-$20,000 class alone had been pardoned. There is no way of knowing how much the officials and agents made from this big business of pardoning.

As he went about restoring his government and rebuilding his way of life, the white Southerner, however optimistic, could hardly ignore the distractions and potential forces for intervention in his midst. For one thing, there was the army of occupation. Nothing offended the warriors of the Lost Cause more than the presence in their towns and villages of companies and regiments of the victorious army—including blacks, many of them former slaves—to remind them of their humiliation. Caleb Forshey, founder and superintendent of the Texas Military Institute, declared the presence and influence of the Union army "very pernicious everywhere, and without exception." The legislature of Alabama described the federal troops as a "constant source of irritation to the people." In protesting the operation by the federal troops of a military court in his beloved Charleston, Armistead Burt said, "Instead of the scales of Justice, I see displayed before me the sword. . . . Instead of a hall dedicated to justice, I find a military camp." For many, military occupation was worse than defeat on the field of battle.

It is nevertheless remarkable how rapidly, under the circumstances, demobilization of federal troops occurred and with what speed they were removed from Southern soil. In November, 1865, the Secretary of War could report that because of the rapid establishment of civil governments in the South, "the military force of the federal government has been greatly reduced, large armies disbanded, and nearly a million brave men . . . paid and honorably mustered out of service." Within a year there were only 11,000 white and black volunteers still in arms, and the strength of the regular army stood at 54,000. Indeed, by June 1, 1866, there were only 200 officers and 2,973 enlisted men in North and South Carolina; and every black soldier in Mississippi had been mustered out of the service.

Throughout the former Confederate states the number of troops had been drastically reduced. By March 15, 1866, the departments of South Carolina and Florida each had only one black regiment, while all the volunteers, white and black, were mustered out of the military division of Tennessee the following month. In the face of continued insults to the federal authority and in view of the persistence of armed guerrillas and "regulators" in many parts of the South, the removal of federal troops was a magnanimous gesture of good will.

The complaints of many white Southerners that the army of occupation was large and that the many black troops in the South were there for the purpose of insulting and humiliating the former Confederates were without justification. Those who expressed to the Congressional Joint Committee on Reconstruction and to others their bitter resentment of the "occupation" either deliberately misrepresented the situation or merely imagined that the South was being overrun by Union troops. Historians who have spoken of the huge military forces that were kept in the South after the war have had no basis for their assertions. Even casual examination of the report of the Secretary of War for 1865 and 1866 clearly establishes the fact that postwar demobilization was rapid and that only a skeleton military force was in the South by the end of 1866.

Only slightly less military than the army itself was the Bureau of Refugees, Freedmen, and Abandoned Lands, commonly known as the Freedmen's Bureau. Created by Congress just before the end of the war, it was to aid refugees and freedmen by furnishing supplies and medical services, establishing schools, supervising contracts between freedmen and their employers, and managing confiscated or abandoned lands. The commissioner was General O. O. Howard, and most of the assistant commissioners for the several states as well as many of the agents were army officers. In the immediate postwar years they maintained a lively and comprehensive program of relief and rehabilitation.

Within four years the Bureau had issued twenty-one million rations to white refugees and freedmen. It established more than forty hospitals and spent more than two million dollars in treating 450,000 cases of illness. It assisted in the settlement of some thirty thousand persons who had been displaced by the war. It restored, at the insistence of President Johnson, most of the abandoned lands to pardoned rebels. Freedmen received only a small portion of the lands confiscated by the Union during the war. After the passage of the Southern Homestead Act in 1866, the Bureau hoped to assist blacks in obtaining farms under its terms. Although the Bureau would provide free transportation to the new lands and one month's subsistence, freedmen had no means of support while they developed the land. With the exception of a few locations in Florida, Louisiana, and Arkansas, the lands remained unsettled. The "forty acres" were most unattractive—and there were no mules. According to Michael Lanza, the program set up under the Southern Homestead Act failed "because the act was only a mere gesture in the right direction."

The Bureau was especially active in the field of labor. It sought to protect the freedman's right to choose his own employer and to work at a fair wage. Agents consulted with planters and freedmen, urging the former to be fair in their dealings and the latter to work to provide for their families and to achieve independence and security. Many freedmen returned to work under conditions that were greatly improved through the Bureau's assistance in the negotiation of several hundred thousand contracts. In its role as arbiter it established courts and boards that not only mediated disputes between planter and laborer but also settled numerous matters of a civil or criminal nature where one or both parties were freedmen.

Both the President and the former Confederates were especially opposed to the Bureau's exercise of judicial authority. When the Act of 1866, passed over the President's veto, extended the life of the Bureau, Johnson refused to prescribe rules for its handling of cases involving racial discrimination as provided by the law. Meanwhile the Southern whites insisted that Bureau courts were totally unnecessary, and their opposition caused Howard and his subordinates to use the Bureau courts with some caution. Where the Bureau courts did not function, agents of the Bureau were frequently active in attempting to secure justice for freedmen in the regular civil and criminal courts of the community.

The Bureau's greatest success was in education. It established or supervised schools of all kinds: day, night, Sunday, and industrial schools, as well as colleges. It co-operated closely with philanthropic and religious agencies in the maintenance of many educational institutions for freedmen. Howard University, Hampton Institute, and Atlanta and Fisk universities are merely the better known of scores of institutions that received Bureau assistance. By 1870, when the educational work of the Bureau ceased, there were approximately a quarter of a million blacks in 4,300 schools; and the Bureau had spent more than five million dollars on its educational program. Reports indicated that there was a marked increase in school attendance and scholarship and that the record of punctuality and regularity compared favorably with the schools in the North. The Bureau had reason to be pleased with this portion of its work although in a recent assessment, Eric Foner has called the Bureau's educational program "a typical nineteenth century amalgam of benevolent uplift and social control."

Despite the fact that its activities enjoyed a measure of success, the Bureau had not taken over the South. Jealous of their increasing prerogatives of self-government, white Southerners maintained toward the Bureau an attitude ranging from indifference to hostility. State legislatures were inclined to ignore or take lightly any suggestions from Bureau officials that they not enact laws discriminatory against blacks. When agents of the Bureau interfered with the policies of state governments, they were not always safe from the wrath of the federal government as well. For example, the assistant commissioner for Louisiana, Thomas W. Conway, was in such "deep water" with state officials by September, 1865, that Governor J. Madison Wells sought and obtained his removal by Washington.

As the President's hostility to the Bureau became more pronounced in 1866, it became increasingly difficult for it to function effectively. His veto of the bill of 1866 to extend the Bureau's life and enlarge its functions merely strengthened the view of the ex-Confederates that the Bureau was a "curse" and "an engine of mischief." They regarded it as "virtually a foreign government forced upon them and supported by an army of occupation." They tended to ignore its good works and to magnify its shortcomings. Since it stood in the way of states' rights and self-government, white Southerners resolved that it should be resisted. Thus, to former Confederates the Bureau was a symbol of outside interference that every self-respecting white Southerner could be expected to oppose. It can hardly be said that rule by the former Confederates was by any means destroyed by the Freedmen's Bureau. It would be more accurate to say that the former Confederates, with the aid of President Johnson, did much to destroy the effectiveness of the Bureau.

In some ways the former Confederates resented the agents of the Treasury Department as much as they objected to the army or to the Freedmen's Bureau. During the war these agents were authorized by Congress to seize abandoned property in the name of the federal government. In May, 1865, they were instructed to seize any cotton that had been sold to the Confederate government or paid to it in lieu of taxes or made available to it in any other way for its use. The agents were also to collect taxes levied on cotton and were themselves allowed 25 per cent on the returns from their seizures and tax collections.

During the year following the close of the war a horde of Treasury agents made their way through the South. That the federal government would seek to exploit the South's one remaining asset was especially revolting. The fact that many of the agents were corrupt merely added to the contempt in which they were held. But Southerners were not above "co-operating" with the agents, if it was advantageous to do so. Some loyalists, Southerners who declared that they had remained loyal to the Union, went into court and swore that certain Confederate cotton was their own property, and subsequently divided the loot with the agents. Rightful owners sometimes were able to secure possession only after paying a tribute to the agent. Such practices provoked Secretary of the Treasury Hugh McCulloch to assert that every species of "intrigue and speculation and theft" could be found in the South.

The rapid rate at which the "Johnson states" were establishing their governments indicated that all or most of them would be ready to present themselves as completely restored by the time Congress opened in December, 1865. Mississippi held its constitutional convention in mid-August. In the following three months South Carolina, Alabama, North Carolina, Georgia, and Florida held conventions and rewrote their fundamental laws. In taking action on the three matters whose disposition the President required—the Confederate debt, slavery, and secession—they had the least difficulty with the Confederate debt. It had gone up in smoke with the surrender anyway, and most conventions recognized this by merely repudiating the debt. Only in the Carolinas and Georgia was there some hesitation. A strongly worded telegram from the President had a "most happy effect" on the Tar Heels. They reversed their decision to lay the matter on the table and proceeded to take the required action. Telegrams from Johnson and Seward goaded the Georgians into repudiation. Only South Carolina refused to comply.

On the question of slavery several of the conventions sought to save face. Some persons in Mississippi did not wish to convey the idea that they were giving up slavery voluntarily. Others feared that a categorical statement abolishing slavery would eliminate any possibility of compensation. But the North "was not to be trifled with," Judge William Yerger warned his Mississippi colleagues; and they finally passed a resolution abolishing the institution. South Carolina chose to forbid the reestablishment of slavery after asserting that slaves had been "emancipated by action of the United States authorities." Georgia inserted a clause in its new constitution acknowledging the abolition of slavery but added a proviso that the people of the state did not give up their right to ask compensation for slaves emancipated. A Virginia minister told the Joint Committee that while the slaveholders were reconciled to freedom for the slaves, they continued to hold the view that they should be compensated. If some freedmen entertained hopes of getting forty acres and a mule from the federal government, many of their former masters had equally illusory visions of securing compensation for their emancipated slaves.

The former Confederate states displayed almost no embarrassment in repealing their ordinances of secession. States like Arkansas and South Carolina repealed their ordinances without the slightest hesitation or reservation. Alabama, somewhat less unequivocal, indicated that the ordinance was now "null and void" without taking a position on its validity in the past. North Carolina seemed to go even beyond what the President required by declaring that the "supposed ordinance" of secession "is now, and at all times hath been, null and void." This was the external repudiation. In other ways the break with the past was not only more difficult but considerably less clear-cut.

After framing their constitutions the former Confederate states plunged into the task of electing officials and setting up governments. No serious consideration was given to broadening the franchise to include even a few blacks. In August, 1865, President Johnson urged upon Governor Sharkey of Mississippi a token enfranchisement of blacks for tactical purposes. "If you could extend the elective franchise to all persons of color who can read the Constitution in English and write their names, and to all persons of color who own real estate valued at not less than two hundred and fifty dollars, and pay taxes thereon, you would completely disarm the adversary, and set an example the other states will follow," he pleaded. If the Southern States would follow this suggestion, the Radicals "who are wild upon Negro franchise, will be completely foiled in their attempt to keep the Southern states from reviewing their relations to the Union by not accepting their senators and representatives." Neither Sharkey nor any of the other provisional governors paid the slightest attention to the President's suggestion.

The former Confederates, moreover, did not heed the signs clearly visible in the Northern sky. Individuals began to advocate suffrage for blacks as the only effective means by which they could protect themselves. The Republican conventions of Massachusetts, Vermont, Iowa, and Minnesota came out for suffrage for blacks. For many Northerners it was rapidly becoming a prerequisite for the entrance of the former Confederate states into the Union. For Southern whites such a proposition was absurd. They held that blacks were not only unprepared for politics but, because of their innate inferiority, were unfit. And when the very stability of the South was at stake, it would be the height of folly to experiment with suffrage for the former slaves. By October, Johnson conceded that the South must not be pressed on the matter for it "must have time to understand its new position."

On the whole, the basis for the franchise was the same as before the war. In some places Unionists had difficulty in exercising the franchise. A Fredericksburg, Virginia, Unionist flatly asserted that he and his political compatriots were not allowed to vote. Meanwhile, all over the South ex-Confederates were elected to office. The Vice-President of the Confederacy, four Confederate generals, five Confederate colonels, six Confederate cabinet officers, and fifty-eight Confederate congressmen were elected to the Thirty-ninth Congress, which met in December, 1865. At the state level former Confederate military and civilian officers dominated the governments. In both houses of the Louisiana legislature former Confederate officers wore their uniforms. In Madison County, Alabama, a man accused of the murder of a Union general was elected sheriff. In the Mississippi legislature two leading figures, Colonel Reynolds and Colonel Pierson, had commanded regiments in the Confederate army. In Georgia some connection with the rebel service seemed to be the "best indorsement in the eyes of the people." In Louisiana all the candidates for offices, including doorkeepers and clerks, printed their tickets "late of the Confederate army" in support of their bid for office, "and every man was elected from that class."

The bold election of former Confederates, many of whom were unpardoned, hurt what chances Johnson's policy had of immediate success. Despite the fact that the President did what he could to restore many former Confederates to full citizenship, he was greatly embarrassed by the lack of prudence and modesty on the part of the late enemies of the United States. After the North Carolina elections Governor W. W. Holden sent a telegram to President Johnson saying that the results, with so many former Confederates the winners, had greatly damaged the chances for the restoration of normal relations. He also advised the numerous ex-Confederates who had been elected to Congress not to rush to present themselves when the Thirty-ninth Congress was being organized, lest they unduly offend those in the North who wished harsher treatment for the South. He began to insist that Confederate officeholders not take office until they had been pardoned. Thus, he would not recognize Benjamin G. Humphreys as governor of Mississippi and he suspended John T. Monroe as mayor of New Orleans until each had been pardoned.

The business of reconstructing the former Confederate states was safely in the hands of former Confederate leaders in the fall of 1865. Among the governors were South Carolina's James L. Orr, late of the Confederate Senate, and Mississippi's Humphreys, who had served the Confederate cause as a brigadier general. Militia colonels and cavalry captains found opportunities for service as members of the legislatures, as sheriffs, local judges, and the like. Whatever their views regarding reconstruction, the former Confederates could look forward to an important role in the formulation and execution of postwar policies.

The Southern states, therefore, under former Confederate leadership undertook in a variety of ways the stupendous task of recovery. A significant and sympathetic recognition of the prevailing destitution was the enactment of stay laws for the relief of debtors. Mississippi suspended for almost two years its laws covering the collection of debts, while Georgia's Relief Act suspended the sale of property for debt for an indefinite period. In South Carolina Governor Orr persuaded General Sickles to issue an order abolishing imprisonment for debt and preventing foreclosure for twelve months. Meanwhile the legislature authorized the issue of

$300,000 in bonds to purchase corn for the starving population. Fearing the large-scale migration of whites as well as blacks to other parts of the country or to Latin America, several legislatures took steps to encourage immigration of Europeans and of some Northerners. To encourage the flow of capital into their states the legislatures exempted new factories from taxation for a period of years and extended other favors.

Some of the Southern legislatures issued mortgage bonds for the repair of railroads, bridges, and public buildings. They built penitentiaries, asylums for the insane, and hospitals. South Carolina's new penitentiary could accommodate three hundred convicts. They did not forget the Confederate veterans, of course. Benefits provided by the legislatures ranged from artificial limbs to pensions for indigent soldiers and indigent families of deceased servicemen.

The former Confederate states took steps, regarded by many as bold, to establish systems of free public education. And given the framework in which Southerners thought and operated, perhaps they *were* bold. Indeed, more young Southerners than ever before would be able to secure an education at public expense. But the young Southerners would have to be white. In July, 1865, the editor of the Charleston *Daily Courier* put it bluntly when he said, "The sole aim should be to educate every white child in the Commonwealth." A member of the Louisiana legislature said he was "not in favor of positively imposing upon any legislature the unqualified and imperative duty of educating any but the superior race of man—the White race." The new education laws in the former Confederacy reflected these views.

Georgia set up a "thoroughgoing" system of education for free white inhabitants between the ages of six and twenty-one. Texas provided a public school fund "exclusively for the education of all

45

the white scholastics." Florida, whose school superintendent declared that the whites cherished a "deadly hatred to the education . . . of the freedmen," did make a concession. If black males would pay a special tax of $1.25 per year, they could have their own "public" schools! Early in 1867 Arkansas established a system of free public education for whites only. The protagonists of rule by the former Confederates thus not only limited the franchise to whites but effectively excluded blacks from the emerging system of public schools. Blacks were ignorant and therefore not qualified to exercise the duties of citizenship, and the Southern officers in charge of reconstruction were committed to keeping them ignorant.

To finance the programs of public works, veterans' benefits, and education, the legislatures undertook to levy taxes that would not be too burdensome on an impoverished people. They enacted property taxes, poll taxes, sales taxes, and occupation taxes. Arkansas required two days' labor or $6.00 from each male citizen between eighteen and fifty years of age for the upkeep of the streets and roads. Mississippi placed a special tax of 2 per cent on property to finance its program of veterans' benefits. Some states required employers to pay poll taxes for employees who were delinquent. Alabama imposed an annual tax of $10.00 on vendors of newspapers and magazines published in the state; but vendors had to pay an annual tax of $50.00 if they handled magazines published anywhere in the United States outside Alabama. The resourcefulness and ingenuity of the legislators were constantly strained to provide financing for their programs, and they were not always successful. Everywhere there was opposition. Some taxpayers simply could not afford the new levies. Others were opposed to them in principle. The merchants of Charleston were bitterly against the state sales tax, while upcountry landowners organized to resist the new property taxes. In Arkansas many citizens opposed the amendment to the revenue laws that made possible the payment of $5.00 per day and 20 cents per mile to legislators. This opened the way, they insisted, for graft and corruption.

The legislators were indeed not uniformly scrupulous and unselfish in their devotion to the public service. There were graft and corruption among those afflicted with get-rich-quick fever. Others saw no harm in supporting legislation advantageous to themselves and their friends. The Louisiana convention of 1864, meeting years before any blacks or their supporters were in the government, was hardly a model of good government. It ran up a bill of $9,400 for liquor and cigars, $4,394 for carriage hire, and $4,237 for newspapers for delegates. More than $156,000 was appropriated for printing the journal and debates of the convention. By September, 1866, four Arkansas county tax collectors had made no report whatever, and one was known to have absconded with most of his collections.

Until recently historians gave only scant attention to the work of the Southern legislatures in 1865–67 in the general area of social and economic reconstruction. Meanwhile, they gave much more attention to the enactment of laws affecting blacks. This is understandable, for the "black codes" enacted within a year following the Civil War were the greatest concern of the Southern legislatures. They forecast, to a remarkable degree, the future attitude of former Confederates toward the place of blacks in the South and in American life. While there were variations from state to state, they embodied some common features. They recognized the right of blacks to hold property, to sue and be sued, and to have legal marriages and offspring. There were important qualifications, however: blacks were competent witnesses only in cases where one or both parties were blacks; those who intermarried with whites were guilty of a felony, punishable by a long prison term.

Apparently more important to the former slaveholders than the above strictures were the laws covering contracts between black laborers and white employers. Mississippi authorized "any person" to arrest and return to his employer any black who quit before the expiration of his contracted term of labor. For this the person was to receive $5.00. Most states had stern provisions against enticing or persuading a black to desert his legal employment before the expiration of his contract. There were also apprentice laws that gave preference to former owners in hiring minors whose parents were not providing for their support. A final feature of the labor provisions of the black codes was the vagrancy laws. In Mississippi all persons not lawfully employed by January, 1866, were to be arrested as vagrants and, if convicted and unable to pay the fine of $50.00, were to be hired out to the person who would pay the fine and require the shortest period of labor in return. Similar laws were enacted in other states.

Other state laws and town ordinances were designed to maintain what the legislators considered due subordination of the freedmen. They were to handle no firearms or other weapons, and they were to possess no alcoholic beverages. In Opelousas, Louisiana, no black person was allowed to come within the limits of the town without special permission of his employer. Many communities required blacks to be off the streets by a specified hour, while others had laws against blacks using "insulting gestures" or "exercising the function of a minister of the Gospel" without a license. Most of the laws employed such terms as "master" and "servant" and clearly implied a distinction that consigned blacks to a hopelessly inferior status. Small wonder that Professor John W. Burgess concluded in 1902, "Almost every act, word or gesture of the Negro, not consonant with good taste and good manners as well as good morals, was made a crime or misdemeanor, for which he could first be fined . . . and then consigned to a condition of almost slavery for an indefinite time, if he could not pay the bill." And Herman Belz has observed that the works by Burgess and his contemporary, William Archibald Dunning, were not soon superseded, in part because subsequent historians preferred to examine social and economic issues instead of constitutional and legal issues. Perhaps it was also because subsequent historians were reluctant to challenge the constitutional and legal arguments set forth by Burgess and Dunning.

The enactment of these black codes confirmed the North's worst fears. Reformers believed that the former Confederates were attempting to re-establish slavery. Businessmen were discouraged from investing in an area where labor was still to be dominated by the planter class. Republican politicians saw in the black codes an important vehicle for the reconstitution of the Democratic party of the South. Northerners would convert the state of Mississippi into a frog pond, declared the Chicago *Tribune,* before they would permit the black codes to "disgrace one foot of soil in which the bones of our soldiers sleep and over which the flag of freedom waves." These first fruits of reconstruction were a "deplorable harvest," declared Horace Greeley, and the sooner the North could gather the tares, "plough the ground again and sow new seed the better." Some condemned Mississippi's law prohibiting freedmen from acquiring farm lands, while others called the restrictions on the competency of blacks as witnesses an "outrage against civilization." To an increasing number of Northerners, reconstruction in the South by the former Confederates was the undoing of Appomattox.

But there were also some white Southerners who were convinced that their compatriots had gone too far in enacting their black codes. They were not unaware of the North's many "anti-

Negro" laws, including vagrancy laws, suffrage restrictions, and laws against intermarriage. The North was *in,* however, and would sit in judgment over the South. Writing in the Charleston *Daily Courier,* a local critic declared that "under the circumstances it would have been better to have made no such ostentatious legal and judicial distinctions between the races, but to have modified slightly the common law. . . . This would have been less expensive and onerous to the people and certainly less offensive to those whose renewed antagonism it were folly to invoke." The black codes had brought reproach upon the state of Mississippi, declared the editor of the Columbus *Sentinel,* and the men who enacted them were "as complete a set of political Goths as were ever turned loose to work destruction upon a state. The fortunes of the whole South have been injured by their folly." Former Governor Sharkey of Mississippi told the Joint Committee that his state's ban on freedmen's acquiring farm land was "foolish." A recent authority on Mississippi reconstruction has concluded that the black code "was not approved by the best thought of the state."

The spirit that lay behind the black codes and other reconstruction measures of the former Confederates was a disquieting feature of "home rule." The optimism inspired by the Johnson policies swept many Southerners into a feeling of confidence bordering on arrogance that they could not or would not suppress. Provisional Governor B. F. Perry of South Carolina had said that the government of his state was a "white man's government and intended for white men only." All the new governments seemed to agree. In his inaugural address in December, 1865, Governor R. M. Patton of Alabama said, "In the future, as had been the case in the past, the state affairs of Alabama must be guided and controlled by the superior intelligence of the white man." During the fall of 1865 the Jackson, Mississippi, *News* carried on its masthead the unequivocal statement, "This is a white man's country—President Johnson."

The violence directed against blacks on almost every hand indicated how determined the former Confederates were to maintain this white supremacy. Organized bands of white hoodlums had systematically and regularly terrorized the black population since the end of the war. Emancipation had removed the freedman's immunity from wanton and indiscriminate violence at the hands of the "superior race." Thus, the road stood all but wide open, as Wilbur J. Cash has said, "to the ignoble hate and cruel itch to take him in hand which for so long had been festering impotently in the poor whites." There was an open season on blacks; groups like the Regulators, Jayhawkers, and the Black Horse Cavalry were committing the "most fiendish and diabolical outrages." In Gallatin, Tennessee, and the surrounding area these bands of outlaws became so formidable and bold that the commander of the United States troops in the Department of Tennessee was compelled to dispatch a company of troops there as well as to several Kentucky communities. These so-called protective societies were popular with both the general public and the governments in the former Confederacy. In 1866 Thomas Conway told his New York readers that "the freedmen are treated harshly, unmercifully, unjustly. The public mind is not informed of one hundredth part of the wrongs endured by the patient freedmen."

The hostility to the education of freedmen was a part of the scheme to keep the whites superior. Within the first two years after the war Southerners themselves not only did little to educate blacks but they also resisted the efforts of others. The opposition to the Freedmen's Bureau was based, in part, on resentment against its education program. Other organizations and individuals interested in educating blacks were vigorously opposed. White teachers from the North, called by Robert Morris "An Army of Civilization," were ostracized and occasionally run out of the community. Freedmen's schools were often burned or razed. In dozens of other ways blacks were discouraged from seeking education. While many whites insisted that they were not opposed to the education of the freedmen, they did little or nothing to make it possible. Meanwhile they resented the presence of "white cravatted gentlemen from Andover" and "pretty Yankee girls" who ventured South to fill the void in the South's educational program. Already the pattern was emerging: bitter resentment of "outside interference" that would contaminate the freedmen and yet no effort by white Southerners to improve conditions.

The attitude of many Southerners toward the federal government and the Confederacy was a source of distress to those who hoped for an early reconciliation. Benjamin Truman, President Johnson's secretary, described the Southern attitude toward Washington as "indifferent." Carl Schurz asserted in 1866 that treason was not yet odious in the South. On the streets of New Orleans Confederate flags were peddled openly. In Alabama Governor Parsons called the flags "sacred souvenirs of the courage and endurance of those who went forth to battle under their folds." In New Orleans the St. James Hotel restaurant featured "Stonewall Jackson soup" and "Confederate hash," while in Richmond a new magazine, *The Land We Love,* was avowedly dedicated to glorifying the Lost Cause in verse, story, and song. The Confederacy was beaten, but it refused to die. The spirit of the South and the principles underlying it were very much alive. More than that, those who had fought against the Union were in control, pursuing most of their prewar policies as though there had never been a war. This was reconstruction, Confederate style!

4

Confederate Reconstruction under Fire

During the spring and summer of 1865 Thaddeus Stevens had tried to come to terms with the President, but to no avail. The member of Congress from Pennsylvania could be vindictive and harsh, and he was showing these qualities in the fall of 1865. There was work to be done—states to be restored and freedmen to be protected. No one was doing it. No one was forcing the rebels to pay the cost of the war. No one was taking steps to make certain that secession and war would never again be perpetrated against the Union. Stevens was disgusted. "Dead states cannot restore their existence," he told the House of Representatives in December, 1865. "The future condition of the conquered power depends on the will of the conqueror. . . . Congress must create States and declare when they are entitled to be represented." If it did not do its duty, it would "deserve and receive the execration of history and of all future ages."

Congress never accepted the reconstruction role of the President conceived by Lincoln and followed by Johnson. And when the presidential policy had the effect of bestowing on ex-Confederates positions of honor and trust, many Northerners became convinced that a lenient presidential policy was wrong and that Congress was right when it demanded harsher measures. The argument that

"Reconstruction." Drawing by Thomas Nast for the cover of
Harper's Weekly, August 15, 1868.

(Photograph, courtesy Mrs. Dorothy Porter, Howard University.)

Extract from the Louisiana constitution, with portraits of members of the convention and assembly, 1868.

Congress was the duly constituted agency to determine the status of the seceded states and to establish the conditions for their return to the Union was a telling one. When it could strengthen the hand of the Republican party, it was also an irresistible argument from the view of practical politics. How to check the President's course of action and ultimately how to take over the program of reconstruction became the prime concern of an increasing number of congressmen in the fall of 1865.

This explains the increasing intensity of the Northern criticism of developments in the South. Thus the black codes became the object of special attention and criticism, and every mistreatment of blacks and every act of white Southern arrogance became the occasion for bitter strictures by men in the North. "Now is the critical time," declared Wendell Phillips. "The rebellion has not ceased, it has only changed its weapons. Once it fought; now it intrigues; once it followed Lee in arms, now it follows President Johnson in guile and chicanery." When the President's emissaries to the South reported on conditions there, Northern leaders rejected the moderate observations of General Grant and Benjamin Truman and warmly received the adverse criticisms of Carl Schurz. Meanwhile, editors like Horace Greeley of the New York *Tribune* and E. L. Godkin of the *Nation* gave full play to every report from the South confirming their view that Confederate reconstruction was a giant step back toward slavery.

The freedmen themselves provided much grist for the mill of Northern critics. All across the South in the months following the war's end they met in convention and declared that they were being victimized by the merciless and inconsiderate policies of the former Confederates. Before the end of 1865 blacks held more than a dozen mass meetings and conventions that deliberated on the freedmen's plight and called on the President and Congress for protection.

Richmond blacks asserted that "invidious political or legal distinctions, on account of color merely . . . is inconsistent with our own self-respect." Those in Nashville were distressed that the federal government had left them without protection after knowing what services they had rendered "to the cause of the preservation of the Union and the maintenance of the laws." North Carolina blacks asked that "all the oppressive laws which make unjust discriminations on account of race or color be wiped from the statutes of the State." Similar pleas came from Jackson, Mississippi; Alexandria, Virginia; Charleston, South Carolina; and the several other places where blacks met. Invariably they asked for the franchise and insisted that on the basis of their contributions to the national welfare they were entitled to it.

Although the former Confederates had not completely formulated their policies by the time the Thirty-ninth Congress met, the advocates of stronger restoration measures had seen enough. They were convinced not only that no former Confederate state was entitled to have its representatives sit in Congress but that Congress should assume its lawful responsibility of taking over reconstruction.

Congress made short shrift of the Southern congressmen—impudent claimants, Stevens called them—by refusing to seat them, thereby serving official notice that it would not recognize the reconstruction program of the President. It then proceeded to set up the Joint Committee of Fifteen, composed of six senators and nine members of the House of Representatives, "to inquire into the condition of the States which formed the so-called Confederate States of America." It was to report whether any were entitled to be represented in Congress, and until such report was made and acted on by Congress, no member was to be received from any of the former Confederate states.

Counting among its membership twelve ardent Republicans and chaired by W. P. Fessenden of Maine, the Joint Committee was a natural forum for airing all the shortcomings of the President's reconstruction policies and justifying the need for a congressional program. The work of the committee is significant not only because it largely determined the course of future reconstruction policies but also because it was one of the first of the large-scale investigations that were to become important in the work of Congress in later years. It called 144 witnesses, including 77 Northerners living in the South, 8 blacks, and 57 white Southerners. Many of the Northerners were army officers and Freedmen's Bureau officials. Southerners appearing before the committee ranged from "loyalists" like John Minor Botts to prominent Confederate leaders like Alexander Stephens and Robert E. Lee.

The committee was especially interested in collecting information regarding the treatment of Northerners and blacks by white Southerners, the necessity for the Freedmen's Bureau and the federal troops in the South, and the attitude of former Confederates toward the federal government. Regardless of whether the committee "stacked" its witnesses, as has been freely charged, there can be no doubt that it was pleased by the testimony presented by most of the witnesses. They testified that the army and the Freedmen's Bureau, though abused and maligned, were necessary and that there was widespread hostility to the Union. "A freedman was shot on one of the plantations" in the Colleton District of South Carolina, "but by whom has not been ascertained. A woman was tied up by the thumbs, and kept so for more than an hour." "The spirit of the whites against the blacks in Virginia is much worse than it was before the war." When the work of blacks was unsatisfactory, they were "bucked and gagged" by seating them on the ground, "drawing their knees up, running a stick through over the arms and under the knees, and tying the hands in front, making them utterly immovable. Then a gag is put in the mouth and tied at the back of the head." So the testimony went, more than seven hundred pages of it, a dreary recital of inhumanity.

The testimony "forced" the committee to conclude that it was "madness and folly" to have permitted as much ex-Confederate rule as existed under the presidential policies. It insisted that adequate safeguards should be provided "before restoring the insurrectionary States to a participation in the direction of public affairs."

The provision of "adequate safeguards" became a major preoccupation of the Joint Committee in its latter days. How could the North, for example, prevent the Southern states from picking up twelve new seats in Congress as a result of counting each disfranchised freedman as a whole person instead of three-fifths of a person, as in the days of slavery? What kind of suffrage in the South would insure the proper kind of rule in the former Confederate states and their proper representation in Congress? These and other questions the committee attempted to answer through bills proposed by the group or by individual members.

Stevens, as early as January, 1866, sought to provide adequate safeguards against the "madness and folly" of Confederate reconstruction by asking approval of a resolution that, in determining congressional representation, would exclude *all* persons who had been denied the franchise because of race or color. But the resolution was defeated in the Senate, in part by men like Sumner who thought it compromised human rights. Stevens' real intention was to use the resolution as a lever to force black suffrage upon the

South. While he was deeply committed to the principle of black suffrage, some of his colleagues who favored it did so out of expediency. Neither blacks nor the Republican party in the South would be safe unless blacks had the vote. This argument was advanced by an increasing number of Northerners, regardless of whether they lived in communities that made any significant concessions to blacks on the question of civil rights.

Among the proposals that came from the Joint Committee was a bill to extend the life and enlarge the functions of the Freedmen's Bureau. When Congress sustained the President's veto on February 21, 1866, the Radicals—the group supporting a far-reaching program of congressional reconstruction—were more convinced than ever that they needed greater strength. The closely reasoned, hard hitting logic of the presidential veto indicated to the advocates of congressional reconstruction what they were up against in battling with the President. The proposed bill, he declared, created too much patronage, required a tax burden that was oppressive, called for military courts in time of peace, and was unnecessary, unwise, and unconstitutional. Johnson was a formidable adversary, and the Radicals began to become aware of it. In their desperate effort to build strength and achieve their aims, they sought the passage of the Civil Rights Act. But the President vetoed this measure on March 27. Two weeks later it was passed over his veto. The Act extended citizenship to "all persons born in the United States and not subject to any foreign power . . . of every race and color, without regard to any previous condition of slavery or involuntary servitude." It also declared that such citizens were to have the same right to make contracts, sue, hold real and personal property, and to enjoy "full and equal benefit of all laws and proceedings for the security of person and property, as is enjoyed by white citizens." This, in turn, fired and encouraged those who were opposed to rule by the former Confederates to the point that they were able to gather sufficient support for the passage in July, 1866, of a new Freedmen's Bureau bill over the President's veto.

If the Radicals regarded rule by the former Confederates as inimical to their political and humanitarian interests, the President regarded their assault on it as a personal affront to him. He therefore was not satisfied with vetoing bills designed to interfere with that rule. He went a step further and registered his strong antipathy to the sponsors of such legislation. In his Washington's Birthday speech, on the day after Congress had sustained his veto of the Freedmen's Bureau bill, Johnson heaped abuse on his adversaries. He called out the names of Stevens, Sumner, and Wendell Phillips as men opposed to the Union. When a voice from the crowd cried, "What about John W. Forney" (the Radical secretary of the Senate and editor of the Washington *Chronicle*), the President shouted, "I do not waste my ammunition on dead ducks."

The ensuing weeks increased the strain as Congress passed bills designed to intervene in the South and the President vetoed them. He contended that the proposed laws would break down the barriers that preserved the rights of the states. Congress contended that such laws were necessary to salvage the victory at Appomattox, which presidential reconstruction was dissipating. But the leaders of Congress began to doubt the ability of these laws to withstand the constantly changing political complexion of the lawmaking body itself. There were even graver doubts concerning the constitutionality of some of this legislation, particularly the new Civil Rights bill. To guard against the possible demise (either through repeal or adverse judicial review) of this "cornerstone" of congressional intervention, the Joint Committee brought forth on April 30, 1866, a set of resolutions that, with revision, became the Fourteenth Amendment.

The first section of the proposed Amendment defined citizenship and enjoined the several states from abridging or violating the rights of citizens to life, liberty, property, and equal protection of the laws. The second section proposed to reduce the representation in Congress of any state denying male inhabitants the franchise, in the proportion which the number of such male citizens bore to the total number of adult male citizens in the United States. A third section excluded from seats in Congress, the electoral college, and other federal offices all persons who, after serving in the federal government under oath, had served in the rebellion or supported it in any manner. The final substantive section upheld the validity of the federal public debt while calling for the repudiation of the Confederate debts and all claims involving compensation for emancipated slaves. The bill promising readmission of the Southern states upon ratification of the Amendment was tabled and allowed to die in both houses by mid-July, 1866. The attitude persisted, however, that no state would be admitted until it had ratified the Amendment.

There were some, like Sumner, who fretted that the proposed Amendment did not provide adequate guarantees of suffrage for blacks. Sumner said that without a provision for such suffrage the Amendment was as bad as the leg of mutton served to Samuel Johnson at dinner, "ill-fed, ill-killed, ill-kept, and ill-dressed." Some others, in Northern states where blacks could not vote, feared that the Amendment went too far, by indirection at least, in supporting suffrage for blacks in the North as well as in the South. But most talk of such suffrage in the North was discouraged, while the Radicals insisted that the Amendment would open the way for the prompt and orderly readmission of the Southern states. Within a few weeks after Tennessee ratified the Amendment its senators and representatives were seated in Congress. This was an impressive beginning for leaders like Stevens who hoped that more Northern Radicals would be elected to Congress on the strength of a new and successful congressional policy in the South. But, as the Radicals were to discover, Tennessee did not point the way for the South despite Governor Brownlow's success in getting that state to ratify the Fourteenth Amendment.

The consideration of the Fourteenth Amendment by Congress proceeded in an atmosphere of increasing doubt regarding the wisdom and justice of presidential reconstruction in the South. In Memphis, for example, there was rioting from April 30 to May 2, growing out of conflicts between black soldiers and white peace officers. After several jostling incidents, white mobs joined the police in an indiscriminate attack on the black population. At the end of three days General George Stoneham, in command of federal forces in the district, was able to establish order. By that time forty-six black men, women, and children had been killed, and more than eighty had been wounded. One white man had been injured. Four churches and twelve school buildings of blacks had been burned. General Stoneham reported that after the first day blacks had nothing to do with it except "to be killed and abused." Two days later the Memphis *Avalanche* boasted, "Soon we shall have no more black troops among us. Thank heaven the white race are once more rulers of Memphis."

Reaction outside Memphis was immediate. The Tennessee legislature, goaded by Parson Brownlow, placed Memphis police under state commissioners. General Stoneham set up a military board to conduct an investigation. Freedmen's Bureau officials also looked into the matter. The House of Representatives sent a special three-man committee, headed by Elihu B. Washburne, to conduct an on-the-spot inquiry. One pregnant black woman told how a group of white hoodlums robbed her while one of them raped her. Another told how white men murdered her husband by shooting him in the head several times as he lay ill. After hearing 170 persons, white and black, the committee concluded that the white mob had been "actuated by the deadly hatred of the colored race," and that its deeds were almost without parallel in the history of nations.

Violence continued, and each incident confirmed the view of Northerners that drastic action should be taken in the South. The riot in New Orleans on July 30 was regarded by some as the last straw. The conflict there grew out of the attempt of some Radicals to disfranchise certain Confederate veterans and, perhaps, to give the vote to some freedmen by reconvening the convention of 1864 in which there had been no representation of Confederates. When a procession of blacks stopped to cheer the assembly on July 30, a riot ensued. Approximately thirty-four blacks were killed, and more than two hundred were injured. Four whites lost their lives; ten policemen were injured. Few if any Northerners regarded this as merely another election riot in traditionally violent New Orleans. It was, perhaps, no more than this, with the additional factor that an issue in this election was suffrage for blacks. To most Northerners the riot was another step back toward slavery and another attempt of the former Confederates to intrench themselves.

There was the usual congressional investigation, and the findings were as sensational as they were unsavory. At the height of the riot, it was learned, a white lad, less than fifteen years old, was seen chasing a black man and brandishing a pistol. He explained to an interrogator that the convention had been reconvened to take away his vote. An unarmed musician with the Seventy-third Regiment told how he was shot by a member of the police force although he had been promised that he would not be harmed if he surrendered. Others told how they saw blacks shot down in cold blood, and whites, known to be Radicals or friends of blacks, shot or injured in some other way. General Sheridan reported that some of his men who saw the affair from first to last declared that "at least nine-tenths of the casualties were perpetrated by the police and citizens by stabbing and smashing in the heads of many who had already been wounded or killed by policemen." He said that it was not just a riot, but "an absolute massacre by the police . . . a murder which the mayor and police . . . perpetrated without the shadow of necessity."

It is almost impossible to exaggerate the Northern revulsion to incidents like the Memphis and New Orleans riots and numerous other altercations of less magnitude. Small wonder that the Fourteenth Amendment seemed more and more indispensable to the establishment of a just peace in the South. "The hands of the rebel are again red with loyal blood," shouted the New York *Tribune;* and the rebels were daily becoming stronger. At the National Union Convention which met in Philadelphia on August 14, they were very well represented; and they enjoyed a status and prestige that many felt they did not deserve. They had the initiative, however, and they kept it throughout the convention, which indorsed the Johnson policies and listened to an impressive message from the President. A few days later a delegation from the convention called on the President. In his remarks to the group he referred to Congress as a body representing only some of the states. Meanwhile, Southerners continued to have the "shackles upon their limbs and are bound as rigidly by the behests of party leaders in the National Congress as though they were in fact in slavery."

In September the Radicals staged a convention of "Southern loyalists" in the same city. It was denounced by Southerners and Democrats as a "black and tan convention," and a congregation of "nigger worshippers." And, as the earlier convention had praised the President's policies, this one condemned them and called for an end to rule in the South by the former Confederates. Speakers lashed out at the President's policies, one calling him a tyrant. Albion W. Tourgee, the Ohio lawyer who had settled in North Carolina on what he was later to call "A Fool's Errand," spoke out in favor of suffrage for blacks. But not all the delegations were willing to go that far. The presence of the black leader Frederick Douglass as a delegate from Rochester was a source of much embarrassment to some who could not bring themselves to indorse either equality or suffrage for blacks.

Already the President had taken his case to the people in the attempt to secure the election of members of Congress who approved his reconstruction program. The ill-fated "swing around the circle" began August 28. In the company of Secretary of State William H. Seward, Postmaster General Alexander W. Randall, General Ulysses S. Grant, and others, Johnson went through Baltimore, then to Philadelphia, several New Jersey towns, and New York City. From there he went to Albany, Buffalo, Erie, Cleveland, Detroit, Chicago, St. Louis, Indianapolis, Harrisburg, and back to Washington. In the principal cities as well as at whistle stops he never failed to inveigh against Congress, attacking the Civil Rights Act and the Fourteenth Amendment as well as the supporters of these measures.

Johnson accused his opponents of preaching more bloodshed and civil war. He said that they had neither charity nor wisdom. He asserted that were Andrew Jackson and Stephen A. Douglas alive they would support his policies. His careless and irresponsible harangues in Philadelphia, New York, and elsewhere were embarrassing to his friends and revolting to his critics. His undignified exchanges with boisterous hecklers and his ill-tempered comments directed toward all who differed with him played into the hands of his enemies. In Chicago banners waved proclaiming "No Welcome to Traitors," and in Indianapolis and Pittsburgh the President was literally driven from the platform. He did his own cause no good whatever, and long before November it was widely conceded that the congressional elections would substantially improve the position of the Radicals. While the Radical victories were not overwhelming, they were in many places decisive. In Indiana the Radicals won eight out of eleven seats in Congress. In New York they won nineteen of the thirty-one seats. And so the President's position deteriorated with the victories of his opponents.

The election results seemed to indicate that the Radicals would be in a position to demand the ratification of the Fourteenth Amendment by the former Confederate states. Perhaps they would demand much more. The South despaired, and it found in the President a source of great consolation. Reversing an earlier decision to be conciliatory to Congress and to advise the South to accept the Amendment, his message to the second session of the Thirty-ninth Congress opened the old wounds and criticized that body for failing to admit Southern members. Thus, the Southern states were emboldened, even in the face of superior Radical strength, to continue their policy of rejecting the Fourteenth Amendment.

Before the end of 1866 Texas, South Carolina, Georgia, Florida, North Carolina, Arkansas, and Alabama had rejected the Fourteenth Amendment. In the first months of 1867 Virginia, Louisiana, and Mississippi turned it down. Many former Confederates agreed with Governor Walker of Florida when he said, "we will be taxed without representation, we will quietly endure the government of the bayonet . . . but we will not bring as a peace offering the conclusive evidence of our own self-created degradation."

If the Southern states needed any consolation for their action, they found it in the equivocation of the Northern states on the question of ratifying the Fourteenth Amendment. Aside from Connecticut and New Hampshire, both of which approved it within one month, most of the other Northern states either dragged their feet or gave no immediate consideration to the Amendment. Few Northern states got around to considering it before the beginning of 1867. In some states—Pennsylvania, for example—debate over ratification was bitter, and both the wording and content were severely criticized. One opponent objected because the Amendment would make blacks the political and social equal of whites. Another saw in it a desperate effort by the Republicans to secure their political ascendancy through extending suffrage to blacks. Gradually, in the winter and spring of 1867 the Northern states ratified the Fourteenth Amendment, but not before they had set a bad example for the Southern states. Congress and its Northern supporters concluded that greater pressure would have to be exerted on the South to secure ratification. There was now sufficient strength in Congress to force this and some other changes on the South. This is what Congress proceeded to do in the late winter of 1867.

5

Challenge by Congress

After the election of 1866 several persons had scores to settle with Andrew Johnson. Some were insulted by remarks he had made. Others were outraged by what they regarded as his abuse and misuse of power. Stevens could not forget that the President had shouted "Hang Thad Stevens" to large crowds in Cleveland and St. Louis. The editor of the Boston *Commonwealth* was so enraged over the Johnson policies that he advocated the abolition of the presidential office. Charles Sumner, anxious to destroy presidential power within the framework of the Constitution, said, "Anything for human rights is constitutional." These were the spokesmen for the group that now gained the initiative in the fight against Johnson.

The erosion of presidential authority had proceeded steadily since the accession of Andrew Johnson. The persistent rejection by Congress of representatives and senators chosen in the former Confederate states emphasized the impasse that had developed. But the open conflict between Congress and the President and the decisive victory of the anti-Johnson forces in the election of 1866 insured the ascendancy of Congress. Given the temper of the campaign and the exultation of the Radical leaders after their victory, it is not surprising that the leaders in Congress proceeded to make good their domination as soon after the election as possible. Immediately upon the opening of the second session of the Thirty-ninth Congress, numerous bills were introduced that looked toward strengthening the position of Congress in reconstruction and, consequently, limiting the political power of the former Confederate states. One way this could be done was by giving blacks the vote. This means of broadening the franchise, already an old and highly controversial issue, was raised again in December. Sumner's bill providing for suffrage of blacks in the District of Columbia passed both houses after the usual acrimonious debate; but the President promptly vetoed it. The strength of the Radicals was clear in the prompt and decisive manner in which Congress overrode the veto.

In January, 1867, Congress insured the early enactment of a program of reconstruction by providing that the first session of the new Congress could begin in March instead of the following December. The general principles of congressional reconstruction were outlined in the act of March 2, 1867, "to provide for the more efficient Government of the Rebel States." The historic bill had begun its journey through Congress a month earlier. In the Senate it had been slightly modified by a group of apprehensive Republicans and Democrats. In its final form it divided the former Confederate states into five military districts: (1) Virginia; (2) North Carolina and South Carolina; (3) Georgia, Alabama, and Florida; (4) Mississippi and Arkansas; (5) Louisiana and Texas. Each district was to be commanded by an officer not below the rank of brigadier general with an adequate military force to maintain the peace and enforce the law. Each commanding officer was authorized to supervise the election of delegates to state conventions that were to write constitutions and set up new governments. Adult males, regardless of color, who were not disfranchised for participation in the rebellion, were eligible to vote for delegates, and the new state constitutions were to provide for similar enfranchisement. When a majority of persons qualified as electors had ratified a constitution, when Congress had approved it, and when the state had ratified the Fourteenth Amendment, the state could be admitted to the Union and its representatives and senators seated in Congress.

The President was outraged by this assumption of complete responsibility for the reconstruction program by Congress. But he held his temper and in a carefully worded message gave his reasons for vetoing the Reconstruction Act. He described it as a measure "without precedent and without authority, in palpable conflict with the plainest provisions of the Constitution, and utterly destructive to those great principles of liberty . . . for which our ancestors have shed so much blood." The President said that blacks had not asked for the privilege of voting. Yet the bill "not only thrusts it into their hands, but compels them, as well as the whites, to use it in a particular way . . . without pausing here to consider the policy or impolicy of Africanizing the southern part of our territory, I would simply ask the attention of Congress to that manifest, well-known, and universally acknowledged rule of constitutional law which declares that the Federal Government has no jurisdiction, authority, or power to regulate such subjects for any State." He declared that by forcing the right of suffrage out of the hands of whites and into the hands of blacks the Congress had clearly violated this principle. The message fell on deaf ears, and the veto was promptly overridden in both houses.

The work of Congress had only begun with the passage of the first Reconstruction Act. On the same day, it passed the Tenure of Office Act to prevent the President from summarily dismissing cabinet members, such as Secretary of War Stanton, who were in sympathy with the new reconstruction program. It was also a device to strip the President of the great power he could wield through the use of the patronage. This bill, specially designed by Thaddeus Stevens to control and humiliate Johnson, had been introduced by him in early December, 1866. Also, on March 2, 1867, the Command of the Army Act became law. This measure severely limited the military powers of the President by requiring him to issue all military orders through the general of the army. Later in the month, on March 23, Congress passed the second Reconstruction Act, spelling out the details by which the military commanders were to reconstruct the Southern states. This involved the registration of voters who could take an "ironclad oath," the election of delegates, the assembling of conventions, and the adoption of state constitutions.

When some opposition to the reconstruction measures developed in the summer, Congress reassembled and passed a third act on July 19 that empowered registration boards to deny registration to persons who were not taking the oath in good faith. Alabamans defeated their proposed constitution by registering and then not voting on the constitution one way or the other. This feat led to the enactment of the fourth reconstruction measure in March, 1868. Thenceforth, a majority of the votes actually cast would be sufficient to put a new constitution into effect, even if a large number of registered voters stayed away from the polls when the constitution was up for consideration.

The South's first reaction to the new measures was not so much the sharp tactic of the Alabamans or even the violence directed against blacks and their Northern supporters. The former Confederates were stunned, almost numb. No one had heeded Johnson's warnings and vetoes. The North seemed as wrathful as Sherman's men had been in 1864, and the President and the white Southerners wrung their hands as they wondered what they should or could do. Perhaps the Reconstruction Acts would be rendered ineffective by the courts. White Southerners decided to try their hand at this orderly process of obstruction. In *Mississippi v. Johnson* the provisional governor of Mississippi tried to enjoin the President from enforcing the reconstruction measures. In April, 1867, the Supreme Court declined to interfere. In *Georgia v. Stanton* the governor of Georgia made a similar attempt, whereupon the Court declared that it had no jurisdiction. In *Ex parte McCardle* an attempt was made to nullify the military authority that Congress had assumed in the Reconstruction Acts, but the Supreme Court declined to consider the matter because Congress had repealed the act allowing the appeal of such cases from the circuit court to the Supreme Court.

The President was similarly frustrated, but his actions further disquieted the Radicals. He not only seemed to be giving advice to the former Confederates but was reported, on good authority, to have considered the possibility of advising that thousands of former Confederates to whom he had granted amnesty in his proclamation of September 7, 1867 enroll as voters. Perhaps the fear of removal from office caused him to reject this possibility. The President did, however, hope that he would be vindicated in the fall elections of 1867. Perhaps the people would finally register their revulsion against the very idea of so many unlettered blacks exercising the franchise. Some states seemed not to be alarmed. But Ohio rejected a suffrage amendment for blacks by 38,000 votes, and elected a Democratic legislature. The Democrats were likewise victorious in Connecticut. Pennsylvania went Democratic by a small majority. In New York the Democrats won by 47,000 votes. Even where Republicans were victorious, it was by a small majority; and some of their major proposals were defeated. New Jersey refused to delete "White" from its suffrage requirements, and Maryland adopted a new law that gave the vote to whites only.

These actions emboldened the President to denounce suffrage for blacks with new vigor in his message of December, 1867. The blacks of the South, he said, not only had no regard for the rights of property, but were "utterly so ignorant of public affairs that their voting can consist in nothing more than carrying a ballot to the place where they are directed to deposit it. . . . Of all the dangers which our nation has yet encountered, none are equal to those which must result from the success of the effort now making to Africanize the half of our country." This was a clear warning to Sumner and the advocates of suffrage for blacks that their proposal was not only unwise but that it would be opposed by the President in every possible way.

This bold presidential stance, together with the Democratic show of strength in the elections, doubtless fired the Radicals in their determination to get rid of the President. There had been talk of impeachment since the fall of 1866, and in the following year a move was made to carry it out. On January 7, 1867, a House resolution directed its Judiciary Committee to inquire into the conduct of the President and report whether he had been guilty of "high crimes and misdemeanors." In June the committee, by a vote of 5 to 4, decided that there was no ground for impeachment, but on the insistence of the minority the case was reopened and the committee continued to take testimony. Although the committee then "found" that the President's conduct warranted impeachment, its report was rejected by the House, 108 to 57, with sixty-seven Republicans voting with the majority. Not satisfied, the President's enemies persisted.

The hysterical fringe feared a dark plot by the President and his

Southern friends to block congressional reconstruction. The hostile, vindictive element concluded that it was time to give the President the ultimate humiliation he deserved. Various other elements thought the President's usefulness had come to an end. These and others found justification for impeachment in the dismissal of the Secretary of War, Edwin M. Stanton. This, they concluded, was a clear violation of the Tenure of Office Act. In August the President had suspended Stanton, and in December Johnson sent to the Senate, in accordance with the provisions of the Tenure of Office Act, his reason for the move. The Senate rejected the reason by a vote of 35 to 6; and on the next day, January 14, 1868, Grant, who had been acting Secretary of War, relinquished the office to Stanton. In February the President dismissed Stanton and appointed General Lorenzo Thomas, the Adjutant General, to the post. Stanton refused to vacate the office and issued a warrant for the arrest of Thomas. On February 22 the President sent to the Senate the name of Thomas Ewing of Ohio as Secretary of War; but since it was a holiday, the nomination was not received by the Senate until February 24. It was never acted upon. By that time Congress was concerned with another matter: the possible impeachment of the President for "the violation of a law of Congress and other offenses."

It was a moment of triumph for Thaddeus Stevens when he rose in the House on February 24, 1868, to begin a speech that, because of his weakened condition, the clerk had to finish. He made his point, however. He called on the House to restore democratic government to a "free and untrammeled people." This could be done only by removing the President, "the great political malefactor" who, at every turn, frustrated the will of the people. A committee was named to draw up the articles of impeachment. Nine of the eleven articles related to the removal of Stanton, a tenth had to do with Johnson's speeches, while the eleventh, an omnibus article, was an over-all condemnation of the President. In Stevens' words Johnson was thus "surrounded, hampered, tangled in the meshes of his own wickedness—unfortunate, unhappy man, behold your doom."

The tone set by Stevens brought a reaction against the Radicals that was to increase as the weeks passed. The press, even when sympathetic to the Radical cause, was shocked by Stevens' strictures. The *Nation* called his indictment of the President "painful reading." The New York *Herald,* somewhat less sympathetic, said that Stevens had the "boldness of Danton, the bitterness and hatred of Marat, and the unscrupulousness of Robespierre."

But while Stevens was in no physical condition to manage the impeachment trial, the prosecution did not suffer from lack of talent. The chairman of the impeachment managers was John A. Bingham of Ohio, formerly opposed to impeachment but now convinced that the country could be saved only by the removal of Johnson. Even more important was the talented, resourceful, vindictive Benjamin Butler, whose disdain for the President matched that of Stevens. He was to be the star counsel for the prosecution who would, by his own declaration, handle the impeachment like a case against any horse thief. The other managers, James F. Wilson, Thomas Williams, and John A. Logan, all faithful Radicals, gave assurance that the prosecution was in safe hands.

The managers pressed their case almost too vigorously. Butler said that the President was trying to overthrow Congress and establish absolute control. To indicate how desperate the situation was he waved a nightshirt allegedly stained with the blood of an Ohio carpetbagger who had been flogged by Mississippi ruffians. Thereafter, whenever Republicans urged legislation to establish greater federal control over the South, opponents would accuse them of "waving the bloody shirt." In the spring of 1868 it was used for one purpose, that of purging the government of its despised President. He was a Napoleon, a Caesar, a Cromwell! But even many Radicals recognized him as a powerless enemy whose influence was steadily waning. The *Nation* was correct in observing that he had been "completely disarmed, tied neck and heels," having lost the confidence of the South and won the utter disgust of the North.

Almost from the beginning it was clear that those who sought removal of the President were overplaying their hand. Although they had dropped the earlier absurd charges that Johnson had been involved in the plot to assassinate Lincoln, they were having difficulty in holding the sympathy of the public. Against the effective defense set forth by the President's able group of attorneys the managers found it difficult to make a water-tight case against Johnson. The *Nation* called Benjamin Curtis' defense of Stanton's removal "lucid and powerful." The New York *Herald* called William S. Groesbeck's defense speech "most eloquent." The work of William Evarts and Henry Stanberry in behalf of the President was equally impressive. The managers for impeachment had no arguments to match those of the counsel for the defense, and public sentiment seemed to drift toward support of the President.

When the vote was taken in the Senate on Monday, May 16, excitement and tension were almost unbearable. Over the weekend there had been much speculation and, perhaps, much pressure on the senators who were undecided as well as on those whose views were not known. On the eleventh article in the bill to convict the President the vote was 35 for and 19 against. This was one vote short of the necessary two-thirds. There was exultation among the Democrats and extreme depression among the Radicals. "The country is going to the devil" was the pronouncement of Thaddeus Stevens, yielding at last to the ravages of disease and old age. With little hope of seeing his dreams fulfilled he died in mid-August.

The general sigh of relief when the trial was over belied any widespread conviction that the country was going to the devil. The crisis was over and, for better or worse, the country had been saved from the great strain of removing a President from office. Even in the eyes of many Radicals the country had not gone to the devil. Political reconstruction of the South was already moving forward according to the congressional plan, and the prospects for new economic growth in the North and in the South were very bright indeed.

Neither the President nor his supporters seemed to be able to stem the tide of congressional reconstruction. In June, 1867, Johnson had instructed the commanding generals that those taking the oath of loyalty were the judges of their own honesty, and boards of registration were not to question their declarations. In the following month he removed General Philip Sheridan from the command of Louisiana and Texas and appointed General George H. Thomas, a Virginia Democrat, and then, in late November, his loyal supporter Winfield S. Hancock. Acting Secretary of War Grant pleaded with the President, "in the name of a patriotic people who have sacrificed hundreds of thousands of loyal lives," not to remove Sheridan. "General Sheridan has performed his civil duties faithfully and intelligently. His removal will only be regarded as an effort to defeat the laws of Congress. It will be interpreted by the unreconstructed element in the South . . . as a triumph." But Johnson, unimpressed, proceeded to remove not only Sheridan but several other commanding generals in the South. Soon he replaced General D. E. Sickles in the Carolinas with General E. R. S. Canby. It was widely believed, as Grant had predicted, that these and other shifts were made in order to soften congressional reconstruction in the South. Even so, it would take more than a shift of commanding officers to undo what Congress was doing, and it became more and more apparent that Congress would have its way even if its way was not always the best.

The new phase of reconstruction launched by the acts of 1867 was momentous in the history of the nation. One result of the legislation was to enfranchise approximately one million blacks. Most—but not all—of them were illiterate. Although thousands had voted earlier in the century, those Southern states that had once permitted blacks to vote had all disfranchised free blacks by 1835. Thus, in 1867, there were few, if any, blacks who had previously voted in a Southern state. Meanwhile, only those whites— easily a million or more—who could qualify to take the test oath were enfranchised. Not all these were literate, perhaps as many as 35 per cent being unable to read or write. Upon the shoulders of these two groups and of the Northern residents in the South rested the political reorganization of the former Confederate states.

From the fall of 1867 through the following year the Southern states, under the supervision of the commanding generals, went through periods of registration, held conventions, and wrote new constitutions in compliance with the Reconstruction Acts. This was no mean undertaking. With the traditional political leadership largely disfranchised, the commanding generals had to find registration officials and oversee numerous details as well as deal with the many problems related to administering the loyalty oath. When the registration had been completed in the ten former Confederate states, approximately 1,363,000 persons had qualified as voters. Of these, 660,000 were white and 703,400 were black.

These registration figures of both blacks and whites are remarkable. Most blacks had little knowledge of governmental machinery, but they manifested a strong desire to learn and participate. They had to overcome fears of reenslavement and reprisals by their employers and former owners for assuming their new roles as citizens. The registration figures of whites compared favorably, under the circumstances, with the total number of whites, 721,100, who had voted in the election of 1860. All whites who registered were required to take the "ironclad oath"; and even making ample allowance for Northerners and Union army personnel who registered in Southern states, the number of native whites who qualified and registered is impressive. Some were convinced that it was their duty to participate if they could qualify. Others registered in order to have a large total registration and, then, by refusing to vote, to contribute to the defeat of the new constitutions, which had to have the support of a majority of the *registered* voters, until the fourth Reconstruction Act was passed in 1868.

These proceedings in the South took place as the nation braced itself for the excitement of the quadrennial presidential campaign and election. This was not just another observance of an important and time-honored practice. It was the first time since the war that the Democratic party had had an opportunity to restore its position as a truly national party and to throw off the odium of secession. The Republicans, on the other hand, had another opportunity to test their strength as the party of union; and as the Southern states ratified the Fourteenth Amendment, the Republicans could measure their strength in those areas undergoing *Republican* congressional reconstruction. The nation in general would watch with peculiar interest every development in the South that was even remotely related to the national political picture. The reentry of the former Confederate states, the part played by the black electorate, and the comparative strength of the two parties in the South proved of particular interest in the election of 1868.

The Republicans, with great political sagacity, nominated General Ulysses S. Grant. He was a celebrated war hero, the symbol of Union and conciliation without any close identification with the extreme Radical wing of the party. He had been vilified by the President when he refused to replace Stanton as Secretary of War. This endeared him to Johnson's enemies. Moreover, he held no strong economic views that would interfere with the Republican determination to maintain a close alliance between government and business. Johnson hoped to capture the Democratic nomination and thus rescue himself from the humiliation he had suffered through impeachment, but the Democrats would have none of him. Chief Justice Chase, popular among the Democrats for his handling of the impeachment trial, hoped to be named by the Democrats when it became clear that he would not get the Republican nomination. E. L. Godkin, forthright editor of the *Nation,* wrote that "what in other men is a craving for the presidency seems to have been in Chase a lust for it." Chase wrote numerous letters to important editors and others indicating his availability. His views on the vote for blacks and, perhaps, his popularity among certain Northern businessmen caused the Democrats to turn finally to Horatio Seymour, the wartime governor of New York.

The Republicans waged their campaign on their war record and on the alleged treachery of the Democrats. They warned the country that a Democratic victory meant the complete undoing of the reconstruction program then in progress. The Democrats, hopelessly divided on economic matters, denounced the military despotism of congressional reconstruction and called for state regulation of the suffrage question. Johnson, disappointed and dejected, sat out the campaign as did many of his friends. Violence was widespread in the South, and campaign funds flowed freely in the

North. In the end the Democrats were no match for the financial resources of Henry and Jay Cooke, the cartoons of Thomas Nast in *Harper's Weekly,* and the Republicans' claim that they had saved the Union. Grant was victorious in twenty-six states, with an electoral vote of 214 to 80 for Seymour, who carried eight states. The popular vote was much closer—3,012,833 votes for Grant and 2,703,249 for Seymour. The Radicals had their President, but the show of strength by the Democrats could not be ignored.

Six weeks after the election the outgoing President issued his last proclamation of amnesty. After his second general amnesty proclamation of September, 1867, only about three hundred ex-Confederates remained on the list of exceptions. On July 4, 1868, the President's third proclamation had pardoned all persons except those who were under indictment for treason or some other felony. Now, at Christmas, 1868, the President proclaimed a universal amnesty that extended pardon to practically all former Confederates, including Robert E. Lee and Clement Clay.

As if to protect the freedmen from the growing political power of the pardoned former Confederates, Congress once again turned its attention to the suffrage question. Few were satisfied with the temporary suffrage arrangements in the reconstruction legislation or with the vague provisions in the Fourteenth Amendment. In 1868 numerous suffrage amendments were introduced in each house, and in January, 1869, the House of Representatives passed a resolution that became the basis for the Fifteenth Amendment. After joint consideration by both houses it passed the Senate with some alteration, but the House fretted over the changes. It was not until late February, 1869, that the new Amendment was ready for submission to the states. The opposition of the Southern Democrats and a considerable number of citizens elsewhere was not sufficient to prevent its ratification; and the declaration that the right to vote "shall not be denied . . . on account of race, color, or previous condition of servitude" became a part of the Constitution on March 30, 1870. Already, however, in the former Confederate states, if not in many other parts of the Union, blacks were voting and holding office.

6

The South's New Leaders

The Act of March 2, 1867, was specific about the qualifications of those who were to have a voice in the new program of reconstruction. Constitutions were to be written by delegates "to be elected by the male citizens of the state, twenty-one years old and upward, of whatever race, color, or previous condition, who have been resident in said state for one year . . . except such as may be disfranchised for participation in the rebellion or for felony at common law." It was no easy task to administer satisfactorily these provisions of the Act. The commanding generals in the Southern military districts were hard pressed to find competent and qualified registrars to enroll the electorate. They used Union Army officers and Freedmen's Bureau agents; and a few of them used some African Americans. Travel into remote areas was difficult, and in some instances weeks elapsed before registrations were received, compiled, and made ready for elections.

Some of the commanding generals felt a deep responsibility to provide a little political education for those voters who had never had the experience or the opportunity to participate in politics. Several of them gave explicit instructions to registration officials to provide the freedmen with adequate information regarding their political rights. Freedmen's Bureau officers and agents en-

gaged by the generals to work in the registration program helped
the new voters understand their rights and duties. When Bureau
officials had no political literature of their own to distribute, they
disseminated materials prepared by the Union League, which was,
as we shall see, easily the most active organization in the political
education of African Americans.

When the criteria for becoming electors were applied to the
people of the South, three groups qualified. One group was the
vast majority of blacks whose loyalty to the Union was unques-
tioned and who merely had to prove that they were not felons and
had lived in the state one year. Another was the Northerners who
had taken up residence in the South. If they met the residence
requirements, they were enrolled. Finally, there were the native
white Southerners who qualified to take the "ironclad oath," and
who were scrutinized with the greatest care. The rank and file
among these groups was to be the center of the controversy that
raged over the ensuing decade. Out of these groups were to come
the leaders who bore the majority responsibility for both the good
and the evil flowing from the difficult task of rebuilding the
South.

The entrance of African Americans into the political arena was
the most revolutionary aspect of the reconstruction program. Out
of a population of approximately four million, some 700,000 qualified as voters, but the most of them were without the qualifications to participate effectively in a democracy. In this they were
not unlike the large number of Americans who were enfranchised
during the age of Jackson or the large number of immigrants who
were being voted in herds by political bosses in New York, Boston,
and other American cities at this time. They were the first to admit
their deficiencies. Beverly Nash, an unlettered former slave sitting
in the South Carolina convention, expressed the views of many

President Andrew Johnson

Thaddeus Stevens,
representative from Pennsylvania

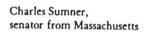

Charles Sumner,
senator from Massachusetts

(U.S. Signal Corps photographs,
Brady Collection, National Archives.)

THE FIRST
AFRICAN AMERICANS
TO SERVE IN THE
UNITED STATES CONGRESS

Joseph H. Rainey
of South Carolina, who entered
the House of Representatives,
December 12, 1870

(U.S. Signal Corps photograph,
Brady Collection, National Archives

Hiram Revels
of Mississippi, who entered
the Senate February 23, 1870.

(*Harper's Weekly*, February 19, 1870.)

when he said: "I believe, my friends and fellow-citizens, we are not prepared for this suffrage. But we can learn. Give a man tools and let him commence to use them, and in time he will learn a trade. So it is with voting. We may not understand it at the start, but in time we shall learn to do our duty."

Like Nash most blacks were illiterate. A slave existence could hardly be expected to prepare one for the responsibilities of citizenship, especially when there were laws, as there were in all slave states, banning the teaching of slaves. Even if blacks had been free, as were more than 200,000 in the slave states before the war, laws forbade their being taught to read and write. Indeed, when they came out of slavery many of them did not know their own names; many did not even have family names. It goes without saying that a considerable number had not the vaguest notion of what registering and voting meant.

None of this is surprising. It had been only two years since emancipation from a system that for more than two centuries had denied slaves most rights as human beings. And it must be remembered that in these two years the former Confederates, in power all over the South, did nothing to promote the social and political education of the former slaves. What is surprising is that there were some—and no paltry number—who in 1867 were able to assume the responsibilities of citizens and leaders.

Among South Carolina's African American leaders was state treasurer Francis L. Cardozo, educated at Glasgow and London, who had been a minister in New Haven and, after the war, was principal of a school for blacks in Charleston. Robert B. Elliott, born in Massachusetts, trained at Eton College in England, and elected to Congress in 1870, was urbane and articulate. J. J. Wright, a state supreme court justice, had studied at the University of Pennsylvania and had been a respected member of the Pennsylvania bar before moving to South Carolina after the war. Congressman James Rapier's white father sent him to school in Canada, and when he returned to his native Alabama after the war he had not only an ample formal education but a world of experience gained from travel and work in the North. Florida's secretary of state, Jonathan C. Gibbs, graduated from Dartmouth College and had been a Presbyterian minister for several years when reconstruction began. Among the African American leaders of North Carolina James W. Hood, assistant superintendent of public instruction, and James H. Harris, an important figure in the 1868 constitutional convention, were educated, respectively, in Pennsylvania and Ohio. Many others, among them Henry M. Turner of the Georgia legislature, Hiram Revels, United States senator from Mississippi, and Richard H. Gleaves, member of Congress from South Carolina, had much more than the rudiments of a formal education when they entered upon their official duties.

Significant among African American leaders were those who were almost wholly self-educated. Robert Smalls of South Carolina pursued his studies diligently until he had mastered the rudiments. Later he went to the United States House of Representatives. In Mississippi, John Roy Lynch regularly took time off from his duties in a photographer's studio to gaze across the alley into a white schoolroom, where he kept up with the class until he had mastered the courses taught there. When he became speaker of the Mississippi house and later a member of Congress, he relied on this earlier training. Before Jefferson Long went to Congress from Georgia, he had educated himself and had become a merchant tailor in Macon. There were numerous other self-educated African American leaders, including John Carraway and Peyton Finley of Alabama, James O'Hara and A. H. Galloway of North Carolina, and James W. Bland and Lewis Lindsay of Virginia. From this educated element came the articulate, responsible blacks who contributed substantially to the writing of the new constitutions and the establishment of the new governments in the former slave states.

Most of the African American leaders were ministers. A fair number taught school. Some were employees of the Freedmen's Bureau or another federal agency. Here and there one found one who had been trained in the law. There were, of course, farmers; and there were some artisans engaged in a variety of occupations. The economic interests and aspirations of the black leaders varied widely. It would be wrong to assume that they had no economic interests or that they had no views regarding the economic future of the South.

One of the really remarkable features of the African American leadership was the small amount of vindictiveness in their words and their actions. There was no bully, no swagger, as they took their places in the state and federal governments traditionally occupied by the white planters of the South. The spirit of conciliation pervaded most of their public utterances. In his first speech in the South Carolina convention Beverly Nash asserted that the Southern white man was the "true friend of the black man." Pointing to the banner containing the words "United we stand, divided we fall," Nash said, "If you could see the scroll of the society that banner represents, you would see the white man and the black man standing with their arms locked together, as the type of friendship and union which we desire."

Blacks generally wished to see political disabilities removed from the whites. In South Carolina several of them presented a resolution asking Congress to remove all such disabilities, and it was passed. In Louisiana they requested that former Confederates be permitted to vote but, for the time being, not to hold office. In Alabama James T. Rapier, a black delegate to the constitutional convention, successfully sponsored a resolution asking Congress to remove the political disabilities of those who might aid in reconstruction. In Mississippi a Democratic paper, the Jackson *Clarion*, admitted that in their general conduct black members "have shown consideration for the feelings of the whites. . . . In other words, the colored people had manifested no disposition to rule or dominate the whites, and the only Color Line which had existed, grew out of the unwise policy which had previously been pursued by the Democratic Party in its efforts to prevent the enjoyment by the newly-emancipated race of the rights and privileges to which they were entitled, under the Constitution and laws of the country." In South Carolina Beverly Nash declared that in public affairs "we must unite with our white fellow-citizens. They tell us that they have been disfranchised, yet we tell the North that we shall never let the halls of Congress be silent until we remove that disability."

Blacks attempted no revolution in the social relations of the races in the South. Francis B. Simkins in his "New Viewpoints of Southern Reconstruction" has accurately observed that "the defiance of the traditional caste division occasionally expressed in an official reception or in an act of the legislature was not reflected generally in common social relations." As a rule blacks conceded to the insistence of whites that they were a race apart; and they made little or no attempt to invade social privacies. They did not even attempt to destroy white supremacy except where such supremacy rejected blacks altogether as human beings, and there was almost nowhere any serious consideration given to providing legal approbation of interracial marriages. While blacks sought equality as human beings, they manifested no desire to involve themselves in the purely social relations of whites as individuals or as groups. "It is false, it is a wholesale falsehood to say that we

91

wish to force ourselves upon white people," declared the near-white P. B. S. Pinchback of Louisiana.

Nor did any considerable number of blacks seek to effect an economic revolution in the South. Henry McNeal Turner, the fearless African American leader who was almost universally disliked by white Georgians, did what he could to assist the whites in recovering their economic strength. In the Georgia convention he secured the passage of two resolutions that indicated a remarkable willingness to stabilize the economic life of the white community. One sought to prevent the sale of property whose owners were unable to pay their taxes; the other provided for the relief of banks. In South Carolina black leaders such as Robert DeLarge and Francis Cardozo supported relief measures with the full knowledge that whites would benefit as much as blacks.

The movement of Northerners into the South after the Civil War is a part of the exciting drama of the migrations that had seen the continent populated from ocean to ocean and had taken Americans, new and old, wherever opportunity beckoned. The movement into the South was greatly stimulated by the favorable observations of scores of thousands of Union soldiers who had seen action on Southern battlefields. Some were mustered out of the army while still in the South and, despite some Southern feelings of hostility against them, decided to adopt the South as their home. Others, back in their Northern homes, waited only for the first opportunity to return to the South. By the fall of 1866, for example, more than five thousand Union soldiers had settled in Louisiana alone. The movement was also stimulated by the large number of industrialists and investors who saw in the underdeveloped South an important new economic frontier. Those committed to the view that the South's recovery from the war would be accompanied by an era of unparalleled expansion began to move into the region, bringing with them their own resources, and often the resources of others, with which to build railroads and factories and to purchase farm land and other properties.

Many federal agents—some from the Department of the Treasury, others from the Freedmen's Bureau—settled in the South and called it home. Northern teachers, men and women, braved numerous indignities at the hands of hostile whites in order to teach blacks, and they cast their lot with the South. There were those from the North, moreover, who saw new political opportunities in the South. They hoped to use the newly enfranchised element and the problems arising out of reconstruction to achieve political power and economic gain. For them the South was a "happy hunting ground" that they could not resist. As to any frontier, there went to the South the adventurers, those who wanted to "get rich quick," and ne'er-do-wells who were fully prepared to embrace *any* cause, including Radical Reconstruction, that would benefit them.

These were the people who have been called "carpetbaggers" for more than one hundred years. This opprobrious term, used as early as 1846 to describe any suspicious stranger, was applied indiscriminately to all Northerners in the South during reconstruction. It has generally implied that as a group they had nothing in the way of worldly possessions and were thoroughly unprincipled in their determination to fleece and exploit the South until their carpetbags fairly bulged with the possessions of Southerners and they were forced to acquire new coffers in which to place their ill-gotten gains. They have been described as a group at work on a grand master plan to Africanize the country. One historian described them as "gangs of itinerant adventurers, vagrant interlopers" who were "too depraved, dissolute, dishonest and degraded to get the lowest of places in the states they had just left." These descriptions fall far short of the mark. They impugn the integrity and good intentions of thousands whose motives were otherwise. Even more important, perhaps, is the fact that such descriptions show no understanding of the variety and complexity of the motives underlying the migrations and no appreciation for the economic and political relationships that grew out of such motives.

There is no evidence that even the considerable number of African American migrants from the North were interested in "Africanizing" the country. Indeed the term was an extravagance, a flourish—like "Negro rule"—used to express disgust. The other common descriptions are equally inaccurate. As Thomas Conway pointed out a few months after the war, many Northerners, including the teacher, preacher, merchant, husbandman, mechanic, laborer, and discharged Union soldier, were ready to move South. He had persuaded Northern men to take $3,000,000 into the South to purchase land, make loans, and advances on crops. Their only fears were whether there was sufficient law and order to maintain security for their investments. But they went South, and they continued to go all during the reconstruction period. In November, 1865, Sidney Andrews observed that already several Massachusetts men were in business in Charleston; and he estimated that at least half the stores on the principal streets of the city were run by Northern men.

The careers of Captain H. S. Chamberlain and General John T. Wilder, both of Ohio, illustrate the kind of activities in which numerous so-called carpetbaggers were engaged. When Chamberlain was mustered out of the Union army in Knoxville, Tennessee, in 1865, he at once entered the iron and coal business in Knoxville and is regarded by some as the real founder of the modern iron industry south of the Ohio. In 1867 Chamberlain joined with General Wilder, late of Wilder's Lightning Brigade of Ohio, to organize the Roane Iron Company, which bought large tracts of coal and iron land and engaged extensively in the operation of coke works, iron mines, and furnaces. Together they became involved in many industrial and financial ventures, including the Dixie Portland Cement Company, the Brookside Cotton Mills of Knoxville, and the First National Bank of Chattanooga.

That all so-called carpetbaggers were not simply Radicals with no consideration for the welfare and development of the South can be seen also in the life of Willard Warner, planter, politician, and iron manufacturer. Born in Granville, Ohio, and educated at Marietta College, Warner served in the Union army and went to the Ohio senate in 1865. Two years later he moved to Alabama, and with his ample resources engaged in cotton planting for several years. He became active in Republican politics and served in the United States Senate from 1868 to 1871. Then he organized the Tecumseh Iron Company and served as president and manager until 1873. For this venture more than $100,000 was supplied by his Northern associates. Later he moved to Tennessee, where he had extensive investments and blast furnaces. The overthrow of reconstruction seems not to have affected this "carpetbagger," for as late as 1900 the Conservatives (the Democrats) in his adopted state elected him to the Tennessee legislature.

If some historians have reviled Northerners who settled in the South after the Civil War, their Southern contemporaries were inclined to be grateful to them for their contributions to Southern development. Clinton A. Cilley, born in New Hampshire and a Harvard graduate, settled in North Carolina in 1866. After a career in the law, including several years as a judge of the Lenoir Superior Court, he was called in 1900 "one of North Carolina's ablest lawyers and finest citizens." General Wilder, the iron manufacturer, was very popular among Southerners, including former

Confederates. During the Spanish-American War the governor of Tennessee named the training camp near Knoxville "Camp Wilder," in honor of the carpetbagger from Ohio. Lieutenant B. H. True of the 136th New York Volunteers, who settled in Georgia in 1865, was consistently popular with his new neighbors; they not only supported his newspaper, the *Appeal and Advertiser,* but elected him, as the "celebrated farmer from Morgan County," to the State Agricultural Society.

The interest of such men and groups of men in the political future of the South was real. With so much at stake in the way of investments and with full appreciation of the economic potential of the South they could not be indifferent to the uncertain political winds that were blowing across their adopted home. Their interest transformed itself into a strong desire to attain certain specific political goals for the South. One was the achievement and maintenance of law and order. They had seen enough hostility and lawlessness in many Southern communities to cause considerable uneasiness about the safety of their investments. They wanted governments that would insure this safety; and if they could facilitate the establishment of such governments, they would certainly do so. Another was the maintenance of a close alliance between government and the business community. They had seen the importance of such an alliance in numerous developments in Washington during the war and in the effective service that several state governments in the North had rendered the business community. Favorable banking and insurance laws, tax exemptions or rebates, land grants and other assistance to railroads were among the favors the government could and would, under certain desirable circumstances, grant to business and industry. If at all possible, Northerners would see that this was done in the South.

Finally, most Northerners in the South were convinced that

their goals could best be attained through a vigorous, well-organized Republican party throughout the South. This was, after all, the party responsible for the intimate relationship between government and business on the national level and in several Northern state governments. They knew that there was little chance of luring the former Confederates into the Republican party and that the Democratic party would oppose at every turn whatever Republicans attempted to do. Southern Democrats tended to equate Republicans with abolitionists and thus to regard them as the destroyers of the South's cherished economic and social system. Northern Republicans had to look to others in the South for political support.

A Republican in the South did not have to belong to the Thaddeus Stevens-Charles Sumner wing of the party to reach the conclusion that suffrage for blacks was not only desirable but imperative. For the conclusion was inescapable that the party's strength would come from blacks and from whatever support they could secure from loyal native white Southerners. They did all they could to promote the enfranchisement of blacks and draw them into the Republican party. This did not mean, however, that the so-called carpetbaggers were interested in "Africanizing" the South. Even when they undertook to "Northernize" the South, there was no revolution in the general social relations between blacks and whites. B. H. True, a New Yorker living in Georgia, said that he was as friendly toward blacks as anyone, "but there is an antagonism which we all have against the race; that I cannot get rid of; I do not believe any man can." Had these Radicals been radical on social questions, they would have opposed the laws against intermarriage that were enacted during the Radical regime. They would also have stood for one system of public schools open to all races, but their infrequent expressions in favor of such

97

a system were feeble indeed. These matters—unlike suffrage for blacks—were not among their primary interests, and they gave them scant attention.

It was only natural that Northerners in the South could wield political influence and exercise power far out of proportion to their numbers. They were the best prepared to step into the vacuum created by the disfranchisement of the former Confederates. They had training and experience in political and economic matters that neither blacks nor loyal native white Southerners had. They clearly knew what their interests were and how best they could be secured. Finally they had the support of the powerful, victorious party that was in control of affairs in Washington. While their influence in the South was not always decisive or even critical, it was invariably a factor in the determination of affairs, present and future, in the Southern states.

No group of postwar Southern leaders has been reviled or castigated—or misunderstood—more than loyal native white Southerners, commonly known as "scalawags." The term came in all likelihood from Scalloway, a district in the Shetland Islands where small, runty cattle and horses were bred. It was used in western New York before the Civil War in referring to a "mean fellow, a scape grace." In the South the term was used by the opponents of reconstruction to describe those they regarded as the lowest, meanest element in society. These were the Southerners who could swear that they had never voluntarily given aid, countenance, counsel, or encouragement to persons in rebellion and had exercised or attempted to exercise the functions of no office under the Confederacy. They were largely men who had opposed secession. The votes against secession in some state legislatures, together with the known sentiment against such drastic action, indicate that a considerable number of white Southerners dragged their feet or refused to have any part in the Confederate cause. Many had for years smarted under a system that gave every advantage to the planter class, to which very few of them belonged. They bitterly resented the course of action, pursued by the planter class, which had led to a war that, from their point of view, became more and more a "poor man's fight."

It is impossible to determine how many so-called scalawags were qualified to participate in reconstruction under the terms of the several acts of Congress. Likewise it is impossible to determine the extent to which those who took the "ironclad oath" were actually eligible to do so. After June, 1867, those who took the oath were, as President Johnson had indicated to the commanding generals, judges of their own honesty. Since the machinery as well as the personnel of registration was of questionable efficiency, it is entirely possible that many who were clearly not eligible registered anyway. There were some eligibles who refused to register, and many who were not eligible advised the loyal Southerners to have no part in the Radical regime. Others advised the eligibles to register and then defeat the Radical effort by voting against it. "If we are to wear manacles," said Governor Perry of South Carolina, "let them be put on by our tyrants, not ourselves."

But there were those in the South who counseled loyal Southerners to participate in the new reconstruction program and then to restrain any excessive or revolutionary tendencies that might militate against the best interests of the South. The fact that blacks were to participate did not degrade white Southerners or diminish their influence unless they purposely abandoned the field to blacks. The New Orleans *Picayune* told its readers that promptness in registering and voting would convince the North "that we mean to take care of our own affairs." The Savannah *News* gave similar advice when it declared that Georgia expected every man to do his duty and register without delay to show his reverence for his "noble commonwealth." The Charleston *Daily Courier* echoed the same view: "That you should register is an imperative duty which each man owes to himself, to his community and to his state."

A curious assortment of native Southerners thus became eligible to participate in Radical Reconstruction. And the number increased as the President granted individual pardons or issued new proclamations of amnesty. It became increasingly difficult to make a distinction between the views of the loyal white Southerners and the views of those whose citizenship was being restored. On political and social questions they ranged from the radicalism of James W. Hunnicut of Virginia, who stood for the full legal and social equality of blacks and whites, to the conservatism of Milton Candler, a Georgia senator who claimed that blacks were not citizens and therefore were not eligible to hold office. Certainly the majority of these loyal white Southerners could not be described as Radicals in the sense of embracing the policies and programs for blacks set forth by the Radicals in Congress. Often they advocated segregation of blacks and whites in educational and other institutions. Often they spoke as vigorously for the rights of the South as did any former Confederate. Their primary interest was in supporting a party that would build the South on a broader base than the plantation aristocracy of ante-bellum days. They found it expedient to do business with blacks and so-called carpetbaggers; but many returned to the Democratic party as it gained sufficient strength to be a factor in Southern politics.

These were the people who were called scalawags by their adversaries. They hardly deserved the name, nor did they deserve the numerous other opprobrious labels pinned on them by hostile critics. Wade Hampton called them "the mean, lousy and filthy kind that are not fit for butchers or dogs." Another called them "scaly, scabby runts in a herd of cattle." Even the historians have joined in the verbal assault on these loyal native Southerners. One describes scalawags as "vile, blatant, vindictive, unprincipled." Perhaps during the period of their ascendancy the scalawags committed many offenses against the social order; for the graft and corruption they must take at least a part of the blame. But their most serious offense was to have been loyal to the Union during the Civil War or to have declared that they had been loyal and thereby to have enjoyed full citizenship during the period of Radical Reconstruction.

It is extremely difficult to determine the strength of the three groups that dominated the South during Radical Reconstruction. There was constant fluctuation in the show of strength, particularly among the native white Southerners and the Northerners living in the South. And there was constant defection, with blacks dropping out of the picture under Ku Klux Klan or other pressures, with Northerners leaving or going over to the Conservatives, as the opponents of Radical Reconstruction were called, and with "loyal" white Southerners deviating from or deserting the Radical cause altogether. The best that one can do is look at the comparative numerical strength of the three groups and draw some inferences from the observation. A likely time for such a comparison is 1867–68, when the several state conventions wrote the new constitutions required by the Reconstruction Acts (see table).

The figures in the table illustrate several significant points. In the first place, except for South Carolina, African Americans enjoyed no numerical domination in the conventions. The only other state in which they were nearly a majority was Louisiana, where by agreement they were to constitute 50 per cent of the delegates. Thus "Negro rule," as reconstruction has been erroneously de-

CHAPTER 6

MEMBERSHIP OF STATE CONVENTIONS, 1867–68

State	Black	White			Total	Percentage		
						Black	White	
		Native	Northern	Total			Native	Northern
Alabama	18	59	31	90	108	17	55	28
Arkansas	8	35	23	58	66	13	52	35
Florida	18	12	15	27	45	40	27	33
Georgia	33	128	9	137	170	19	74	7
Louisiana	49	*	*	49	98	50	*	*
Mississippi	17	29	54	83	100	17	29	54
North Carolina	15	100	18	118	133	11	75	14
South Carolina	76	27	21	48	124	61	22	17
Virginia	25	33	47	80	105	24	31	45
Texas	9	*	*	81	90	10	*	*

* Further breakdown unavailable.

scribed, had an inauspicious beginning and, indeed, was never to materialize. Second, the so-called carpetbaggers were in the minority in every state except Mississippi. Many were so preoccupied with personal undertakings, or with setting up schools and churches, that they had no time for public service. Their position, however, was adequately represented by those new settlers who did find time to serve. Finally, the native whites had a larger numerical representation in the conventions than is usually recognized. Dominating several conventions, such as those in Alabama, Georgia, and North Carolina, and having substantial numbers in others, they were prepared to play a significant part in the deliberations and in the administration of affairs in their states.

Although leadership in the South came from these three groups, at least in the early days of congressional reconstruction, it does not follow that the leaders invariably worked together in promoting a Radical program. Their motives, values, and goals were not the same and their effort to work together was often strained because of these differences. Far from entering into any conspiracy to degrade and destroy the Southern way of life, they frequently worked at cross purposes. At times the position of the African American leaders approached that of the crusading abolitionists. Meanwhile, the so-called carpetbaggers were frequently preoccupied with building up the alliance between the business community and the Republican-controlled state government. All too often, moreover, the loyal white Southerners talked and acted like the conservative former Confederates whom they presumably opposed. Co-operation was at best loose and irregular, forced at times only by the threat of their common destruction. It was under these circumstances that the three groups of leaders forged a program for the reconstruction of the Southern states. How such a program actually emerged is one of the fascinating chapters in American history.

7

Constitution-making in
the Radical South

Early in January, 1868, the Reverend James Lynch, a black delegate to the Mississippi constitutional convention, listened atten-
tively to the proceedings. He was more than literate, and his years
in the ministry had provided him with poise as well as valuable
experience. The delegates were organizing the convention. One
white member moved that the word "colored" be added to the
name of each black delegate. In a flash the man who was later to
serve as Mississippi's secretary of state was on his feet. When he
was recognized, Lynch moved to amend the proposal to include
the requirement that the color of each delegate's hair should also
be added. It would seem that constitution-making in the Radical
South was not to be without its problems, large and small.

All over the South during 1867 and 1868 the new leaders grap-
pled with these problems as they framed constitutions and established governments under their new organic laws. There was much
heckling from the sidelines by critics, members of the old order,
who refused to concede that anything good could come out of conventions composed of carpetbaggers, scalawags, and blacks. South
Carolina whites, furious that the convention was held at all, called
the new constitution "the work of sixty-odd Negroes, many of
them ignorant and depraved, together with fifty white men, out-

casts of Northern society, and southern renegades, betrayers of their race and country." In North Carolina the convention, with 15 blacks out of 133 delegates, was described as "Ethiopian minstrelsy, Ham radicalism in its glory," containing "baboons, monkeys, mules, Tourgee [a white Northerner], and other jack-asses." Louisiana whites called their new constitution the "work of the lowest and most corrupt body of men ever assembled in the South. It was the work of ignorant Negroes co-operating with a gang of white adventurers, strangers to our interests and our senti-ments."

None of these strictures included a discussion of the merits or demerits of the new constitutions. They were the tirades of a people less concerned with the quality of government than with who exercised the powers of government. Their discussions con-tained no substantive criticism of the new governments, and they attempted to make their case against the new constitutions simply by name-calling. Today, of course, it is not enough to condemn the conventions for what the delegates wore, how black or white they were, or whether or not they had been slaves. The work of the conventions and the governments they created must be judged on the basis of a substantive evaluation of how well they served the states and the people.

In their constitution-making the new leaders of the South tried, first of all, to frame organic laws that would facilitate the readmis-sion of their states to the Union. In compliance with the congres-sional mandate, none of them placed any racial restrictions on the exercise of the franchise. Some of the states, like Alabama and Georgia, simply extended the suffrage to "every male citizen of twenty-one years old or upward." Others, like Florida and South Carolina, were more specific in their compliance with the Recon-struction Acts by extending the suffrage to adult male citizens "of whatever race, color, nationality, or previous condition." Alabama and Louisiana made specific exceptions of those who had been disfranchised by the Reconstruction Acts and the Fourteenth Amendment. The other conventions presumably felt that the federal government had made adequate provisions for the disfranchisement of those groups. It will be recalled that some of the African American delegates urged the speedy end to the disabilities suffered by former Confederates.

Even in the face of the disfranchisement of specific individuals, the framers of the state constitutions had no inclination to impose permanent suffrage restrictions on any groups. There was, rather, a clearly implied hope that the disabilities would be temporary and that in time universal suffrage would prevail. When P. B. S. Pinchback and his Louisiana colleagues, who protested the disfranchisement of former Confederates, said, "We are now and ever have been advocates of universal suffrage," they spoke for many in the constitutional conventions. Property qualifications for voting and holding office were removed, in part to preserve the enfranchisement of large numbers of impecunious blacks and whites who supported the new regime. It was more than this, however. It was also a reaction against the practice of the well-to-do planters in the ante-bellum period of monopolizing political power and excluding even many whites from the higher privileges of citizenship.

There was no unanimity, however, in the demand for universal suffrage. In Alabama the debates on the suffrage provisions of the new constitution were protracted and bitter. In Georgia the stipulation that all voters should be eligible for holding office was stricken from the constitution, thereby laying the basis for the later expulsion of all African American members from the state legislature. When universal suffrage was adopted by a substantial majority in the Mississippi convention, twelve white delegates handed in their resignations. On the following day two others resigned. The Jackson *Clarion* called them "a noble band whose names will long be remembered by their countrymen." In Texas former Governor A. J. Hamilton led the fight for universal suffrage in order to obstruct the disfranchisement of the late rebels. In an uphill struggle he secured the adoption of a provision enfranchising all adult male citizens," without distinction of race, color, or former conditions," provided they had not been disqualified under the Constitution of the United States and until any such disqualification had been removed by Congress. Universal suffrage thus came gradually to the former Confederate states for the first time, but not without a struggle.

Closely connected with the granting of universal suffrage was the establishment of a system of universal public education. Before the war there had been a good deal of talk in the South about public education, but very little had been done about it. Even in North Carolina, where a superintendent of public instruction had been at work since 1852, there was little interest in public schools, and very few existed. In other Southern states the situation was much worse. In the first years after the war there was a more vigorous effort to establish public schools, but these were for whites only. There had been no desire to provide education for blacks and no belief that they could benefit from it anyway. The feverish educational work among blacks carried on by the Freedmen's Bureau and a dozen religious and philanthropic agencies had convinced few white Southerners that blacks should be educated.

It is difficult to exaggerate the eagerness of blacks at the close of the war to secure an education. Their several conventions held in 1865 drew up resolutions requesting the states to provide educational facilities for them. Most of the states turned a deaf ear.

When Florida in 1866 made special provisions for the education of blacks by imposing a tax of $1.00 on each black male between twenty-one and forty-five and 50 cents per month for each pupil, black parents seized the opportunity to send their children to school. Meanwhile scores of thousands of blacks were availing themselves of their only educational opportunity in the schools set up by the Freedmen's Bureau, religious societies, and philanthropic agencies. Booker T. Washington said that the desire and effort to learn was so great that anyone who did not witness it would have difficulty comprehending it. Washington further observed, "It was a whole race trying to go to school. Few were too young, and none too old, to make the attempt to learn. As fast as any kind of teachers could be secured, not only were day-schools filled, but night-schools as well."

The avid desire of blacks for learning combined with other factors after 1867 to produce a system of public education in the Southern states. One was the anxiety of the poorer whites to overcome their own educational disadvantages. The ante-bellum planters had steadfastly refused to support public education in the belief that only those who could afford it should be educated. They sent their sons and daughters to private schools or had them tutored at home. Without help the poorer classes were unable to educate their children. Another factor was the widespread commitment of Northerners in the South to the idea of universal education. Many were themselves the products of Northern public schools, and they hoped to see similar systems established in the South. As anxious to "Northernize" the South in this respect as in any other, they were ready with unqualified support for any effort toward education in their new home.

There was, furthermore, the old American ideal that the responsibilities of citizenship, of voting and holding office, could be exercised intelligently only by an educated citizenry. This was the view of those who advocated universal education in New York, Massachusetts, and other Northern states during the 1830's and 40's. It was also the view of those who advocated it in the South in 1867 and 1868. "Give us the right of suffrage; establish a school system that will give us an opportunity to educate our children; leave ajar the door that leads to peace and power; and if by the next generation we do not place ourselves beyond the reach of mortal man, why, then take them away from us if not exercised properly," W. H. Grey, declared to his colleagues in the Arkansas convention. In South Carolina African American delegate A. J. Ransier said, "In proportion to the education of the people so is their progress in civilization." To the majority of the delegates to the constitutional conventions universal public education seemed fully as important as universal suffrage and, indeed, indispensable to it.

Each state provided in its new constitution for free education of all persons of school age, usually five to twenty-one years. While many whites had the most serious reservations about educating blacks, no convention seriously considered the possibility of altogether excluding them from public education. Most states merely provided for the education of all children. Some added, significantly, "without partiality or distinction" or "without distinction or preference." Whether statements like these were in support of racially mixed schools was a burning question in every Southern state. Conservative Arkansans feared that the schools to be established under their new constitution would permit "indiscriminate social intercourse between whites and Negroes." In Alabama several of the native white members of the convention demanded specific provisions for separate schools, but they were not successful. They continued in their efforts and were rewarded late in 1868 by a move on the part of the State Board of Education, which had legislative power. In what may be regarded as a forerunner of the pupil-placement law that was to become popular in the South in the 1950's, the board declared that mixed schools would be permitted only on the unanimous consent of the parents or guardians of the children involved.

In each convention there were heated debates over mixed schools. Native whites generally opposed the education of blacks and whites together. Northerners did not seem to be particularly excited over the question, apparently being more interested in the education itself than in whether the schools were racially integrated. At the time, racially integrated schools were not widespread in the North. Most blacks who spoke on the subject favored mixed schools and offered two reasons. They felt that any racial distinction violated the principles of democracy and the provisions of the Fourteenth Amendment. They also feared—and rightly so—that separate schools would ultimately result in an inequitable distribution of the educational funds, with their schools receiving a smaller and inadequate share. In South Carolina a black delegate, J. A. Chesnut, spoke in favor of an integrated, voluntary educational system and added that "if there be a hostile disposition among the whites, an unwillingness to send their children to school, the fault is their own, not ours."

The opposition to racially mixed schools was tempered by the fact that many Southern Democrats, who called themselves Conservatives, believed that the equality required by the Fourteenth Amendment meant unsegregated education. Indeed, this is why General Beauregard and several of his Louisiana colleagues came out in favor of mixed schools as late as 1873. In most conventions the proposals to make constitutional provisions for separate schools were tabled, the advocates themselves realizing that the Radicals in Congress would probably reject a state's application for readmission if it had laws enforcing racial segregation. The only state that could get away with such legislation was Tennessee, which was not subjected to congressional reconstruction. Thus, in 1867 it enacted a school law providing that separate schools for whites and blacks were to be opened throughout the state.

Those who advocated racially mixed schools had almost as much difficulty in securing legislation favoring their position as did the segregationists. Only in South Carolina and Louisiana could the integrationists win any kind of victory. After much debate the South Carolina convention wrote into the constitution a provision that "all the public schools, colleges, and universities of this state, supported in whole or in part by the public funds, shall be free and open to all the children and youths of this State, without regard to race or color." This disappointed and distressed Governor Robert K. Scott, a Pennsylvanian and a former colonel in the Union army. In his next message to the legislature he asked for the enactment of a law providing for separate schools, deeming this "a matter of the greatest importance to all classes" of the people. The Charleston *Daily Courier* commended the governor for his "moderation in tone, no doubt resulting from his knowledge that the end of Radical rule is in sight." The legislature, however, did not heed the governor, and the constitutional provision for racially mixed schools remained until 1895. When separate schools did come to South Carolina, in practice in the late sixties and by law after the overthrow of Radical Reconstruction in 1877, they were, under the existing organic law, unconstitutional. The constitutional ban on racially segregated schools was not repealed until 1895.

Louisiana's constitutional provision for mixed schools was even more unequivocal than South Carolina's. It said, in part, "There shall be no separate schools or institutions of learning established exclusively for any race in the state of Louisiana." There was vigorous opposition both in and out of the convention. Judge W. H. Cooley called it "another attempt to establish, by law, the social equality of all classes and color." The New Orleans *Times* said the effort by the "Congo Convention" to introduce "amalgamation" into the public schools would never work and, worse, "may serve to destroy the public school system . . . and should be kept in mind as an additional reason for a strong united effort upon the part of our citizens to defeat a constitution so iniquitous and repulsive." These views did not prevail. The view that prevailed by a vote of 71 to 6 was expressed by that delegate who said he voted "*yes* with the profound conviction that the Constitution secures to all people of this State equal justice." Racially integrated schools remained public policy as late as 1875, when the legislature declared in one of its acts that "there shall be no distinction of race or color in the admission, management or discipline" of the State Agricultural and Mechanical College.

The fear of education for blacks, widespread among conservative whites, stemmed not merely from a lack of faith in the educability of blacks, or a dread of racially mixed schools. They also feared the cost. Free universal education was expensive and especially onerous when the chief beneficiaries paid little or no taxes. The conventions boldly provided for the support of public schools by special taxes, by certain fines from the courts, by literary funds maintained from the sale of public lands, and by other sources. In addition to income from public lands, escheats, and a possible poll tax, Alabama set aside one-fifth of all state revenue for the support of its public schools. Arkansas provided a property tax in each county, township, or school district "for maintaining an annual three months school in each school district, where the public school fund was not of itself sufficient." White property owners were outraged. Although the Mississippi constitution did not call for racially mixed schools, the Jackson *Daily Clarion* denounced the public school provision because "a fund will be raised by taxing the property of the people to build up a gigantic system of 'Public Education,' under the control of imported amalgamationists." All over the South the cry against direct taxation for educational purposes was almost as loud as the cry against the education of blacks or the possibility of racially mixed schools.

Of the many other matters the several constitutional conventions took up none was more critical than the question of land. Many observers, North and South, watched with great interest the disposition of this matter. Would blacks now take their forty acres by expropriation, even if there were not enough mules to go around? Many were relieved, therefore, when no program materialized for the confiscation and redistribution of land. South Carolina blacks hoped the federal government would lend them money with which to purchase land, but, considering such an eventuality unlikely, the convention created a commission to purchase land and resell it to blacks. In Mississippi a committee of the convention recommended that the state take some steps to relieve the widespread destitution. There was no suggestion of land redistribution, although many blacks privately hoped it would come. But planters opposed any kind of relief, and no commanding general desired to press the point. Everywhere some convention members sought to extend relief to the poor; and their actions in this regard were generally more successful than the efforts to facilitate the acquisition of land by blacks. Exemptions from taxes of $500 to $1,000 in personal property and $1,000 to $2,000 in real property further attest the desire for the stability that might be provided by land and equipment. Abolition of imprisonment for debt further relieved the poorer classes.

Closely allied with the desire to obtain land was the desire to provide a constitutional basis for a wide range of social welfare programs. Florida authorized the courts of the state to provide for those inhabitants "who by reason of age, infirmity or misfortune, may have claims upon the aid and sympathy of society." North Carolina, in establishing a state board of public charities, described "beneficent provisions of the poor, unfortunate, and orphans" as "one of the first duties of a civilized and Christian State." Most states made provisions for the establishment of homes for orphans, the insane, and the deaf and the dumb. Loud objections to such institutions were raised by planters and other large taxpayers who would bear the burden of support but would receive little or no benefit from them. They called public welfare programs irresponsible extravagance, nests of graft and corruption, and vehicles by which the Radicals could squander public funds. Through their resistance to taxation they would do all they could to nullify such programs throughout the former Confederacy.

Perhaps the least controversial provisions of the new constitutions were those having to do with the establishment of private corporations and the expansion of the states' industrial and natural resources. Most constitutions contained articles authorizing the formation of corporations under the general laws of the states. As peace came to the former Confederacy, these provisions were adequate to encourage the establishment of new industries, new railroads, and other enterprises. Few went as far as Alabama in setting up a Bureau of Industrial Resources, under a commissioner who was to collect statistical information on productive industries and agricultural and geological resources and disseminate it to the people of the United States and foreign countries. Other states moved in this direction once their new governments were established.

If there had been any question whether qualified Southern

whites should register at the beginning of Radical Reconstruction, there was no question what they should do once the constitutions were written. Some delegates were so incensed over certain provisions that they refused to sign. There were sixteen such persons in Alabama and fifteen in Arkansas. In the Texas constitutional convention the division and strife within the Republican party had become so bitter that a committee of delegates issued a formal denunciation of the document. Composed of Radicals, Northern whites, and blacks, the group declared that the conservative element had betrayed every loyal voter, white and black. In several important respects the Conservatives had won the day. In other states delegates denounced the constitutions on the grounds that they created social equality and that they did not reflect the views of the leading elements or represent their interests. Under the circumstances it can hardly be argued that the so-called Radicals in the state conventions were alone responsible for drawing up constitutions opposed only by former Confederates. In every convention most of the constitutional provisions were bitterly debated on all sides, and many delegates not only refused to accept them but fought them as earnestly as did any former Confederate. In each state, moreover, the conservative element organized itself to oppose ratification. In Alabama their technique was to "sit out" the vote, thereby assuring defeat of the constitution. Since, under the terms of the Reconstruction Acts, a state constitution had to be ratified by a majority of the *registered* voters, the Alabama document was defeated because more than half the registered voters stayed away from the polls. This was a grievous blow to the Radicals in Congress, who enacted a new law providing that a majority of the vote cast was adequate for ratification.

In the other states the Conservatives sought to defeat the new constitutions by outvoting the supporters. In Mississippi an all-out campaign against the constitution, especially in the Black Belt, resulted in its defeat by a vote of 56,231 to 63,860. The Republicans charged that the defeat had been accomplished through terrorism and fraud. Once more it was Congress that solved the problem. A bill provided that Mississippi was to be admitted when she ratified the Fifteenth Amendment, and the constitution was to be resubmitted. The constitution was ratified by a large majority, but the provisions disfranchising the former Confederates were defeated. In Arkansas most of those who were opposed to the constitution voted at polls supervised by the military, and General Gillem reported to Congress that the constitution had been ratified by a majority of 1,316. Despite bitter opposition in Georgia the constitution was ratified by a majority of 17,699. The situation was substantially the same in the other states.

Seldom have new governments been created under circumstances as difficult as those in the South in 1867 and the years that followed. The new constitutions were written by people with little experience in such matters, indeed with little experience in exercising any kind of political power. They had to do their work in an atmosphere of incredible hostility; and they had to comply with conditions imposed upon them by Congress that merely aggravated this hostility. The constitution-makers did not embrace revolutionary doctrines concerning the structure of economic life or government, but many features of the new constitutions were decidedly radical. Universal suffrage, free public education, and numerous welfare and charitable programs were new departures for the former Confederate states. None of these innovations won favor among the former Confederates, who hated both the radical measures and the men who promoted them.

The new constitutions were never discussed on their merits. Instead, the opponents wrung their hands and grumbled about the disappearance of the white man's government, the rise of black domination, and the terrible burdens imposed by ignorance and irresponsibility. Meanwhile, those who forged the new constitutions found themselves in such a critical struggle for survival that their energies were diverted to the task of perfecting a political organization. They needed such an organization if they were to weather the onslaught of an opposition with formidable economic resources—land and control of much of the black labor—and an opposition that was now regaining its political strength.

In spite of the preoccupation of one side with recrimination and of the other with political survival, the new constitutions did have considerable merit as satisfactory instruments of state government. The fact that for a generation no serious constitution-making was undertaken in the South is the best proof of this fact. If the constitutional fathers of the Radical South did not possess genius in statecraft, they showed good judgment in drawing on the experience of other governments and adapting this experience to the peculiar conditions of the South. In doing so they provided the South with structures of government that not even their bitterest adversaries could honestly condemn.

Putting the new governments into operation and maintaining them in the face of bitter and persistent opposition required the utmost skill. To be sure, the newly reconstructed states had some federal military support which, in sufficient strength and properly used, could have helped a great deal to sustain them. The generals in command of the five military districts were expected to carry out the provisions of the Reconstruction Acts; and if this required the use of armed force they had the authority to do so. But they were also to supervise the orderly transfer of the new state governments to worthy civilian hands, and this implied the reduction

"TIME WORKS WONDERS."

(Harper's Weekly, April 9, 1870.)

Thomas Nast imagines the reaction of the former president
of the Confederacy to the new occupant
of his old Senate seat.

(*Harper's Weekly,* May 31, 1879.)

RELIEVING ("BAYONET") GUARD
U.S.A. "Keep the Peace at the Polls."
C.S.A. "We'll KEEP it!"

Former Confederates collaborate with the Ku Klux Klan in policing
Southern elections. Cartoon by Thomas Nast.

and final elimination of military authority. The withdrawal of military support from the reconstruction governments did not proceed rapidly enough for the enemies of these governments, but it proceeded much too rapidly for the comfort of the governments themselves.

The strength and influence of the military forces in the South between 1867 and 1877 have frequently been exaggerated. Even during those years the opponents of congressional reconstruction in their bitter tirades sought to convey the impression that hordes of federal soldiers were stalking through the land on a permanent "Sherman's March." They made the most out of incidents in which persons seeking to obstruct the execution of the congressional program were tried before military tribunals. They were forced to admit, however, that not all the federal troops were reprehensible characters. Some local observers were inclined to think that some members of the army of occupation were too friendly. In South Carolina, for example, the troops were regular army men who got along well with the local population. If anything, they tended to favor the whites and oppress the blacks.

Federal troops were present in the former Confederate states to assist the commanding generals in the task of setting up the new governments. Once this was done, they retired to a less conspicuous role or were withdrawn altogether. As the reconstruction governments became established, the commanding generals relinquished their authority. This usually occurred shortly after the first general election following the ratification of the state constitution or shortly after the inauguration of the new government. Despite the claims of contemporary opponents of Radical Reconstruction or their modern followers, federal military activity in the former Confederacy during the period was negligible.

As in other parts of the country, most of the federal troops in the South during the period of congressional reconstruction were at regular forts or barracks, such as Fort Jefferson, Florida; Fort Pulaski, Georgia; Fort Macon, North Carolina; and Fortress Monroe, Virginia. In November, 1869, there were only 1,112 federal soldiers in Virginia, including those at Fortress Monroe. In Mississippi there were 716 officers and men scattered in many places, with 129 at Vicksburg and 59 in Natchez. More than three-fourths of the 4,612 in Texas were on the frontier trying to cope with the Indian problem. Two years later there were 342 in Atlanta and 54 in Savannah. By that time there were only 315 in Virginia. The number of federal troops in the South steadily declined until by 1876, outside the regular military installations, there were mere remnants of federal military authority in only South Carolina, Louisiana, and Florida.

Indeed, it was the hasty withdrawal or significant reduction of federal troops and the threats of the opposition to overthrow the reconstruction governments that led the state and local officials to set up their own military organizations. No sooner had Powell Clayton been inaugurated as governor of Arkansas than he and the Republicans realized that without military support the Democrats would overthrow them. They must have a militia that would be "ready to strike early and to strike hard" if they were to survive, one panic-stricken Republican spokesman exclaimed. Arkansas was merely one of the new governments that sent an urgent request to Congress to repeal the law forbidding the former Confederate states to organize and use militias. The proposed bill to repeal the law aroused bitter debate, with the opponents of Radical Reconstruction insisting that the proposal was one more attempt to reverse American doctrine and to place power in the hands of an ignorant and selfish minority. The Radicals won the day, however, and in March, 1869, the law was repealed so far as it applied

CHAPTER 7

to North Carolina, South Carolina, Florida, Alabama, Louisiana, and Arkansas. The Radical position was still dangerously insecure in Virginia, Texas, Mississippi, and Georgia. In the following year those states, too, were authorized to organize militia forces; but Virginia and Georgia never acted under the authorization.

In some states, the situation was so desperate that the authorities did not wait for congressional permission to organize state troops. In Florida a militia was organized and armed in June, 1868, although it was never used. Governor Brownlow of Tennessee also organized a militia that served more as a warning to his enemies than as an actual fighting force.

After Congress had acted, there was a feverish organization of militia in the former Confederate states. From 1870 to the end of the period in 1877 these forces were used with varying frequency in Texas, Louisiana, Mississippi, North Carolina, and South Carolina. They contained large numbers of blacks, and they were usually referred to as the "Negro militia." But they were by no means exclusively black. Persons of known loyalty of whatever race were welcomed into the militia. Conservatives were usually rejected, and when they protested against this discrimination, they accused the governments of preferring blacks to keep the whites under control. Whites were used, however, not merely as officers but as enlisted men when they could be trusted and could be induced to join in the task of supporting and protecting the Radical governments. It was not always easy to find such whites, even among the so-called scalawags.

These local forces were employed in a variety of ways. They were called into active service whenever there were rumors that Conservatives were planning to overthrow a state government. They were used to maintain peace during periods of Ku Klux Klan activity. They were most in evidence during hectic political campaigns when the Radicals feared that the Conservatives would try to dissuade Republicans, by force or otherwise, from going to the polls to vote. The opposition to them was always strong, and their presence frequently precipitated violence. The governments were convinced, however, that troops were indispensable to the stability of political life in the former Confederacy. This was not always the case, and the effect of the militia's activities was not always salutary.

The new reconstruction program was essentially political, and its success or failure depended on the kind of political support the state governments could maintain. The local whites, even when they could qualify for participation, were an unknown quantity. The utterances and attitudes of many of them in states such as Georgia and North Carolina raised doubts among the Radicals about the kind and extent of real support they could be expected to give. Even if they were staunch Unionists, it was not clear that they would also be staunch supporters of the congressional program. The realistic Radicals hoped for the best from the local whites; but they began to realize that the blacks, if properly trained, were their best hope for building and maintaining a strong political organization that would keep the Radicals in power.

The task of building a political organization out of an untutored black electorate was stupendous. It involved educating them to appreciate the strategic importance of their own political strength and to understand that the Republican party was their only friend in the South. The opponents of congressional reconstruction were not as certain in 1867 as they were to be later that the disfranchisement of blacks was a good thing. Some of them, therefore, hoped to win them to their side and "vote them" on the side of the Conservatives. In Georgia, South Carolina, and Alabama community efforts were made to bring blacks into the Democratic fold. The numerous expressions of friendship for them by former Confederates were enough to increase the apprehensions of the Radicals regarding their own political future.

Even before the new governments were established, the Radicals began building a following among blacks. The vehicle for this effort was usually, although not always, the Union League. Founded in Philadelphia in 1862 to stimulate and promote support for the Union, its leaders discovered new opportunities for service at the war's end. Already by 1865 a powerful political arm of the Radical wing of the Republican party, it was ready to do what it could to further the postwar program of the party. An apparently promising field of endeavor was among the freedmen. Within months after Appomattox the Union League was busy with its program of political education among the freedmen in the former Confederate states. During his trip through the South in May, 1865, as an emissary of President Johnson, Chief Justice Salmon P. Chase observed this activity and reported to the President that "everywhere throughout the country colored citizens are organizing Union Leagues." By the time Congress launched its program in 1867, the League's own program was well under way.

Some of the employees of the Freedmen's Bureau already in the South were active in promoting the work of the Union League. Among them were John M. Langston and W. J. Armstrong. In addition, the League sent special emissaries such as Senator Henry Wilson and Representative William D. Kelley to organize the freedmen. In time many other League organizers made their way into the South. Frequently they worked closely with the agents of the Freedmen's Bureau to promote Republicanism among the former slaves. The results produced the nearest thing to a real organization that the Republicans ever had in the South.

The usual procedure of the Union League to get its program

going was for a representative of the organization to go into a community and begin enrolling blacks in a branch of the League. Then the organizer would initiate the enrollees into the secrets and mysteries of the Union League. This was followed by what one organizer called "their quiet instruction . . . into their rights and duties." Invariably such instruction touched on the point that they had been liberated by the Republican party and that they should vote Republican in order to preserve their freedom. They were catechized on the meaning, importance, and methods of registering and voting. They were warned about the danger of "falling into the trap" laid by former Confederates who might try to win their votes by "kindness, fraud, or intimidation." They were also urged to stand up for their rights and to conduct themselves as the equals of their former masters.

The extent to which blacks were urged to assert their rights as the social and political equals of whites depended on the zeal of the League or Freedmen's Bureau organizers. Some, like Wager Swayne, were most energetic. Swayne not only distributed Republican literature among blacks, but he also electioneered and left nothing undone to get them to exert their political strength. Others, by temperament or conviction, were not quite so zealous. The reaction in the South to the political activity of members of the League or of Bureau agents was, however, the same regardless of the intensity of their activity.

The criticism of the League's activities was general and widespread throughout the South. Conservatives accused the League of urging blacks, through inflammatory speeches and elaborate oathtaking, to support their friends and oppose their enemies. Their enemies were, of course, their former masters who sought, through the Democratic party, to deliver them back into slavery. The League was accused of voting the freedmen like "herds of senseless cattle." Some chapters of the League were even accused of committing acts of violence against the former Confederates. Whatever their offenses happened to be, they were greatly exaggerated by the excited and outraged whites who were disfranchised by the same legislation that placed the vote in the hands of the freedmen. As the League's program of political education met with a measure of success, the opposition increased its objections and called for countermeasures to destroy the political power that was being put into the hands of blacks.

Even before the Ku Klux Klan struck a fatal blow at the political structures erected by the Union League, the transplanted organization had begun to decline. It had no long-range program, even in the area of politics, for Southern blacks. By the time it completed its initial task of political education in connection with launching the new Radical governments, the leaders of the League themselves were interested in other things. They hoped and believed that the organizations they had set up could perpetuate themselves and that if they needed help, they could get it from the newly formed militia. Meanwhile the more important Union Leaguers found important roles either in state or national political activities or in the new economic activities that were becoming more and more attractive. In the first stage the League had achieved striking success. It was the absence of effective League machinery or, indeed, any machinery for sustaining the political organization and for developing some economic independence that served to bring about the eventual downfall of the Republican party and, consequently, of the new governments in the South.

8

Reconstruction—Black and White

The elections held in the former Confederate states following the writing of the new constitutions were preceded by strenuous campaigns. Conservatives, already gathering strength from new amnesties and individual pardons and from defections in the ranks of the loyal native Southerners, were making a last-ditch stand to defeat Radical Reconstruction. One of the first efforts to defeat it was an appeal to African Americans to join the Democratic party. In many communities they were invited to Democratic party conventions and rallies. "Let every white man and honest black man in the State fall into the Democratic ranks and make a crushing charge upon the shattered cohorts of scalawags and carpetbaggers," counseled the Montgomery *Advertiser.* The appeal won few converts. Failing to entice blacks into their ranks, they took a stand against suffrage for blacks. In Virginia, Colonel R. E. Withers, late of the Confederate army and an unsuccessful Conservative candidate for governor, said that he was the standard-bearer of the white man's party. "I do not ask the support of the Negroes, nor do I expect it, for I consider them unfit to exercise the right of suffrage." The Conservatives were determined never to accept Radical Reconstruction, and every move they made in the ensuing months and years proved this. Although unable to place one of their number in any of the gubernatorial chairs in these first elections, they sent representatives to the legislatures in practically every state. In 1868 they had a majority in both houses of the Georgia legislature. In Florida they were a respectable minority of almost one-third.

But the strength of the Conservative opponents of Radical Reconstruction is not to be measured merely by the numbers of those who regarded themselves as Conservatives. At times they supported Northerners or loyal Southerners, when they had assurances that such persons would adhere to policies and programs that were essentially conservative. For governor of Virginia they turned from Colonel Withers to the Northerner Gilbert Walker, who had long been a resident of Norfolk and who was about as conservative as any Virginian. Walker was elected. In Georgia many Conservatives supported the successful gubernatorial candidate, Rufus B. Bullock. Although he was born in the North, Bullock had come South before the war and had served in the Confederate army. In time, however, even while Radical Reconstruction continued, the Conservatives succeeded in electing their own members governors and leaders in the legislatures. Witness, for example, the accession in 1870 of Robert B. Lindsay, a Democrat, to the Alabama governor's chair. Lindsay's counterparts were rising all over the South within a very few years after the beginning of Radical Reconstruction.

It is in the context of a vigorous, threatening opposition that the new reconstruction in the South must be observed. The opposition was resourceful and versatile, at times throwing its own candidates into the field, at other times coalescing with loyal Southerners for some common goal or co-operating with Northerners when that tactic served its ends. It generally opposed suffrage for blacks but at times supported this radical measure where control of the black vote seemed likely. Likewise, it supported certain economic measures sponsored by the Radicals but clearly benefiting the Conservatives. Indeed, it is somewhat inaccurate to call this group the opposition. With its extensive resources, enormous prestige, and ample experience in the field of public affairs it was a formidable force in the South in the postwar years. Even while laboring under political disabilities these men could easily make themselves felt all over the South. And as their disabilities were removed, the Radicals found them even more difficult to cope with.

As each new government was established in the South, the Conservatives usually observed the occasion by making dire predictions of the evils that would flow from it. In Alabama they set aside the day for fasting and prayer to Almighty God for the deliverance of the state "from the horrors of Negro domination." They seemed not to be consoled by the fact that the attorney general and the president of the new Board of Education were Conservatives and former officers in the Confederate army. One editor exclaimed, "We must render this either a white man's government, or convert the land into a Negro man's cemetery." But since Conservatives were as anxious as everyone else to have their states readmitted to the Union, they held their heavy fire until admission had been achieved.

The first task of the new governments was to secure the ratification of the Fourteenth Amendment, one of the conditions for readmission laid down by the Reconstruction Acts. By midsummer, 1868, seven states—Alabama, Arkansas, Florida, Georgia, Louisiana, North Carolina, and South Carolina—had organized their governments and ratified the Fourteenth Amendment. Congress, therefore, readmitted them to the Union on the condition that suffrage for blacks forever remain a part of their fundamental laws. Problems related to the suffrage provisions of their constitutions and other details delayed the readmission of Virginia, Texas, and Mississippi, all of which came back into the Union in 1870.

Immediately upon the readmission of their states the Conservatives, calling themselves variously the Democratic party, Conservative Union party, or the Democratic and Conservative party, began their running attack on the new administrations. Overthrow would come soon, they felt, if they worked hard enough at it. When federal authority was withdrawn from Georgia after it was readmitted, the Conservative Democrats opened fire on the three African American senators and twenty-nine representatives in the state legislature. After the failure of a move to expel the black senators as a group, the legislature began to attack them individually. It began with the most vulnerable black member, Aaron Alpeoria Bradley. This colorful figure had moved from New York to Savannah at the close of the war. Soon he became a leader among the blacks of his adopted home and was elected to the constitutional convention of 1868. He was expelled after a majority of the members cited him for "gross insults" to them. He then organized the blacks in Savannah and won a seat in the legislature, but the senate moved his expulsion on the grounds of an alleged criminal conviction in New York. When Bradley was not permitted to defend himself, he resigned.

The senate then challenged the eligibility of its other two African American members. For one hour they sought to establish their claim to their seats, but they were unsuccessful and were forthwith expelled by a vote of 24 to 11. The twenty-nine black members in the house were not safe from the attack; and in August, 1868, resolutions to expel them were passed by a vote of 83 to 23, with the black members abstaining. Only four remained, and this was because their fair complexion made it impossible to prove that they were African Americans.

In September, 1868, the Georgia legislature formally declared all black members ineligible to sit in that body. But they were prepared to fight. Henry McNeal Turner, the most articulate—and most disliked—black member, published and circulated throughout the state his impassioned defense, which the legislature did not print in its minutes, of the right of African Americans to their seats. "It is very strange," he said, "if a white man can occupy on this floor a seat created by colored votes, and a black man cannot do it. . . . It is extraordinary that a race such as yours, professing gallantry, chivalry, education, and superiority, living in a land where ringing chimes call child and sire to the Church of God—a land where Bibles are read and Gospel truths are spoken, and where courts of justice are presumed to exist . . . that with all these advantages on your side, you can make war upon the poor defenseless black man."

The Republicans appealed to the state supreme court for relief. The court in a 2 to 1 decision declared the blacks eligible, but there was serious doubt that the legislature would respect the decision. In October 136 African Americans from eighty-two counties met in Macon to protest the action of the legislature. They described their condition as intolerable and pleaded for federal relief. Governor Bullock transmitted their appeal to Congress together with his own view that the legislature was illegally constituted. The Committee on Reconstruction of the United States House of Representatives investigated the matter and heard blacks tell of numerous outrages against them. The United States Senate, meanwhile, refused to seat Joshua Hill, who had been elected by the Georgia legislature in July. The case against Georgia lawlessness was building up.

Congress, reconvening from the heated elections in November, was in a state of indecision over what to do about Georgia. Finally, when the state legislature rejected the Fifteenth Amendment in March, 1869, Congress went into action. Georgia was immediately put under military rule once more, and the ratification of the Fifteenth Amendment was made a condition for readmission. General Terry expelled twenty-four Democrats from the legislature on the ground that they were disfranchised by the Fourteenth Amendment. He then filled their places with Republicans and restored the African American members to their places. The legislature ratified the Fifteenth Amendment, recognized the African American members, and voted back pay for them. In a remarkable display of magnanimity a black member introduced and secured the passage of a resolution providing for the compensation of the displaced white representatives. On January 10, Georgia was admitted to the Union for the second time under Radical Reconstruction. No other former Confederate state put on such a display of incorrigibility.

No group has attracted more attention or has had its role more misrepresented by contemporaries and by posterity than Southern blacks during Radical Reconstruction. The period has been described as one of "Negro rule," as one of gross perfidy with blacks as the central figures, since the reins of misgovernment were supposedly held by black militiamen. Blacks were not in control of the state governments at any time anywhere in the South. They held public office and, at times, played important parts in the public life of their respective states. But it would be stretching a point to say that their roles were dominant, and it would be hopelessly distorting the picture to suggest that they ruled the South. It was in South Carolina that they had the greatest numerical strength. In the first legislature there were eighty-seven blacks and forty whites. From the outset, however, whites controlled the state senate and in 1874 the lower house as well. At all times the governor was white. There were two black lieutenant governors, Alonzo J. Ransier in 1870 and Richard H. Gleaves in 1872. There were other black leaders. Samuel J. Lee was speaker of the House in 1872 and Robert B. Elliot in 1874. From 1868 to 1872 Francis L. Cardozo was secretary of state, and from 1872 to 1876 he was state treasurer. Jonathan J. Wright, a member of the Pennsylvania bar before coming to South Carolina, sat on the state supreme court for seven years, but he was the only African American to achieve a judicial position of that level in any state.

Despite their large numbers, 437,400 compared to 353,800 whites in 1860, blacks in Mississippi did not approximate a numerical domination of the state government. In the first reconstruction legislature there were 40 black members out of a total of 115. According to John R. Lynch, black speaker of the house in 1872, "Of seven state officers, only one, that of Secretary of State, was filled by a colored man, until 1873 when colored men were elected to three of the seven offices." They were A. K. Davis, lieutenant governor, James Hill, secretary of state, and Thomas W. Cardozo, superintendent of education. Of the situation in 1873 Lynch declared, "Out of seventy-two counties in the State . . . electing on an average twenty-eight officers to a county, it is safe to assert that not five out of one hundred of such officers were colored men." Vernon Wharton, after a careful study of the problem, concludes that "although Negroes formed a majority of the population in thirty counties in Mississippi, they almost never took advantage of their opportunity to place any large number of their race in local offices." Doubtless, the principal factor in their not taking advantage of their numerical superiority was intimidation and threats of reprisal by the white minority.

Several Louisiana African Americans were prominent and influential, but they never approached a dominant position in public affairs. The forty-two in the first legislature were in the minority, as were those in succeeding legislatures. Three served as lieutenant governor: Oscar J. Dunn, 1868–71; P. B. S. Pinchback, 1871–72, who acted as governor for forty-three days in 1872 when Governor Warmoth was ousted; and C. C. Antoine, 1872–76. Others held important offices, including P. G. Deslonde, secretary of state, 1872–76; Antoine Dubuclet, state treasurer, 1868–69; and W. G. Brown, superintendent of public education, 1872–76. Most of the Louisiana black leaders had been free before the war and had enjoyed some educational opportunities. Of the seven blacks in the state senate in 1868 only one, Oscar J. Dunn, had been a slave; and before the war he had purchased his own freedom. Pinchback, a well-to-do former captain in the Union army, had been educated in Cincinnati. He had the physical appearance of a white man but his white skin gave him little advantage in the hurly-burly of reconstruction politics in Louisiana.

In the other state governments the roles of blacks were even less significant. In the North Carolina legislature they constituted barely one-seventh of the membership, and the only black official of any consequence was James Walker Hood, who served as assistant superintendent of public instruction for several years. The first Alabama legislature saw only twenty-six blacks out of a total membership of eighty-four, and there were no important state offices in their hands. The "horrors of Negro domination" from which Alabamans prayed deliverance simply did not exist. James T. Rapier is the only African American who was at all prominent; after serving as assessor of internal revenue in Alabama he went on to Congress. What influence blacks might have had in Georgia was nullified by their expulsion from the legislature. By the time they returned, Radical Reconstruction had been so effectively undermined that there was little chance for them to exert any considerable influence.

Florida had only nineteen blacks in its first legislature, which contained seventy-six members. Their influence was extremely limited. The only high-ranking black in the state government was Jonathan C. Gibbs, who was secretary of state from 1868 to 1872 and superintendent of public instruction from 1872 to 1874. Very few held other than minor offices in the new government in Virginia. Twenty-seven sat in the first legislature, and there were none among the policy-makers in the executive branch of the government. The influence of blacks in Arkansas was meager. At the beginning of the period none held any important offices. In 1871 W. H. Grey was appointed commissioner of immigration, a position he held until 1873. J. C. Corbin, a graduate of Oberlin College, served as superintendent of education from January, 1873, to October, 1874. There were no important black officeholders in Texas, but G. T. Ruby of Galveston wielded considerable political influence, while Norris Wright Cuney, also of Galveston, held several offices, including membership on the country school board and state inspector of customs.

In a different but highly significant category were the sixteen African Americans who served in Congress between 1869 and 1880. Two of them, Hiram R. Revels and Blanche K. Bruce, represented Mississippi in the Senate. Revels was a North Carolina free person of color who had lived in several Northern states and had studied at Knox College in Illinois. By the time of the Civil War he had become an ordained minister in the African Methodist Episcopal Church and had taught school in several places. During the war he recruited blacks for the Union army, founded a school for freedmen in St. Louis, and joined the army as chaplain of a

135

black regiment in Mississippi. At the war's end he settled in Natchez, entered politics, and in 1870–71 filled the Senate seat previously held by Jefferson Davis. Bruce had been born a slave in Virginia. When war came he escaped to Missouri and soon was teaching blacks in Hannibal. After the war he studied in the North for several years and went to Mississippi in 1869. Soon he got into politics and worked up from tax collector to sheriff to county superintendent of schools. In 1875 he went to the United States Senate, where he served a full term. His wide range of interests as a lawmaker is seen in his introduction of bills on the Geneva award for the Alabama claims, aid to education, railroad construction, and the reimbursement of depositors in the Freedmen's Savings Bank.

South Carolina sent six blacks to the House of Representatives, the largest number from a single state. But they were not all in the House at one time. Alabama was second with three. Georgia, Florida, Mississippi, North Carolina, and Louisiana sent one each. Most of these men had some experience in public service before going to Congress. Alonzo Ransier of South Carolina had been a member of the constitutional convention, auditor of Charleston County, and lieutenant governor. John R. Lynch of Mississippi and James T. Rapier of Alabama had served their states in similar fashion. Some were war heroes, like Robert Smalls of South Carolina who had seized the Confederate ship "Planter" in 1862 and delivered it to Union authorities. In addition to representing their constituents in the usual ways, African American members of Congress showed considerable interest in a wide range of national questions. Joseph Rainey of South Carolina and Josiah T. Walls of Florida were strong advocates of federal aid to education. John A. Hyman of North Carolina championed relief for the Cherokee Indians, while all were outspoken in their vigorous support of civil rights legislation. Their responsible conduct moved James G. Blaine, their contemporary, to observe, "The colored men who took their seats in both Senate and House did not appear ignorant or helpless. They were as a rule studious, earnest, ambitious men, whose public conduct . . . would be honorable to any race."

When the new governments were launched, the black legislators and state officers joined the others in developing and carrying forward programs for the rebuilding and improvement of their states. The legislatures implemented the constitutional provisions for welfare and educational institutions, and the governors appointed officials to fill the posts. Six of the ten governors were labeled carpetbaggers, but one of them, Rufus Bullock of Georgia, had adopted that state in 1859 and had served as an officer in the Confederate army. Another, H. C. Warmoth of Louisiana, was born in Illinois but he had "not a drop of any other than Southern blood" in his veins. Mississippi's Northern governor, Adelbert Ames, was shortly elected to the Senate and was succeeded by a native of the state, J. L. Alcorn. Thus, whether Southern legislators and governors were transplanted Northerners or native Southerners depended on the personnel available, and there was constant shifting from one group to the other.

Appointments to public office also depended on available personnel, as well as on the inclinations of the chief executive. Governor Bullock of Georgia was close to many former Confederates and appointed a number of them to office. Indeed, the "Augusta ring" that received so many favors from Bullock was largely ex-Confederate. On the other hand, Governor W. W. Holden of North Carolina was intimate with carpetbaggers and relied on them to carry out his policies. He appointed Milton Littlefield, a native of New York, as state printer, and he saw to it that when he became governor this "Prince of Carpetbaggers" succeeded him as president of the Union League. In Florida Governor Harrison Reed relied heavily on Jonathan Gibbs, the African American leader who was the first secretary of state in the reconstruction government. Later, Reed's successor, Governor O. B. Hart, appointed him superintendent of public instruction.

All the new programs were expensive. Public buildings had to be repaired or rebuilt altogether. Not only did the damage from the war require public attention, but the general lag in public works had to be overcome. Many public roads were practically impassable, and numerous bridges had either been destroyed or had collapsed under constant use without maintenance. In some states departments of public works were established, in others the work of improving public roads and buildings was assigned to various state and county officials. There was much more excitement, however, in the area of railroad construction; and the legislators as well as others, in and out of the government, took a lively interest in such projects. The rebuilding of old roads was encouraged by state aid, usually in the form of bonds or state indorsement of railroad bonds. Charters were granted for the construction of new roads. The activity was feverish, as if railroad building symbolized the emergence of a modern South equal to the North, behind which it had lagged for a generation before the Civil War. But it was feverish for another, more practical, reason. It was a noncontroversial, bipartisan activity in which Northerners, blacks, and every group of Southerners could participate with profit— honestly if possible, dishonestly if necessary.

Every conceivable kind of economic activity was encouraged. Some states, like South Carolina, had land commissioners to facilitate the purchase of land by persons without private financial resources. Some states, like Alabama, had commissioners of industries to encourage the establishment of new industrial and commercial activities. Several states set up bureaus of immigration under a commissioner whose duty was to collect and publish information on matters of interest to prospective investors and settlers. Arkansas placed under the control of its commissioner of immigration all lands in which the state had an interest. He was to make assignments of land to actual settlers and perform other duties that would have the effect of attracting "northern capital and labor to the state." If such projects were not always successful, it was because prospective settlers found more attractive places elsewhere or because of political and social instability in the South or both. But the new governments were attempting to strengthen economic life. And despite the fact that they were denounced for their efforts, settlers and capital flowed into the South in the fifteen years following the war.

The new public school system, too, was expensive. After the states had re-entered the Union, the legislatures began to implement the provisions for free universal education that had been written into the constitutions. By 1870 a public school system was in operation all over the South. Except for South Carolina and Louisiana no serious attempt was made to put into operation a racially mixed school system. South Carolina's effort was wholly unsuccessful and Louisiana's only scarcely better. Two systems of education increased the expenses of a poverty-stricken and educationally backward region. In its first year of operating a school system, Mississippi spent more for education than for all other government activities combined. South Carolina went so far as to provide free textbooks to children who could not pay for them, but it found itself unable to raise sufficient funds to finance its expensive school program. Poverty, the inability of the states to collect taxes, and inefficiency and corruption in many places prevented the successful operation of the schools. The pattern was there, however, and in more instances than is usually admitted the system was operating successfully. In 1870 there were 30,448 children in South Carolina's 769 schools. Six years later there were 123,035 students attending 2,776 schools. Similar increases were to be found in other states and included black as well as white students.

The new governments took other steps, significant in one way or another. They raised salaries and expense allowances of officials and increased the number of officials—innovations that were expensive and sometimes needless. Where constitutional conventions had not done so, legislatures repealed the more objectionable features of the black codes. There were efforts to increase the efficiency of government through a reorganization of the judicial system, the redistribution of powers in towns and counties, and the modification of registration and election laws. The penal systems were modified, although not always improved. In Alabama and Georgia the practice of leasing convict labor for private use, which had actually been initiated by federal officials, became more deeply intrenched. Some states enacted homestead legislation or adapted existing legislation. Finally, there was some effort to enact at the state level the kind of civil rights legislation that Sumner and his friends were seeking in Congress. In 1873 the Arkansas legislature passed a law requiring hotels and places of public accommodation to admit blacks and school districts to provide equal facilities in separate schools.

The mounting costs of government plagued the new administrations from the beginning. There is no point in making comparisons with the ante-bellum governments, for the role of government in the South had undergone a radical change, bringing with it new responsibilities and new costs. The school system, the ambitious public works and railroad building programs, and the many new services were problems with which Southern governments did not have to cope before 1860. The spiral of inflation mounted steadily, adding to the woes of those who attempted to finance the new programs. Extravagance and corruption played their part, too, as the winds of public immorality sweeping New York and Washington took their toll also in the South. Under the circumstances deficit spending was almost inevitable, and state indebtednesses rose to the danger point. Louisiana's public debt increased from $17,347,000 in 1868 to $29,619,000 in 1872. For the same period South Carolina's debt increased from $14,896,000 to $22,480,000. Alabama's debt in 1869 was $8,355,000; in 1874 it was $25,503,000, including railroad bonds. It was essentially the same in the other states, but even as the debt mounted, each state sought ways and means of paying the cost as far as possible. Taxation, of course, became the principal means of financing, although borrowing was a source that was not overlooked.

To finance their operations the Radicals of South Carolina instituted a "uniform rate of assessment of all property at its fair money value," in contrast to the ante-bellum system that was easy on land and slaves and hard on mercantile, professional, and banking interests. Between 1868 and 1872 the average rate was nine mills on the dollar, but because of the decreased valuation of property and the difficulty of collecting, it rose to more than eleven mills by 1876. For the same reasons the rate in Mississippi rose from one mill in 1869 to fourteen mills in 1874. In Louisiana the rate increased from 5.25 mills in 1869 to 21.5 mills in 1872. There were other taxes. Poll taxes, widely levied before the war, were continued and sometimes increased. In North Carolina the poll tax in 1867 was fifty cents. In 1870 it was one dollar. Seventy-five per cent of this tax was to be used to support the public schools, and similar use of it was made in Georgia, Arkansas, and several other states. From time to time there were special taxes, on luxury items such as furs and jewelry, on land and other properties to pay the interest on state bonds, and on businesses and professions to pay the costs of education and special services.

Some states supplemented their tax programs with schemes for borrowing capital, while others, like Georgia, relied largely on borrowing. In Georgia the rate of taxation during the brief so-called Radical regime remained about the same as that fixed by the Confederate reconstruction government in 1866. But the indebtedness of the state mounted steadily, largely as a result of the issuance of bonds. Between 1868 and 1872 the government issued $6,831,000 in bonds, as well as indorsing railroad bonds in the amount of $5,733,000. The most widely recognized purpose for the issuance of state bonds was to finance some phase of railroad development. The usual method was for the state to issue state bonds to the railroad in exchange for bonds of the company. Shortly after the congressional reconstruction of North Carolina began, the legislature undertook to finance the Chatham Railroad in this fashion, followed by similar moves supporting the Williamston and Tarboro Railroad, the Western North Carolina Railroad, and the Northwestern North Carolina Railroad.

In Alabama the state began to give indorsement of the bonds of certain railroads as early as February, 1867. Among the companies benefiting from state action were the Montgomery and Eufala, the South and North, and the Wills Valley railroads. The state permitted the reorganization and merger of old lines and issued charters to new companies. It supported construction of new lines to the extent of $12,000 to $16,000 per mile. Not infrequently, when the railroad defaulted in its payment of interest, Alabama, as well as other states, found it necessary to take over the railroads and operate them in the name of the state. Such activities almost invariably increased the indebtedness of the state from 50 to 75 per cent.

If the ex-Confederate whites scoffed at the very idea of Southern state governments operating without their leadership, they were outraged when the governments proceeded to impose the heaviest burdens on those who were disfranchised. They gave little attention to increasing expenses resulting from new functions assumed by the government or to the inflation that resulted from an expanding national economy and numerous shortages. Their sense of outrage was intensified by a traditional antipathy to high taxes, which they were determined to fight with every resource at their disposal. In some states taxpayers' conventions met to organize opposition to increases. Two such conventions in South Carolina, in 1871 and 1874, protested the enormous rise in taxation—the result of "frauds the most flagrant, and corruption the most dangerous and demoralizing" ever perpetrated by state officials. The second convention, the Orangeburg *Times* said, should protest at Washington "against further taxation, under such a filthy, disgusting, loathsome State government and ask to be made a territorial dependency, or a conquered province, anything rather than the football of [Governor] Moses and his crew." While the convention formally sought a revision of the existing tax law, which was "cumbrous, obscure, and intricate," it was very busy strengthening the determination of many to refuse to pay their assessed taxes. This it did by forming tax unions in the several counties. These organizations were to see that taxes were fairly assessed, collected, and expended. But they became centers of resistance not only to taxes but to the entire Radical regime.

In other states resistance was even more pronounced. In Louisiana a strong Tax Resisting Association was organized in 1872 to co-ordinate the efforts of numerous parish groups that had been active since 1869. In Mississippi some citizens described their taxes as "awful, monstrous, and ruinous" and in various ways indicated their unwillingness to give financial support to the new regime. The result was, of course, a steady decline in revenue accompanied by the inability of the state and local governments to meet their obligations. Many farms and plantations were sold for taxes. In 1869 some twenty-three Wake County plantations in North Carolina containing 7,872 acres were sold for taxes and brought only $7,718. When tax sales brought insufficient revenues, states resorted to the issuance of scrip, which depreciated almost immediately, giving rise to more problems than it solved. In the end the fact remained that the reconstruction governments were unable to raise the funds required for their administration.

Most opponents argued that the troubles of the state and local governments arose from their extravagance and corruption that, in turn, resulted from the abnormalities inherent in "Negrocarpetbag-scalawag" rule. J. G. de Roulhac Hamilton, the historian of North Carolina reconstruction, has gone so far as to say that the presence of blacks in politics was responsible for the "blunting of the moral sense of the white people." It would be remarkable if the very small fraction of blacks in political life in North Carolina could destroy or even blunt the "highly developed political sense" or the "equally high standard of political morality" of the whites of North Carolina. The fact is that such assertions ignore certain very important considerations highly relevant to any understanding of the problems of extravagance and corruption during the reconstruction era.

The national forces conducive to the decline of public morality were powerful, and the South was not immune. Among them was the rapid wartime expansion of the economy that encouraged all sorts of ventures and attracted all sorts of people. Closely connected with this was an expanded role of government in facilitating and stimulating economic expansion. After the war those who had made huge profits were seeking still more, while those who had not were desperate in their determination to make a "killing." Anything was fair game, especially new areas to be exploited, new groups with potential political power, and new opportunities arising out of instability of one kind or another. These are the factors that made it possible for William M. Tweed to flourish as the corrupt boss of New York City during these years. Drawing his strength from his adept manipulation of the lower classes, he and his confederates, Mayor Oakey Hall, Peter B. Sweeny, and Richard B. Connolly, took more than $100,000,000 from the city. The city spent $11,000,000 for the partial construction of a courthouse, $350,000 for carpets, and $179,929 for forty chairs and three tables. It seemed incredible that a large, politically mature city could have succumbed to such crude graft and corruption.

But the situation was essentially the same elsewhere. In 1869 Jim Fisk and Jay Gould conceived a plot to corner the gold on the New York market and to make millions by selling at the proper moment. Taking advantage of the President's innocence in such matters, they drove the price of gold steadily upward with assurances that the federal treasury would not enter the market. Many bribes passed and many honest men were driven into bankruptcy. Finally the federal government offered to sell $4,000,000 worth of gold to end the panic created by the Fisk-Gould machinations. Even closer to the federal government was the Credit Mobilier scandal. Several members of Congress and Vice-President Schuyler Colfax had accepted shares of stock and dividends from this railroad construction company, which in return had received handsome favors from the government. Then there was the scandal of the Whiskey Ring, which was exposed as having robbed the federal treasury of several million dollars in internal revenue and which included President Grant's private secretary. Meanwhile Grant's Secretary of War, W. W. Belknap, was discovered to have regularly sold the privilege of disbursing supplies to Indians to persons who made fortunes by furnishing substandard goods.

Such was the national climate in which graft and corruption flourished. In the Southern states much of the graft was petty. In North Carolina two members of the legislature charged mileage for 154 miles, although they lived in Raleigh, where the legislature met. In Arkansas an African American was paid $9,000 for bridge repairs that reportedly cost only about $500. In South Carolina the legislature voted $1,000 extra compensation for the speaker after he allegedly had lost that amount on a horse race. In Louisiana large amounts of cash from the permanent school funds of the parishes regularly disappeared.

There was big graft also, especially in connection with the states' participation in railroad construction. In North Carolina General M. S. Littlefield headed a lobby of railroad interests that dispensed numerous favors to legislators. And his efforts to bring "railroad development" to the state were indorsed as enthusiastically by Conservatives as by Radicals. In Georgia Hannibal I. Kimball of New York sought and gained legislative favors by a variety of corrupt means. If he wielded influence among the Republicans during their brief tenure, his connections with the Conservatives seemed even closer. When he secured by questionable means the lease of the state-owned Western and Atlantic Railroad in 1870, he could list among his associates the Confederate governor Joseph E. Brown, the Confederate Vice-President Alexander H. Stephens, and respected Conservatives like Ben H. Hill, H. B. Plant, Richard Peters, and John P. King.

Alabama has provided some of the prime examples of big graft during reconstruction. Numerous railroads fed at the public trough by bribing legislators and other officials and through the use and misuse of state funds placed at their disposal. The state literally underwrote much of the construction of railroads during the period, sometimes by subsidizing each mile to be built, sometimes by indorsing the bonds issued by railroad companies. Carpetbaggers and scalawags were not alone in their efforts to advance "railroad development" with state aid. On the boards of the railroads sat many respectable, prominent, ex-Confederate Alabamans. Josiah Morris, the Montgomery banker, was on the board of several roads, including the Mobile and Montgomery and the South and North; and it was his money that John Milner used to bribe members of the Alabama assembly. Robert Patton, Johnson's provisional governor, became vice-president of the Alabama and Chattanooga Railroad, a company whose bonds he had helped indorse shortly before he left the governor's office. In the public financing of railroads, by fair means and foul, there was no marked difference in Alabama policy when the Republicans came into power in 1868 or when a Democratic governor was elected in 1870 or when the Republicans were finally driven from power in 1874. Corruption was bisectional, bipartisan, and biracial.

If no party or race had a monopoly on public immorality, none could boast that it was the sole keeper of the public conscience. In 1872 the Democrats were outraged by the revelations of corruption in high places. But there were some Republicans, like Carl Schurz, Horace Greeley, Charles Francis Adams, and B. Gratz Brown, whose sense of outrage was equally great. It was this group that organized the Liberal Republican party to crusade for clean honest government. The Democrats went so far as formally to support the Liberal Republican platform and its candidates, Greeley and Brown. This combination was no match for Grant, who was easily re-elected. But it frightened the Republicans into relaxing their control over the South. Even before the election many of the remaining disabilities under which former Confederates lived were removed, and President Grant adopted a policy of using federal troops less frequently in Southern elections. When Governor Adelbert Ames sent a desperate plea for federal troops to cope with the chaotic conditions in Mississippi in 1875, Grant, through his Attorney General, refused the request. It was on this occasion that he declared, "The whole public are tired of the annual autumnal outbreaks in the south."

In the South there were frequent tirades against the corruption of the Radical regime. Indeed, this became one of the principal arguments for its overthrow, even when Conservatives were among the beneficiaries of Radical policies. Former Confederate leader James H. Clanton, one of the receivers for the Alabama and Chattanooga Railroad, said that the effect of dishonesty in Alabama was "to drive the capital from the State, paralyze industry, demoralize labor, and force our best citizens to flee Alabama as a pestilence." But some black and white Republicans were likewise distressed over dishonesty and corruption. As early as 1869 a group of Arkansas Republicans denounced those members of the party who seemed to be interested solely in the exploitation of the state. Later in the same year a group, including several African Americans, organized the Liberal Republican party of Arkansas and called on Democrats and former Whigs to assist them in their fight for good government. In 1872 a group of black members of the Florida legislature made a public declaration against corruption. One of them, John W. Wyatt, said, "We want no *Tom Scotts, Jim Fisks,* or *Vanderbilts* in this State to govern us. . . . The great curse of Florida has been dishonest corporations, rings, and cliques, with an eye single to their central interest. . . . The recent expose of the Tammany Ring in New York has satisfied all right thinking men that the power exercised by strong bodies, composed of many corporations, is the most dangerous to the public good and safety."

Thus, the tragedy of public immorality in the Southern states was merely part of a national tragedy. The added misfortune of the South was that it could least afford it, not only because of poverty and political instability, but because already critics in and out of the South were anxious to find excuses to discredit any effort to reconstruct the South. The instances of corruption provided by the Radical regime, even if they were not general or typical, were sufficient excuses for those who needed no convincing that Radical Reconstruction was an unmitigated curse. If the opponents of reconstruction needed an issue on which to base their fight, those in power all too often handed it to them. The leaders of counter reconstruction used it for all it was worth.

9

Counter Reconstruction

The reaction of the former Confederates and their supporters to the taking over of the reconstruction program by Congress could hardly have been unanticipated. When abolitionists had called for an end to slavery in the ante-bellum period, white Southerners had said that the North was making war on their institutions and their way of life. Whenever there had been slave revolts or rumors of them, planters, and even most non-slaveholders, were thrown into a frenzy of preparation for the great upheaval that they seemed to think was inevitable. "We must prepare for any eventuality," they were accustomed to saying; and whether the dangers of which they spoke were real or fancied, they had no intention of being caught short. All too frequently, long before the Civil War came, these fears had erupted with a violence that to some observers made the South appear a dark and bloody land.

Even when the former Confederates were rather firmly in control of Southern state and local governments in the early postwar years, violence was an important part of the pattern of life. In 1866 the head of the Freedmen's Bureau in Georgia complained that numerous bands of ruffians were committing "the most fiendish and diabolical outrages" on the freedmen. The former slaves themselves made many representations to Congress and the President that they were in constant danger of physical harm at the hands of the former Confederates. Northern teachers of freedmen frequently saw their efforts literally turn to ashes as local white opponents set fire to the African American schools; and the reports of the Bureau contain many instances of bodily harm inflicted upon Northern teachers by those in the South who were unalterably opposed to the education of the former slaves. If violence was an integral part of the old order and even of the new order controlled by former Confederates, it was only natural that it would be a prime factor in any move to oppose the still newer order administered by those whom the former Confederates regarded as natural enemies.

The targets of attack now were, of course, the Union League, the Heroes of America in North Carolina, the Lincoln Brotherhood, a Radical group that flourished in Florida, and other similar organizations. The work of the League was especially reprehensible to the former Confederates. In addition to teaching African Americans what their political rights were and instructing them in the mysteries of voting, the League also fired the self-respect of the former slaves by telling them that they were the social equals of whites. To many who had supported the Lost Cause this was worse than the burning of Atlanta and Sherman's path of devastation from that city to the sea. Another target was the several state militias, which, in addition to being charged with the responsibility of keeping the hated Radical governments in power, frequently boasted of having black contingents to participate in the discharge of this responsibility. If Radical governments were to be placed in power by "Negro votes" and were to be kept there by "Negro militias," they invited opposition by every means, including violence, at the disposal of the former Confederates.

The young Tennesseans who organized late in 1865 the frolicking secret lodge that was to be known as the order of the Ku Klux

Klan, or the Invisible Empire, could hardly have been unaware of what they were doing. Even if they were bored and impatient with life, as has been claimed in their defense, this was nothing new for young bloods in the village of Pulaski, Tennessee. Nor were wanton attacks on helpless blacks new. If the young men were looking for fun, they did not have to go beyond the nearest black settlement, and furthermore they would be performing a service to the white community if they whipped blacks to keep them in line. Long before blacks became a political factor and while the governments of the Southern states were still in the hands of the former Confederates, the Klan organization was being perfected and was spreading to many parts of the South. It described itself as an institution of "chivalry, humanity, mercy, and patriotism." Within a matter of months it had selected its name, adopted its ritual, and had begun to terrorize blacks of the area. Soon there were other chapters (dens) with officers bearing such ominous titles as dragons, hydras, titans, furies, and night-hawks.

In the spring of 1867 delegates from several states met in convention at Nashville, placed General Nathan B. Forrest at the head of the organization as the Grand Wizard, and sent its members back to their respective homes fired with a determination to nullify the program of congressional reconstruction that was just getting under way. No longer was it sufficient to frighten or terrorize blacks by ghoulish dress, weird rituals, and night rides. By social and business ostracism of the white Radicals, by intimidation and any effective means of violence conceivable against blacks, by the purchase of votes of any sellers, and by glorifying the white race and especially white womanhood, the Klan grimly moved to wreck each and every phase of Radical Reconstruction.

While the Klan made rapid strides in Tennessee, North Carolina, and Alabama, other similar groups were springing up elsewhere. In Louisiana it was the Knights of the White Camellia. In Texas it was the Knights of the Rising Sun. In Mississippi it was the White Line, and on and on throughout the former Confederate states. Scores of other counter-reconstruction organizations flourished in various parts of the South. Among them were the Constitutional Union Guards, the Pale Faces, the White Brotherhood, the White League, the Council of Safety, and the '76 Association. As the months and years went by, more such organizations came into existence. Old or new, large or small, they had one aim in common: the maintenance and, later, the re-establishment of white supremacy in the South. They had one means in common: any and every kind of intimidation and violence against blacks and their supporters. Even if they were, in some instances, autonomous and even amorphous, these groups were at least held together loosely by the ideals, aims, and methods which they shared with the Invisible Empire.

It would be a historical fallacy to assert that the Ku Klux Klan and its compatriots were organized to combat the Union League and to overthrow Radical Reconstruction. They came on the scene much too early to support such a view and they were, indeed, too much a reflection of the general character of Southern life to require the unique conditions of Radical Reconstruction to spawn them. Radical Reconstruction was, however, a powerful stimulus for such endeavors, and the struggle against it gave the Klan respectability and a dignity that it had not anticipated. The lawlessness of the Jayhawkers and Bushwhackers of 1865 became the holy crusade of the Klansmen of 1868. Within a matter of months it was being claimed that the "instinct of self-protection" prompted the organization of the Klan. "It was necessary," one of them argued, "in order to protect our families from outrage and to preserve our own lives, to have something that we could regard as a brotherhood—a combination of the best men in the country, to act purely in self-defense, to repel the attack in case we should be attacked by these people."

The real stimulus, then, to the growth and expansion of Klan activities was not the attacks on innocent white families by blacks and others but the apparent determination on the part of blacks and their Radical friends to assume and wield political power. For the former Confederates this was indeed an attack as real as any they could imagine. The oath of the Klansmen to aid those fellow members in distress and "pecuniary embarrassment" was liberally construed, while their promise to protect female friends and widows of Confederate veterans drew into the fold many who would not have been attracted for other reasons. They proceeded on the basis of that ancient principle that the best defense was a well-planned offense. At times wearing hoods and robes, at other times without disguise, they rode over the land at night "terrifying, whipping, or murdering whites and blacks who, for one reason or another, were to them undesirable." Offenses of blacks ranged from insolence to voting and holding office. White offenses ranged from participating in Radical governments to associating with blacks on a basis of equality.

Acting "purely in self-defense" assumed curious forms. It involved the murder of respectable blacks by roving gangs of terrorists, the murder of those who rented land, the looting of stores whose owners were sometimes killed, and the murder of peaceable white citizens. On one occasion in Mississippi a member of a local gang, "Heggie's Scouts," claimed that his group killed 116 blacks and threw their bodies into the Tallahatchie River. It was reported that in North Carolina the Klan was responsible for 260 outrages, including 7 murders and the whipping of 72 whites and 141 blacks. In one county in South Carolina 6 men were murdered and more than 300 were whipped during the first six months of 1870. Meanwhile, the personal indignities inflicted upon individual whites and blacks were so varied and so numerous as to defy classification or enumeration. There were the public whippings, the maimings, the mutilations, and other almost inconceivable forms of barbaric intimidation.

If the doctrine of political and social equality of whites and blacks was to be spread by the Union League, then the League was an enemy of the South and deserved any obloquy and violence that could be directed against it. League officials, black and white, were bitterly assailed, their property frequently destroyed, and themselves whipped and sometimes murdered. League members were warned to stay away from the polls on election day if they and their families wanted to remain alive. One newspaper editor, calling for the organization of a chapter of the Klan in every community, declared in 1868 that this was the most effective way for the men of the South "through whose veins the unalloyed Caucasian blood courses" to crush, "with one mighty blow, the preposterous wicked dogma of Negro equality." He left little to the imagination when he exclaimed, "If to every tree in our forest-like streets were attached a rope; and to the ends of each rope a Northern and Southern Radical, gathered from the Loyal League assembled in our courthouse, then might we once more live in peace and harmony." In this spirit the Klan undertook to destroy the main political arm of Radical Reconstruction in the South.

Since the Freedmen's Bureau had been an important factor in the establishment of congressional reconstruction and since it had assisted the Union League in the "political education" of the freedmen, it was viewed by the Klan as another special enemy. Encouraged by President Johnson's opposition to the Bureau and by the widespread opposition among former Confederates to the

Bureau since its inception, the Klan proceeded to drive the Bureau out of the political picture altogether. The attack on Bureau officials was systematic and effective. Sometimes they were simply warned to leave town, sometimes they were flogged. An agent of the Bureau in Tennessee slept for months with a revolver under his pillow, "a double-barreled shot gun, heavily charged at one hand and a hatchet at the other, with an inclination to sell the little piece of mortality with which I am entrusted as dearly as possible." Even after the Bureau had been officially disbanded, former employees were marked objects of the wrath of the Klansmen.

Perhaps nothing aroused the hatred of Klansmen as much as the so-called "Negro militia units." Conservatives called the units a "dangerous offensive design" to spy on those opposing Radical Reconstruction. Those in the state legislatures sought to block appropriations for the militia and, failing in this, to enjoin the expenditure of the funds that had been appropriated. The opposition moved steadily toward outright violence. The names of black militia leaders were recorded in "Dead Books," while in some communities coffins "were paraded through the streets marked with the names of prominent Radicals and labeled with such inscriptions as 'Dead, damned and delivered.'" African American militiamen were attacked individually and stripped of their weapons, including pocket knives. When they learned through spies of the shipment of arms into the state for the use of the militia, the enemies of Radical Reconstruction would intercept the shipment and either appropriate it for their own use or destroy it altogether.

Personal violence against militiamen, white or black, was the favorite weapon of the Klansmen. In South Carolina, Joseph Crews, a white organizer of the black militia, carried on a running fight with his bitter enemies for several years. Finally, in 1875, he was ambushed and killed by a shotgun blast. Frequent raids on the homes of militiamen resulted in property being taken, muti-lated, or burned. In Marion, Arkansas, a black militia captain was murdered on the streets "in broad daylight." After discharging both loads of a double-barreled shotgun into his body, the assailant fired five revolver shots into him and then rode away unmolested. In Mississippi the well-known African American state senator, Charles Caldwell, had commanded a company of black troops that had been ordered to maintain the peace in Clinton. For this deed, Caldwell was lured into a cellar, shot many times there, and then carried into the streets where his body was "grotesquely turned completely over by the impact of innumerable shots fired at close range." Murders, lynchings, drownings were the hazards facing black and white militiamen who undertook to support congres-sional reconstruction in the South.

The more "respectable" members of Southern communities, re-pelled by these excesses, argued that the terrorist organizations had been taken over by the low, irresponsible elements of the pop-ulation. They were composed of "drunken and lawless vagabonds" declared one disgusted South Carolinian. They were "ignorant and without education to the last degree" asserted the Democratic mi-nority of a congressional investigating committee. The Klan fell into the hands of "cut-throats and riffraff, for private gain and ven-geance," one historian has recently claimed.

It is difficult to understand how the flower of Southern man-hood could have surrendered the leadership of the Klan to so irre-sponsible an element of the community. Klan leaders in Alabama were Generals James H. Clanton, erstwhile Whig lawyer, and John T. Morgan, a future United States senator. Mississippi's lead-ing Klansman was General Albert Pike, poet, journalist, and ex-plorer. In North Carolina leaders were Zebulon Vance, former gov-ernor, and William L. Saunders, Confederate colonel and editor of the state's colonial records; and in Georgia, General John B. Gordon, wealthy insurance executive. The Grand Wizard was General Nathaniel Bedford Forrest, the strong man of Fort Pillow. When Forrest denounced lawlessness employed by "bogus" Klans in 1869, the "respectable" element supported his position. He dissociated himself and his outfit from those who were seizing the opportunity to satisfy private vengeance and to disarm harmless blacks who had no thought of "insurrectionary movements." The distinction was not nearly so clear as Forrest attempted to make it. He would have been hard put to distinguish between the "lawful" violence of the Klan and the "unlawful" violence of the disreputable element. The assassination of an Alabama judge by the Klan should be no different in the eyes of the law from the murder of black would-be voters by hoodlums. In the final analysis, the "respectable" organization remains a prime instigator of the use of violence as a counter-reconstruction measure.

Congressional reconstruction would have no chance of success unless it could put down the lawlessness that was rapidly destroying every semblance of political and economic stability in the South. If they were ever to take a stand and fight for their survival, the state governments realized that the time was at hand. Governor William G. Brownlow of Tennessee, among the most vigorous defenders of Radical Reconstruction, was outraged that the violent counter-reconstruction movement should have had its formal inception in his state. These "rebellious elements," he declared, were composed of ex-rebel soldiers and their sympathizers, who were "plotting and planning mischief in every respect." The legislature of 1868 complied with his request to enact a law "to preserve the public peace." These and similar measures in other states came to be known as the "Ku Klux laws." Any person belonging to secret organizations engaged in night prowling "to the disturbance of the peace" or sheltering members of such organizations was to be punished by a fine of not less than $500 and imprisonment for a term of not less than five years and was to be "rendered infamous." Informers were to receive one-half the fines if private citizens and three-fourths if public officers. There were other provisions, including the assessment ranging from $500 to $5,000 for the state school fund on a county permitting a Klansman to reside within its borders and civil damages ranging from $10,000 to $20,000 in favor of the victim of Klan violence.

Other states followed Tennessee's lead, and within two years there was a network of Ku Klux laws extending across the South designed to combat the counter-reconstruction efforts. In the same year Alabama enacted a similar law and added that "the fact of a man's hiding his face and wearing a costume was *prima facie* evidence of guilt." In the following year Arkansas and North Carolina passed Ku Klux laws, with Mississippi and South Carolina following in 1870 and 1871, respectively. Governors sought to speed the process of destroying the Klan by declaring martial law, appointing special constables, and offering rewards for the apprehension of the night riders. On the whole, the laws were ineffective and their enforcement was generally impossible. As the authorities realized this, they became more desperate. Few means were left to bolster governments that were sagging badly under the weight of counter-reconstruction.

One possibility was military power. In Tennessee full control over the state militia was placed in the governor's hands, and Brownlow did not hesitate to use it. Late in 1868 Governor Powell Clayton declared martial law in thirteen Arkansas counties and sent militiamen into the disturbed areas to maintain the peace. In the summer of 1870 Governor William W. Holden of North Carolina ordered a Union veteran, Colonel George Kirk, to raise troops and put down threatened insurrections in several Piedmont counties. Scores of Ku Klux suspects were arrested and several were hanged for alleged outrages. These and similar measures merely stiffened the resistance of the enemies of reconstruction and strengthened the conviction that the Klan was fully justified. Reports of the number and conduct of black troops on a scene of trouble were frequently exaggerated, and even when that was not the case their use was universally condemned by the former Confederates. Unable to predict what dire consequences might flow from the wielding of military power by African Americans and their friends, the Conservatives began to assert that life for them was becoming "unendurable."

As the whites lashed back at the Ku Klux laws and resisted their enforcement with all the resources they could muster, the supporters of reconstruction began desperately to turn to the federal government for support. From the beginning of congressional reconstruction the new governments had kept the authorities in Washington informed of developments. The Northern press followed every incident with lively interest and gave full play to the stream of Ku Klux atrocity stories coming out of the South. At least a portion of the North was becoming aroused. The Republican party in the South was rapidly disintegrating, violence was threatening Northern investments there, and the war and the reconstruction amendments to the Constitution were being nullified by the Klan and its confederates. The Klan was a "hell-born cabal," declared John W. Forney of Philadelphia. It was "another secession snake," the editor of the New York *Tribune* shouted with characteristic directness. Sooner or later, for one reason or another, the federal government would have to take official cognizance of counter reconstruction in the South.

Perhaps no one took very seriously the order of the Grand Wizard in the spring of 1869 that the Invisible Empire was to dissolve, bury or burn its regalia, and destroy its ritual and records. Certainly, the anti-Klan laws enacted by the states did little to discourage the Klan or coerce its dissolution. Nor could the irresponsible violence of the so-called lower elements have filled the Klan with sufficient disgust to cause it to want to dissociate itself from the more extreme counter-reconstruction measures. In the midst of growing criticism and public outrage against the Klan, the dissolution order of the Grand Wizard appears to have been more of a tactical move than an honest effort to reduce the violence associated with the name of the Klan. Such an order, the leaders hoped, would mean that the Klan could no longer be held responsible for hundreds of crimes described in issue after issue of Northern newspapers. And if the work of the Klan was to be effective, whether performed by the white-robed "better elements" or by others, there was no need to invite the criticism of and, perhaps, punishment by those who possessed the means of vengeance. The path to survival and success was underground, and most of those committed to the Klan's objectives followed that path.

The order of dissolution did not, however, divert attention from the Klan. Leaders in Congress became convinced that some measure of federal support was necessary if the reconstructed states were to survive. The enactment of appropriate legislation would provide the ground on which the "Republican party must stand in carrying into effect the Reconstruction," declared Senator John Pool of North Carolina. Without it the "whole fabric of Reconstruction, with all the principles connected with it, amounts to nothing at all, and in the end it will topple and fall." Congress, busily engaged in admitting the last of the Confederate states, soon diverted some of its attention to the defense of the new governments and enacted measures to enforce the reconstruction amendments. At the end of May, 1870, a law was passed designed to protect African Americans in their exercise of the franchise. Persons hindering, obstructing, or controlling qualified electors in their effort to vote were to be fined and imprisoned. The Klan or others in disguise who interfered with anyone in the enjoyment of his constitutional rights were to be found guilty of committing a felony. Federal district and circuit courts were to have jurisdiction, and federal marshals and other officers were to enforce the law.

The first federal intervention was, on the whole, ineffective. Operating underground, the Klan was able to continue its work by threat and by violence. When charges were brought against alleged offenders, witnesses were usually afraid to testify. When they did testify, juries declined to convict. Through the summer and fall conditions in the former Confederate states deteriorated steadily. The Klan was openly active in the Alabama election of August, 1870. Its members paraded in full regalia, despite the Alabama law, the new federal statute, *and* the Grand Wizard's dissolution order of the previous spring. In Mississippi the Klan took on new life in 1870 in order to oppose the establishment of schools for blacks and to resist the new taxes that it regarded as unreasonable. In North Carolina Governor Holden carried on a running fight with the Klan, and when it appeared that he was not strong enough to cope with the organization, he wired President Grant for support. Holden did not receive any reinforcements and consequently was unable to perpetuate his regime. But he had given the President some indication of the difficulties the reconstruction governments were experiencing, and the President would not forget what he had learned.

In a special message to Congress on December 5, 1870, President Grant declared that "the free exercise of franchise has by violence and intimidation been denied to citizens in several of the states lately in rebellion." On the basis of the information that had come to him regarding conditions in the South, the Senate established a committee of seven to inquire into those conditions. The committee not only examined the voluminous reports turned over to it by the President but called before it a large number of witnesses from North Carolina—federal and state officials, Klan leaders, and private citizens, white and black. The five Republican leaders concluded that the state of North Carolina had insufficient force to cope with the Klan. It was indulging in "a carnival of murders, intimidation, and violence of all kinds." The two Democrats on the committee dissented, declaring that the claim of anarchy in North Carolina was "absurdly untrue."

As a result of the majority report Congress was in a mood to strengthen its legislation of the previous year. On February 28, 1871, it amended the Enforcement Act of May 31, 1870. Supervisors of elections were to be appointed by federal courts, and interference with the discharge of their duties was to be a federal offense, punishable by fine and imprisonment. Federal courts were given jurisdiction over the election supervisors and their work.

Before this law could be tested, a new session of Congress had convened, and the sentiment was strongly favorable to a much more vigorous effort to sustain the new governments in the South. A fresh flood of reports of outrages had come to the attention of the President, and he was ready to take the initiative. Numerous altercations and riots in South Carolina were especially disturbing. They confirmed his growing conviction that life and property were insecure and that the carrying of the mails and the collection of revenue were being endangered. In a special message to Congress he indicated that the power of the states to deal with the problem was inadequate and that he was not certain his own powers were sufficient for such emergencies. Therefore, he recommended legislation to facilitate his enforcement of the law. He then issued a proclamation condemning the lawless elements in South Carolina and ordering them to disperse within twenty days.

Almost immediately Congress responded by drawing up a bill, known as the Third Enforcement Act, which became law on April 20, 1871. Opposition to the bill was bitter, and debate was acrimonious. Not only did Democrats oppose it but several important Republicans spoke out with deep feeling. James A. Garfield in the House called the measure "extreme," while Carl Schurz in the Senate said that the bill gave the President power that he, Schurz, was unwilling to confide in any living man. The majority of members of both houses had been persuaded that the President was justifiably alarmed, and they gave him what he asked for.

The new law, known as the Ku Klux Act, declared that the activity of unlawful combinations constituted a "rebellion against the government of the United States." In areas where such combinations were at work the President could suspend the privilege of the writ of habeas corpus and proclaim martial law. Persons having knowledge of conspiracies could be held responsible for injuries done if they made no effort to prevent the conspirators from carrying out their designs. The President then issued a proclamation calling public attention to the new legislation. He warned that while he would be reluctant to exercise the powers granted him, he would use them "whenever and wherever it shall be necessary to do so." It was not until October 17 that he suspended the writ in nine South Carolina counties that had been especially chaotic and violent during the summer of 1871.

In South Carolina and in other states where the President directed his attention federal troops were used to make arrests and to enforce the law. At the trials in Greenville and Columbia many were found guilty and given fines and prison terms. In Mississippi there were trials under the new law as early as June, 1871, but no convictions. In North Carolina there were hundreds of arrests. Some of the accused confessed their guilt and were released upon providing information that implicated others. By the time the law expired in 1872 there had been hundreds of arrests and some convictions. But the South had not succumbed to federal force. "Short memories," "illness of the defendants," and other reliable alibis frequently destroyed the government's cases. The general attitude of witnesses, the accused, and the public was that the interference by the government was unwarranted and that their previous and current actions were fully justified.

Meanwhile, Congress had injected itself into the reconstruction picture in still another way. At the time the Ku Klux Act was under consideration Congress passed a resolution establishing a joint committee of twenty-one members to "inquire into the condition of the late insurrectionary states." There were five Republicans and two Democrats from the Senate and eight Republicans and six Democrats from the House. Senator John Scott of Pennsylvania was designated chairman. Among the more prominent members from the Senate were Zachariah Chandler of Michigan, Francis P. Blair of Missouri, and New York-born Benjamin F. Rice of Arkansas. From the House, the better-known members were Benjamin F. Butler of Massachusetts, Samuel S. Cox of Ohio, and William E. Lansing of New York. Six committee members were from former Confederate states, while Missouri, Delaware, and Kentucky each had one member. On April 20, 1871, the day on which President Grant signed the Ku Klux Act, the joint committee was organized for work. Like its predecessors this committee expanded vastly the investigative role of Congress. A subcommittee of eight was to hold hearings in Washington, and three subcommittees were to hold hearings in various parts of the South.

By the middle of February, 1872, the committee had completed its work and was ready to make its report.

Persons from every segment of the population appeared before the committee. Governors, senators and representatives, state legislators, mayors, and sheriffs; United States Army officers, ex-Confederate generals and other veterans; planters, lawyers, doctors, editors, merchants and artisans; teachers and clergymen; and African Americans "by the score." Wade Hampton and Governor James L. Orr of South Carolina appeared. Former governor Joseph Brown of Georgia, Governor Robert Lindsay of Alabama, and Nathaniel B. Forrest, widely recognized as the Grand Wizard of the Invisible Empire, all gave testimony.

Suspected members of the Klan and former Confederates in general gave little helpful information. Witnesses usually denied membership in the Klan or any knowledge of its activities. Even when they admitted membership in some organization, they could not remember who asked them to join or who were members. General James H. Clanton of Alabama said that he did not think there had ever been an organization known as the Ku Klux Klan in his state. The testimony of General Forrest and others similarly situated was no more helpful. Indeed, when pressed by members of the committee, some of them became voluble, loosing a flood of invectives and profanities against blacks and the committee.

African American witnesses were "more co-operative." Some of them "made good witnesses and told graphic and convincing stories which had the ring of truth," a historian of the Klan has declared. One of them told how he was whipped because he had not lifted his hat when he met a white man on the road. Another related how a black man was killed by a mob after an altercation with a white man. A black woman told how the Klan dragged her husband from their home and lynched him, presumably because he was politically active. Many told of threats and intimidation directed at those who wielded some political influence or who merely voted. Thus, the black witnesses and their white friends emphasized the lawless, political character of the Klan, while the former Confederates feigned ignorance of it or claimed that it confined its role to that of peacemaking and law enforcement.

The division within the committee was not unlike the division among the witnesses. The Democratic members criticized the committee for confining its work to six states—North and South Carolina, Georgia, Mississippi, Alabama, and Florida. They argued that the committee's work and its report had been politically inspired, that any violence in the South had been provoked by the corruption of the Republican party and the irresponsible rule of the new governments. The Republicans, who wrote the majority report, recommended continuing protective measures by enforcement of federal laws. This should be maintained until there was "no further doubt of the actual suppression and disarming of . . . [the] widespread and dangerous conspiracy" that it had discovered. The committee urged the North to be patient while the strong feeling engendered by the war gradually subsided. Meanwhile, the South's "reluctant obedience" to federal authority was hoped for, but "less than obedience" the government would not accept.

The report of the joint committee, covering thirteen large volumes, was one of the most extensive that a congressional committee had ever made. Almost as much was gained from what the report did not say as from what it did say. The bellicosity of some of the former Confederate witnesses and the artful evasiveness of some of the others clearly indicated that many white Southerners had no intention of accommodating themselves to federal control or congressional reconstruction. The earlier decision of the Klan

167

to go underground paid off handsomely, for the members could now say they knew of no organization whose purpose was to resist the law. Even without the committee's saying so, it was clear that counter-reconstruction had been so successful that the new governments in the South could not stand without the most vigorous and direct support of the federal government. And if any of the Republican members had looked to the South for strong party support in the election of 1872, they must have been depressed by what they saw. The reconstruction governments were showing signs of collapse, and the party in power was collapsing even more rapidly.

Counter reconstruction was everywhere an overwhelming success. In the face of violence the Fourteenth and Fifteenth Amendments provided no protection for the African American citizen and his friends. The federal enforcement laws of 1870 and 1871 proved wholly inadequate, especially when enforcement was left to the meager forces that remained in the South at the time of their enactment. African Americans could hardly be expected to continue to vote when it cost them not only their jobs but their lives. In one state after another, the African American electorate declined steadily as the full force of the Klan came forward to supervise the elections that federal troops failed to supervise. Towns, counties, and states went Democratic. Overthrow of existing governments became systematic and inevitable. As early as April, 1868, the Democratic convention of South Carolina had said to the blacks of the state, "It is impossible that your present power can endure, whether you use it for good or ill." Within two years this promise was well on its way to fulfillment in South Carolina and elsewhere.

While the success of counter reconstruction through violence was itself a kind of vindication of violence, it is now clear that reconstruction could have been overthrown even without the use of violence. Except for the exasperation of Grant in 1870 and the Enforcement Acts of 1870 and 1871, the federal government was, more and more, leaving the South to its own devices. Even more important was the enormous prestige that the former Confederates enjoyed. In time they were able to assume leadership in their communities without firing a shot or hanging a single black. What they lacked in political strength they made up in economic power. By discharging or threatening to discharge black employees who persisted in participating in politics, they could reduce the African American electorate to a minimum. By refusing to pay taxes to support the expanded and inflated functions of the new governments, they could destroy Radical Reconstruction in a season. But the former Confederates relied on no one method. By political pressure, economic sanctions, *and* violence they brought Radical Reconstruction crashing down almost before it began.

10

Economic and Social Reconstruction

When New Yorkers and Bostonians spoke optimistically of "Northernizing" the South at the close of the war, they had in mind not merely political and social reconstruction, important as it was to modify the South's way of life in these spheres. They were also thinking of making the kind of arrangements and setting up the kind of relationships that would foster a continuation of the growth and prosperity that had characterized the Northern economy during the war. They wanted to be certain that political reconstruction would facilitate the economic well-being of the country and, more especially, their own ascendancy in the nation's economic life. They wanted to be certain, too, that the reconstructed section would provide the kind of free labor force and the kind of markets that the expanding economy could use with profit.

Down to 1865 the greatest stimulus that the American economy had ever had was the war and the wartime economic policies of the federal government itself. The war—and the prosperity it fostered—disclosed almost unlimited possibilities for the new industrial order. Almost any economic endeavor seemed to thrive during the war. And as peace came closer, the new industrial leaders agreed that the economy, if properly stimulated, would continue to expand, perhaps indefinitely. Their optimism was well founded. A vast productive organization with valuable wartime experience as well as the new technical processes that had contributed to the winning of the war could now be employed to satisfy the growing needs of a peacetime economy. The war's end had made available an enormous quantity of raw materials in the South and West. Under favorable conditions these could be fed into the postwar machines to benefit the new masters of American industry. The war had demonstrated, too, that the government could play an important role in stimulating economic development through its currency, tax, railroad, and tariff policies.

The momentum of industrial development gained during the war continued for another decade. In the last year of the war the first factory in the United States to employ the Bessemer process of making steel was built. In 1868 the open-hearth process was introduced. With these significant improvements in blast furnaces and with advancements in rolling mill techniques, steel manufacturing began to play a vital role in the industrial life of the country. Soon the coal mines of West Virginia, Illinois, and Ohio supplemented those of Pennsylvania in providing fuel for steel and other industrial centers, while the Minnesota ore deposits provided new, high-quality raw materials for the burgeoning steel industry.

Even more dramatic was the growth of the oil industry. At the beginning of the war, oil production, begun only in 1859, was still a novelty. By 1864, as new uses were demonstrated under the pressure of war, there were scores of oil derricks in the area of Titusville, Pennsylvania. Almost overnight the refining of oil became a major industrial activity, attracting huge capital as well as shrewd business acumen in such centers as Erie, Pittsburgh, Cleveland, New York, and Baltimore. Shrewdest of all in the business was John D. Rockefeller, who became an oil refiner at the close of the war and founded the Standard Oil Company in 1870. By 1880 the nation was producing annually about 26,000,000 barrels of oil, and Standard was refining more than 90 per cent of it.

The pattern of industrialization took shape rapidly as one enterprise after another came under the stimulating influence of the psychology as well as the fact of expansion. New sources of power were discovered with the construction of the first dynamo to generate a continuous supply of direct electric current; and by 1879 Thomas A. Edison had perfected a carbon-filament electric lamp. The emergence of an electrical industry was an important stimulus for production of copper. This was reflected in increased activity in the Michigan copper mills and in the search for new sources found, among other places, in Montana and Arizona. Industrialization had its effects, also, on the production of a wide variety of tools and implements, shoes, and firearms, as well as on food processing. The meat-packing industry, which had made great strides during the war, was advanced significantly in the 1870's with the introduction of the refrigerated car.

A tangible force in the nationalization of the country's industrial activity was the growth of railroads and other forms of communication and transportation. Here the state and federal governments both played a vital role. The pattern of subsidy developed by the federal government in the prewar years was continued during the war with the chartering by Congress of the Union Pacific and Central Pacific railroads in 1862. The completion of the first transcontinental line in 1869 merely whetted the appetites of prospective railroad barons, who stepped up their demands for government aid of other lines. Meanwhile, states, including those of the South, did what they could by lending money and making land grants to improve transportation within their borders.

While the Northeast easily led the nation in economic growth, the other sections were far from inactive. Chicago was becoming an important center with the meat-packing activities of Armour, Morris, and Swift, the manufacture of agricultural machinery by the McCormicks, and the parlor-car industry of George Pullman. Minneapolis was rapidly becoming the flour-milling capital of the world, thanks to Charles Pillsbury and George Christian. Other western cities produced furniture, beer, clothes, and many other consumer goods. Farther west there was considerable activity brought on by the building of the railroads and by the population movement caused by gold and silver mining and the successful campaign against the Indians. By 1880 the yields of gold and silver had passed their peak, but by that time Colorado, Nevada, Montana, Wyoming, and Idaho had become centers of coal mining, timber, ranching, and farming activities.

Interest in expansion extended beyond the territory already in possession of the United States. Some Americans in 1866 and 1867 spoke freely of expanding into British Columbia, and a few even went so far as to request the British government to cede that territory to the United States. Despite this interest, Americans were shocked to learn early in 1867 that their government had concluded a treaty with Russia for the purchase of Alaska. It was "a dark deed done in the night," they declared. What would they do with this "Walrussia," or "Seward's Folly," as they derisively called it. It would have been much more to their liking if the Secretary of State had succeeded in purchasing the Virgin Islands, but the *Nation* expressed the opinion of many when it declared that if the national future "be in peril at all, it is not for want of territory but from excess of it." For the time being, Alaska was more than enough for the American territorial appetite.

Most public leaders seemed less interested in expansion than in settling the score with Britain regarding the "Alabama" and other Confederate ships which had been built or fitted out in British ports and which had done so much damage to Union shipping during the war. The treaty negotiated by Reverdy Johnson, the United States minister to England, contained no word of regret or any mention of "indirect damages" caused by the "Alabama" and the others. Consequently, the Senate rejected the treaty by a vote of 54 to 1. It was not until 1871 that a joint commission settled the "Alabama" claims and other differences between Britain and the United States. In the final treaty, the British expressed regret over the "Alabama" and agreed to the establishment of a commission of five members to arbitrate the claims of the United States. In the following year the tribunal concluded that Britain had violated the rules of "due diligence" in permitting the escape of the "Alabama" and two other cruisers and awarded the United States $15,500,000. The United States appeared to be more successful in international disputes than in settling vexing problems at home.

Despite the uncertainties and instability caused by the shifting fortunes of political reconstruction, the Southern states began moving steadily toward economic recovery shortly after the last shot was fired. While it lacked adequate capital and the other ingredients necessary to compete in a complex industrial order, the South was not without its advantages as an agricultural section. Northerners early became aware not only of its needs but of its economic possibilities, and they contributed the capital and experience where necessary to assist the section toward recovery and transformation. Reconstruction brought with it no drastic or even substantial change in the locus of economic power in the South. Neither Congress nor the Radical state legislatures seriously considered measures leading to the redistribution of land. The small planting class continued to dominate that most important asset.

In many instances, as Roger Shugg has clearly illustrated by examining conditions in Louisiana, alleged land redistribution was more apparent than real. The misconception arose from the fact that large landowners continued to own and control many acres which some observers, including census reporters, mistakenly recorded as the property of the small farmers who lived on them; but these, as renters or sharecroppers, had only temporary tenure.

Cheap labor was another economic asset, as abundant and as available in the South in 1865 as it had been in 1850. The four million former slaves had not fled the South or even the plantation; and after a holiday of a few weeks they were back at work under conditions not unlike those that prevailed before the war. Even after the repeal of the short-lived black codes by Radical legislatures the relationship of freedman to planter gave evidence of no social or economic revolution. Blacks and whites who were low-paid workers or disadvantaged sharecroppers combined their energies and talents in the task of promoting economic recovery in the South.

The production of cotton soon reflected the strides toward recovery. In 1860 the Southern crop had reached 5,300,000 bales. It was down to approximately 2,000,000 in the year following the war's end. Then it began its steady climb to 3,000,000 bales by 1870 and to 5,700,000 by 1880, more than the South had ever before produced. In 1886 the tobacco crop, augmented by expansion into the Piedmont, North Carolina and Kentucky, had reached some 470,000,000 pounds, exceeding the 1860 yield by approximately 40,000,000. Recovering, though not as dramatically, were the rice and sugar crops. In South Carolina the *News and Courier* reported that rice production rose steadily from 4,019 tierces in 1866 to 42,677 by 1872. In Louisiana sugar production had materially improved, not only because of optimism arising from the "settlement" of reconstruction, but also because of the acute crop shortage in Cuba. Meanwhile, commercial ventures in the production of fruits, nuts, and vegetables opened new opportunities for the Southern farmer. Peanuts, which had no prewar value as a commercial crop, became important in the economic life of Virginia and North Carolina shortly after the close of the war. No more than 75,000 bushels were produced in 1865. By 1880 production had climbed well above 1,000,000 bushels. Georgia and other states began to produce peaches for the Northern market, and within a decade this was an important cash crop.

The Yankee trader, who reluctantly withdrew from the Southern scene at the outbreak of the war, returned happily soon after the last shot was fired. He provided Southerners with many desperately needed items they could not yet produce. They tended to eye him suspiciously, but unless he was known to be rabidly anti-Confederate, he was accepted with grace—at least for his wares. Often he had old ties among the Southern people, and if he had some capital of his own or was well connected in the North, he was often instrumental in setting up a business or industry in his favorite Southern community.

The North was more than ready to provide, through traders or otherwise, whatever capital and ingenuity the South lacked. This was years before the D. A. Tomkinses and the Richard H. Edmondses fostered a program of self-help in the South. The movement of Northern investors into the South had begun as a trickle before the war. Toward the end of the conflict it began again, as Union soldiers, with a shrewd eye to the future, came to appreciate the Southern potential and made plans to exploit it. Thus, in 1867 General John Wilder of Ohio saw his dream of 1863 fulfilled when his Northern friends responded to his appeal for funds to establish an iron foundry in Chattanooga. In the early postwar years numerous others from the North were looking for investment opportunities in the South. Some put capital in agricultural lands and became planters. Others went into the business of lending money for a variety of new ventures. Still others sought to construct factories in their adopted section. Although their greatest success was to come after 1880, the economic developments in the fifteen years following the war fully justify Holland Thompson's assertion that the New South began with the fall of the Confederacy.

In the Piedmont section of the Carolinas the textile mills began to make the kind of progress vainly urged by William Gregg before the war. In 1860 there were seventeen cotton mills in South Carolina. By 1880 the number of separate mills had decreased to fourteen but the number of spindles had nearly tripled, with the value of the products increasing from $713,050 in 1860 to $2,895,769 by 1880. In North Carolina there were the beginnings of the development that was to make the state a major producer of cotton textiles before the end of the century. In Georgia, Columbus became an important center for the manufacture of cotton. Rising from the ashes of 1865 two cotton factories in Columbus capitalized at $700,000 had 12,500 spindles in 1867. The Athens, Georgia, Manufacturing Company had 3,000 spindles and employed 175 operatives by 1868. In 1860 North Carolina had approximately one hundred small tobacco establishments, employing 1,500 workers. By 1880 more than 6,500 workers were producing $13,800,000 worth of plug, twist, smoking tobacco, and snuff. Within a few years the Dukes were to revolutionize the industry with "ready rolled" cigarettes.

In Virginia the ironworks around Richmond began to surpass their prewar importance, while the efforts of General Wilder were transforming the Chattanooga works into an important source of pig iron and iron products. In Alabama, David Thomas, who had pioneered in the Pennsylvania fields, joined with his son to tap the iron and coal resources in the hills around what was later to be called Birmingham. Soon, others like Truman Aldrich of New York were to enter into agreements with local leaders to make that region one of the main centers of iron and steel production. Numerous other successful ventures resulted from a combination of Northern capital and Southern co-operation. Among them were lumber and flour mills, publishing houses, tanneries, and harness works.

These successful economic developments greatly stimulated the movement of people into Southern towns and cities. The section was soon able to boast of a cityward trend similar to what other sections of the country were experiencing. While Mobile, Memphis, and Vicksburg lost population, Nashville, New Orleans, Atlanta, and Savannah were growing. Textile manufacturing and tobacco processing were making towns out of the previously sleepy hamlets of Charlotte, Durham, Greensboro, and Spartanburg. As the whites moved to urban centers, so did the blacks. There was little prospect that they would secure employment in the new ventures (the mills were for whites, "our people of purest Anglo-Saxon descent"), but they went along hopefully and were there to perform the domestic chores for the white men and women who found jobs in the new stores, factories, and mills.

In all parts of the country, as the great economic transformation took place, the working class became conscious of its problems and needs. The worker no longer could bargain individually with his employer, whom he did not even know. He was unable to rely on his skills to earn an adequate living in a system that had little or no need for special skills. Industrialization tended to reduce even the skilled laborer to the status of a semiskilled or even unskilled worker. This disheartening fact reduced some of the ablest artisans to the level of millions of immigrants, erstwhile farm workers, and others who were unable to boast of any manual accomplishments. If the worker was to secure adequate wages and satisfactory working conditions, he could no longer rely on his own resources. Reluctantly he reached the conclusion that his only recourse was to join with others to seek what he was unable to secure as an individual.

The first national expression of this feeling was the organization in 1866 of the National Labor Union under the leadership of William H. Sylvis, president of the Iron Moulders' Union. The national character of the organization was emphasized by its banner proclaiming, "Welcome to the Sons of Toil of North, South, East, and West." Avoiding radicalism or even militancy in its program for the rights of the working man, it advocated equal rights for all, including African Americans and women, called for a federal department of labor, the elimination of monopoly, and establishment of the eight-hour day. From the beginning the National Labor Union expressed a desire to incorporate blacks into its organization, and at the 1869 convention, with nine blacks present, the Union called on them to organize and to send delegates to the next convention. Blacks, however, were suspicious of the good intentions of the leaders of the NLU. Consequently, they established their own National Negro Labor Union, which had only indifferent success during its short life of about four years. The National Labor Union fared little better. Workers, interested primarily in higher wages and employment security, felt that there was not enough direct action in the NLU program. Membership rapidly declined, and its reorganization into the National Labor party in 1871 did not stem the tide. Within a year it was less than a shadow of its former self.

The Knights of Labor had a longer life and a larger membership than the National Labor Union, but it was not much more effective. From its founding in 1869 it welcomed all who toiled; and it advocated a number of reforms looking toward the general improvement of the social order. While opposing the use of the strike, the knights sought to obtain by other kinds of pressure the eight-hour day, compulsory arbitration, equal pay for men and women, and the abolition of child and prison labor. It accomplished none of these objectives in its first decade of existence; and while its second decade was equally fruitless, it did much to arouse workers to the need for co-operation especially after Terence V. Powderly was elected Grand Master Workman in 1879.

Aside from an increased self-consciousness, labor made no significant advances before 1880. The effective resistance of management made possible by its vast resources, including those of the government, proved too much for the fledgling labor organizations. Unfavorable publicity resulting from the violent tactics employed by Pennsylvania coal miners (Molly McGuires) and others did further damage to the cause. The inability of the leaders to forge a program that would appeal to the unsophisticated rank and file and still be acceptable to most Americans, who were deeply committed to non-revolutionary approaches to progress, proved to be another stumbling block in labor's path.

The most significant setback by labor during the period was experienced by the whole economy, namely, the panic of 1873 and the depression that continued for another five or six years. As economic expansion continued in the postwar years, more and more speculative activity became a part of the general economic picture. Overexpansion and the resulting inflation alarmed the conservative element in the business community. But nothing seemed to check the headlong plunge. Business firms were increasing at a dizzy pace: 431,000 in 1870; approximately 610,000 in the following year. In each of the two years preceding the panic 13,000 miles of railroad were built. But businesses were failing at an alarming rate, and few railroads were paying dividends. As early as 1870 the Conservatives demanded and secured congressional legislation providing that the government would pay its debts in gold or the equivalent. But after the Supreme Court reversed its ruling of 1869 and declared in 1871 that greenbacks were legal tender, the law of 1870 could not check inflation effectively.

The Conservatives were still arguing that the excessive amount of currency in circulation was undermining the economic structure when the crash came in 1873. And little or no attention had been given to other important contributing factors. An unsound international economic situation had been precipitated by wars and revolutions in Europe and the New World. There were glaring defects in banking policies, as banks persisted in lending money on patently unsound ventures and as they shifted commercial paper from one bank to another for speculative purposes. Scandals involving the business community's connections in government tended to undermine public confidence in both business and government. Early in September three major New York investment houses failed—the New York Warehouse and Securities Company; Kenyon, Cox and Company; and Jay Cooke and Company. The Freedmen's Savings and Trust Company, on which the Cookes had dumped much undesirable commercial paper, was unable to survive a run on its deposits; it was one of many banks forced to close. Within a few days the New York Stock Exchange announced that it was taking a ten-day recess to allow the business community to collect its breath and its wits. The road to ruin continued, with more than five thousand businesses failing and eighty-nine railroads defaulting on their bonds before the year's end.

Early in 1874 the panic settled into a full-scale depression that was, until then, the worst in the nation's history. In 1876 there were nine thousand business failures, approximately the same number in the following year, and ten thousand in 1878. Unemployment figures reached staggering proportions, and labor union memberships fell accordingly. Demands for relief were louder than demands for better working conditions or long-range reform. Congress seemed helpless, except in its continued search among proposed currency legislation for a solution to all or most of the economic difficulties. In 1874 it fixed the amount of greenbacks in circulation at \$382,000,000. In the following year it passed the Resumption Act, which provided that in 1879 the Treasury would redeem in coin all legal-tender notes offered in amounts not less than \$50. For the first time since 1862 gold and greenbacks were to be at parity. This, however, did not "prime the pump" of recovery, as had been hoped.

That the labor movement was not completely destroyed by the depression is evidenced by its activity in the late seventies. Union members bitterly resented the introduction of non-union workers into industry by managements hard pressed to reduce production costs. In numerous towns in Pennsylvania, Ohio, and Illinois miners and iron workers resorted to violence to drive out black or immigrant competitors. In businesses where employment remained fairly stable the unions attempted to function as usual and to press their case. In the summer of 1877 they walked off their jobs on the Baltimore and Ohio Railroad to protest wage reductions and the use of the blacklist by the railroad. The strike quickly spread to other lines, and violence flared up in numerous cities as the workers resisted troops called out to subdue them. Through the use of the injunction, the armed forces of states and the federal government, and their overwhelming economic resources, the railroads broke the strike, but not before millions of dollars' worth of damage had been done.

The changes wrought in the social fabric of the nation by postwar political and economic changes were too numerous and complex for any simple description. No aspect of life in the United States escaped the far-reaching effects of social upheaval. Everywhere there was movement, change, transition, transformation. New social and economic classes were coming into being, and almost at once they became important. Millionaires and near-millionaires, those sensational phenomena that made their debut during the war, were becoming sufficiently numerous to develop group characteristics. The great middle class was rising, as the industrial urban community grew in numbers and size and as mercantile and professional groups came to constitute a very significant factor in the life of the city. The industrial workers, constantly becoming more conscious of their role and of their problems, were being strengthened by new recruits from the farms and from abroad, as immigrants resumed their trek to the New World at the end of the war. The sense of movement and change was further heightened by the movement of large numbers into the new mining and farming areas in the West and into the new industrial centers in many parts of the country.

Social movement and change were of a very special kind in the South, at once the most dramatic and the most far reaching. The drama was provided by the entrance into the society of some four million African Americans in a new role. Whites were, of course, constantly asserting that the social status of the blacks was precisely what it had been before the war. Even so, the bitter resentment and objections of the whites could not alter the fact that freedom for blacks, however limited by hostility and rejection, implied some elevation in the social scale. There was a new dignity, a new pride, a new self-respect by which African Americans gave evidence of understanding the marked change in their status. The evidence lay not in the caricatures that white writers have labored to draw of supercilious blacks with hats, gloves, cutaways, and umbrellas, but in their quiet, undramatic attempts to assume their responsibilities as members of an advanced and changing social order.

As the whites of the South fretted over changes in the social status of blacks, their own society was itself undergoing significant changes. White skin remained the badge of superiority, but while no white Southerner was willing to disregard this as the sacred cornerstone of Southern life, those whites at the top found their positions nevertheless challenged. They were forced to share their command with the politicians—"scalawags" and "carpetbaggers"—whom they frequently despised. The greatly transformed business community now included, in addition to white Southerners, some Northern financiers and industrialists who inevitably became a part of the Southern social scene. Like the trader before him, the Northern investor could look forward to some degree of social acceptance unless he was known to be particularly hostile to the Southern way of life. By 1880 through happily placed investments or through marriage, Northerners had begun to experience a near transformation into Southerners. They frequently became as vigorous as the ex-Confederates themselves in defense of the Lost Cause. In this regard a significant Southern victory had been won.

Social values were inevitably affected by the many changes taking place in the economic and political spheres. The spirit of reform that had touched so many Americans and so many phases of life before the war gave way to the more practical considerations of trying to get ahead in a rapidly changing and complex world. Everywhere the emphasis was on material things, and the scandals of the Grant administration clearly demonstrated the extent to which the moral fiber of the country had been affected by this emphasis. It was difficult to find an area of reform that elicited the enthusiastic support of many Americans. The slaves had been freed, and there was an increasing feeling that not much more could be done for them. Native Americans were being maltreated both by settlers in the West and by officials of the federal government. But the sympathetic response of the American public to their plight was extremely limited. The growth of cities intensified the older urban problems and created many new ones, but there was as yet no disposition to grapple with them.

There were no really significant developments in American religion. The popularization of the Darwinian theory of evolution presented a challenge to the churches, but by 1880 they had evolved no thesis that could make peace with the evolutionists. Mrs. Mary Baker Eddy published *Science and Health* in 1875, but two decades passed before the Church of Christ, Scientist had any appreciable following. Among African Americans there continued the process of organization of separate churches that began before the war. The African Methodist Episcopal Church and the A.M.E. Zion Church could boast of several decades of growth before 1865. Their growth quickened noticeably during reconstruction. Other black Methodists began to withdraw from their white affiliations, and by 1870 the Colored Methodist Episcopal Church had been organized. Black Baptists continued to increase in numbers, and their position was greatly strengthened by the consolidation that finally led to the establishment of the National Baptist Convention in 1886. Meanwhile the white Baptists, Methodists, and Presbyterians, who had split into Northern and Southern organizations during the sectional controversy of the 1840's, remained as far apart as ever.

Education was one of the few areas where the spirit of reform remained strong during the postwar period. An important factor in the growth of educational facilities and opportunities was the widespread belief that education was a means of self-advancement in the highly competitive economic world. Public school facilities increased everywhere, although cities led rural areas and the North led the other sections. In higher education the changes were more dramatic. New colleges and universities, beneficiaries of the millionaire philanthropists, were opening almost yearly. Vassar, Smith, Wellesley, Cornell, Johns Hopkins, Minnesota, and California led the list among institutions of higher education. Meanwhile the older ones joined with the new ones in developing approaches and techniques for exploring the frontiers of knowledge as well as for disseminating what was already known.

The "enlightenment" of the American people during the period cannot be measured only by the growth of colleges and universities. The great impact of these institutions was reserved for a later generation. A more accurate reflection of current intellectual activities and tastes could be seen in the literary output and reading habits of the American people. Among the periodicals, *Harper's Monthly Magazine* and the *Atlantic Monthly* continued to flourish, while E. L. Godkin's *Nation,* launched in 1865, created a new mood in its advocacy of honesty in government and civil service reform. In the South new periodicals, such as *Scott's Monthly Magazine, The Land We Love,* and the *Southern Review,* emphasized the importance of a regional approach to literary and intellectual matters. In the newspaper world, the great era of personal journalism epitomized by Raymond of the *Times,* Greeley of the *Tribune* and

Bennett of the *Herald* was rapidly coming to a close, while the new era of Pulitzer and Hearst had not yet begun.

We must not overlook the fact that Mark Twain made his first national impression during the reconstruction era and that *The Gilded Age,* which he wrote in collaboration with Charles Dudley Warner, dealt with most of the fundamental problems of the period. In the same mood, Walt Whitman continued to sing the praises of his country and William Cullen Bryant closed his career as a social critic nagging at the conscience of America. In the South writers like John Esten Cooke, Sidney Lanier, and Henry Timrod wrote verse that not only praised the Southern land but, at times, rose above the sectional issue. An example of this can be seen in Lanier's "Centennial Cantata," written expressly in observance of the centennial of national independence. African Americans, moreover, were mindful of the centennial of independence. For the occasion, George Washington Williams, a recent graduate of the Newton Theological Institution, delivered an oration in Cincinnati, "The American Negro, from 1776 to 1876." In time this effort would inspire him to write his *History of the Negro Race in America,* which appeared in 1882.

For the most part, Southern writers devoted most of their talents to glorifying and defending their particular past. In 1866 E. A. Pollard's *The Lost Cause* appeared, and only two years later the first of Alexander Stephens' two volumes, *Constitutional View of the Late War between the States.* In the same year Frank Alfriend published his *Life of Jefferson Davis.* George W. Cable, Joel Chandler Harris, and Thomas Nelson Page had begun to write, but in 1880 the important years of their careers were still ahead of them.

But the serious writings of the period received scant attention from the American reading public. Cheap magazines and newspapers circulated freely even in the remote areas, and sensational "dime novels" were already popular by 1870. In 1866 Horatio Alger began to write his stories for juveniles. By 1880 Harlan P. Halsey had begun to publish his interminable dime novels in the "Old Sleuth" series. Americans as a whole were much more conversant with the works of Alger and Halsey than with the works of Twain and Lanier. This was something that Charles W. Eliot at Harvard and Andrew D. White at Cornell could not change even in a generation.

11

The Era Begins To End

Thanks to the fictional accounts of reconstruction by novelists and the near-fictional accounts by influential writers in other categories, the many misconceptions and distortions regarding the period are tenaciously persistent. A significant ingredient in the distortion is the neglect of the period immediately following the close of the Civil War. At this juncture the former Confederates had complete control of their own states. White manhood suffrage was the basis of the franchise; violence against the Freedmen's Bureau, the philanthropists from the North, the United States Army, and the former slaves was rampant. And, except for representation in Congress, the former Confederates had the destiny of their section in their own hands. A failure to give consideration to the effect of such a state of affairs and to the consequences that resulted from it conveys, consciously or unconsciously, a misrepresentation of the early postwar years that makes impossible any clear understanding of what followed.

Another misconception flows from careless assertions regarding the nature and extent of so-called Radical Reconstruction. Such assertions, conveying the impression that the years following 1867 were characterized by a uniformly oppressive regime imposed by the Radicals on all the former Confederate states, must be modified and qualified. Tennessee was never subjected to Radical Reconstruction under the provisions of the legislation of 1867; and former Confederates were always eligible and, indeed, did participate in the affairs of government there. In Virginia the vigorous activity of the Conservatives not only delayed the beginning of Reconstruction under Congress for more than two years but also prevented effective domination by the Radicals after congressional reconstruction began.

Georgia was so completely under the control of native whites with conservative proclivities that the readmission of the state was delayed for two years. The state's insistence on outlawing the collection of debts due prior to January 1, 1865, the expulsion of blacks from the legislature, and the refusal to abide by the congressional enactments of 1867 clearly demonstrated the virility of Georgia's resistance, which carried over into the brief period of Radical Reconstruction. The conspiracy of the former Confederates in Alabama to defeat the ratification of the new constitution and the increasing strength of the Conservatives in the affairs of government meant that congressional reconstruction there would be greatly weakened by the opposition.

It is well to remember, moreover, that the so-called Radicals in the former Confederate states were not in full agreement regarding the program of reconstruction. Many of the native whites who held office were as opposed to the idea of equality for blacks as were many of the disfranchised former Confederates. It was the native whites who insisted on segregated schools and laws against intermarriage. Nor was there agreement among the Radicals regarding the proposed social programs of the reconstruction governments. Debates over the establishment of orphanages and insane asylums were often sharp and bitter, and decisions to subsidize railroads and public works were reached only after exten-

sive wrangling among the lawmakers. Even in the matter of enfranchising African Americans the only considerations that
seemed to command acceptance of them as voters were the clear
mandate of the Congress and the practical necessity of doing so in
order to remain in power. As the white electorate grew through
amnesties and individual pardons, the disagreements among those
in power increased and the extent and nature of the reconstruction
program were substantially altered even further.

Still another widely held misconception is that the reconstruction period was of long duration. It is usually regarded as having
lasted for at least a decade, and most of the criticism of the "excesses" of Radical Reconstruction implies that these excesses were
all the more unbearable because of this "long" period of time. The
contention is that not until Hayes withdrew the troops in 1877
was Radical Reconstruction "overthrown" and the Southern states
"redeemed." The fact is that few troops were left in the South in
1877 and only three states could be considered "unredeemed" by
this time. When James M. Smith, Democrat, was inaugurated as
governor of Georgia in 1871, he spoke of the "long and cheerless
night of misrule" from which the people of Georgia were emerging. This "unhappy" period had lasted for less than two years, a
portion of which time the legislature was controlled by Democrats
and all of which time native whites, with strong Confederate sym-
pathies, were dominant.

The period from their admission as "reconstructed" states to the
time of Democratic or Conservative victories may be regarded as
the maximum extent of so-called Radical control of the former
Confederate states. While these periods varied from state to state,
they were less than a decade except in Florida, South Carolina,
and Louisiana. A recent historian of reconstruction observed that
Virginia "escaped simon-pure Radical rule entirely." Indeed, the

Radicals, feuding among themselves, were unable to win the first election after the readmission of Virginia, with the result that the Democrats became the controlling party in 1870, the very year of readmission. In North Carolina the Radicals lost their grip in 1870, after two years of difficult and uncertain rule. In the same year, Tennessee went Conservative, ending a four-year period as the first state of the former Confederacy to be reconstructed. The Democrats won Texas in 1873 and Alabama and Arkansas in the following year. Mississippi capitulated in 1875. Thus, within ten years after the surrender at Appomattox—including two years of native white rule—eight states had been "redeemed," and their redemption had been effected within a range of a few months to seven years after their readmission to the Union.

The strong local opposition that severely limited the scope of reconstruction and made possible the early "overthrow" of "Radical Rule" in many communities and states was greatly facilitated by developments outside the former Confederate states. Many of the Northern leaders who had pressed for the reconstruction legislation of 1867 had passed from the scene, while others had lost their ardor for reform, becoming generally indifferent or transferring their interests to other matters. Thaddeus Stevens was dead, and there was no replacement for his relentless advocacy of the Radical cause. Carl Schurz had shifted from his caustic attacks on the South in 1868 to a point in 1870 when he could say that the "exigencies of a great public danger have ceased to exist." Within a few months he was attacking the "insane Ku Klux legislation" of the Radicals and was beginning to show revulsion against Republican corruption North and South. George W. Julian, no longer fired by abolitionist principles, seemed more interested in political reform in general and in the improvement of public morality in particular. Edward Atkinson, long associated with the

Boston reformers, shifted his attention to business interests and promoted conciliation with the South for admittedly business considerations.

Former advocates of strong measures against the South turned their fire on those attempting to carry out the strong measures. Whitelaw Reid, the journalist who had found the South arrogant and defiant in 1865, was much more charitable five years later. That he had invested heavily in Louisiana plantations could possibly have affected his attitude. James S. Pike, the Radical journalist who advocated Negro suffrage in 1865, lampooned Radical Reconstruction in *The Prostrate State*, published in 1873. Robert F. Durden, however, has clearly proved, by examining Pike's journals and notebooks, that he was more interested in discrediting the Grant administration and in giving vent to his long-held racist views than he was in an accurate portrayal of conditions in South Carolina. If padding his report at some points and omitting significant on-the-spot material at others would serve his purposes, he was not above doing so. The result was a highly colored, distorted picture that discredited reconstruction at the time and survived as one of the "standard" accounts of the reconstruction period.

Even when Northern supporters of the Radical program in the South were convinced that fraud and corruption were destroying chances of effective reform there, they did little or nothing. Despite the lively interest in the activities of the Klan and in the "outrages at the South," Northerners did little more than go through a ritualistic wringing of their hands. As the Red Shirts flourished in South Carolina, the Knights of the White Camellia in Louisiana, and the Klan in many places, the demand for new legislation was relatively slight. When, finally, President Grant and Congress brought forth the Enforcement Acts of 1870 and

1871, they were bitterly assailed in some Northern quarters. Senator Lyman Trumbull of Illinois thought that the powers given the federal government would be "destructive at once of the State Governments." To suspend the writ of habeas corpus by executive action would be a "monstrous thing," declared Representative Daniel Vorhees of Indiana. The mood of Radical Reconstruction had been replaced by one "more understanding" of the South and, perhaps, more sensitive to constitutional scruples and economic interests.

Northern animosity, the only kind that would have made any difference in the course of reconstruction, was rapidly receding. In many places in the North a conciliatory attitude had replaced the bellicose posture. In 1870 Edward King, in *Scribner's Monthly Magazine,* said that white Southerners were as loyal to the idea of the Union as were any citizens of New York. Northern business interests were stepping up demand for a policy of leniency toward the South and for the restoration of sectional peace. The New York *Commercial and Financial Chronicle* attacked Radical Reconstruction because it exacerbated the difficulties between the North and South and, consequently, delayed the resumption of normal business relations of the sections. As Paul H. Buck has said, "Where economic interests jibed . . . men of business were men of peace." In every section of the country, these men became the staunch advocates of conciliation in the period following the Civil War. Those having common railroad interests or crop-marketing interests or investment interests could and did easily extend their hands across sectional lines and join in the task of working together for the common good.

More and more one heard in the North statements of conciliation that echoed on the other side of the sectional line. "Let the South alone," a Northern businessman would say. "The Negro and the Southern white man must be left to solve their own problems," a prominent Southern leader would say. "Let us work to improve the South within the framework of the Southern social system," the policy of the new Northern philanthropy seemed to imply. Meanwhile, the earlier notion that the South was indeed different was revived. And if there were those who persisted in trying to understand it, an increasing number seemed resigned to live with the difference. Northernization was no longer a crusade or even a policy. Acceptance was the spirit that came to dominate Northern spokesmen and leaders.

Acceptance involved, most of all, Northern acquiescence in the Southern view of blacks. Southerners dominated all expressions of opinion regarding the qualities and characteristics of blacks. As Sterling Brown has observed, the "authoritative" white Southern writers described them in seven categories: the Contented Slave, the Wretched Freedman, the Comic Negro, the Brute Negro, the Tragic Mulatto, the Local Color Negro, and the Exotic Primitive. These writers aggressively advanced the concept of the inherent inferiority of blacks. And, as Rayford Logan has pointed out, Northerners seemed quite content with the white Southerners' contentions in this regard, thus giving the Lost Cause a notable victory in "the market place of free ideas" in the North.

The action of the several branches of the federal government in some areas and their inactivity in others did much to hasten the end of the very policy established by Congress in 1867. After the impeachment of the President, Congress itself was fairly inactive on the reconstruction front. There was, of course, some discussion on the floor in 1869 and 1870 of the numerous counter-reconstruction measures adopted by Southerners. The Acts of 1870 and 1871, designed to "enforce" reconstruction came much too late to be an effective deterrent to the stern opposition to reconstruction that had crystallized all over the South. The growing Democratic minority in both houses found support among new Republican leaders like James G. Blaine, and they defeated in 1874 and 1875 the passage of bills designed to increase the federal supervision of elections. When Senator Sumner pressed for the enactment of a civil rights law in 1872 and 1874, he was defeated. When the Civil Rights Act finally passed in 1875, following Sumner's death, some of its most important provisions, including that calling for desegregation of public schools, had been deleted. This excision had been vigorously advocated by the leaders of the Peabody Fund. The spokesmen for this agency, established in 1867 to provide financial support for Southern schools, made it clear that they favored racially segregated schools in the South. The Civil Rights Act remained a dead letter, for the most part, until the Supreme Court removed it from the statute books in 1883 by declaring it unconstitutional. Speaking for the Court, Justice Joseph P. Bradley said that the Fourteenth Amendment did not authorize general legislation for the protection of civil rights.

Meanwhile, Congress had been taking steps to facilitate the entrance of the former Confederates into the political arena. Almost from the beginning of Radical Reconstruction Congress had been under pressure to modify its test oath law in order to make possible the seating in Congress of certain former Confederates who had been elected. By the summer of 1868 Congress began to yield by voting to admit to the House R. R. Butler from Tennessee, who was not qualified to take the regular "ironclad oath." In July, 1868, a general bill to modify the test oath was passed. Now, those freed by Congress of political disabilities could take an oath of allegiance that did not involve their past conduct. But the fight to repeal the test oath continued, and in 1871 a bill became law without President Grant's signature. He made it clear that his opposition to the law was based on the fact that it was not actually a repeal of the test oath but a measure to relieve some from taking the oath while still requiring it from others. Within the next five years some nine bills to repeal the ironclad oath had died in Congress. By 1884, when Congress finally passed an act repealing it, there were scarcely any former Confederates who suffered political disabilities.

President Grant, even when mindful of the implications for the Republican party of strong reconstruction measures, had little real enthusiasm for the Radical program. He used his pardoning power freely between 1869 and 1877, thereby greatly contributing to the growing strength of white Southerners who were busily using their political and economic power to overthrow Radical rule. In 1871 he encouraged Congress to enact a measure providing for general amnesty. The act that passed the following year and the subsequent special acts reduced the number of disqualified Southerners to less than three hundred. While the President was moved in 1870 to call for legislation to outlaw the Klan and other similar groups, he was most reluctant to use his own powers to deal with the problems of the South. Thus, in 1874 he refused to send federal troops to Mississippi to assist the Ames government in maintaining law and order because he believed that the great majority of the public "are ready now to condemn any interference on the part of the government." It was not that he condoned what was going on in the South. He called the riots in Louisiana "bloodthirsty butchery" and said that the 1875 elections in Mississippi had been achieved by fraud and violence that would "scarcely be a credit to savages." But he was restrained from intervention by the honest conviction that such action would do more harm than good. Former Confederates continued to believe, therefore, that while Grantism might mean a kind of laxity in public morality, it also meant a welcome leniency in the enforcement of reconstruction.

Even the federal judiciary seemed to give more encouragement to the opponents than to the proponents of Radical Reconstruction. In its decisions of January, 1867, in the Test-oath cases, the Supreme Court gave the supporters of reconstruction nothing to cheer about. Justice Field, in *Cummings* v. *Missouri,* said the state law requiring a prospective officeholder to swear that he had always been loyal to the United States was unconstitutional because it demanded punishment for activities that were not punishable at the time they were committed and was, therefore, an *ex post facto* law. In *Ex parte Garland,* Justice Field declared that the petitioner could not be required by Congress to take the test oath in order to be permitted to practice as an attorney, since he had already received a full pardon from the President for his Civil War activities. Both decisions came from a Court that was divided five to four, a ratio representing fairly accurately the cleavage existing in the country as a whole over the questions of reconstruction.

The Court seemed reluctant, however, to enter into the reconstruction controversy. When the state of Mississippi sought an injunction to prevent the President from enforcing the Reconstruction Acts of 1867, the Court declined to interfere with the President in the performance of his official duties. This was essentially the position of the Court later in 1867 when the states of Mississippi and Georgia sought to enjoin the Secretary of War from carrying out the provisions of the Acts. In 1869 the Court had an opportunity to rule on the constitutionality of the Reconstruction Acts in a case in which a Southern editor, William H. McCardle, was arrested and held for trial by a military commission established by the Acts. When his petition for a writ of habeas corpus was denied, he appealed to the Supreme Court. Meanwhile,

Congress, fearing an adverse Court decision, passed an act withdrawing the appellate jurisdiction of the Supreme Court in such cases. The Court then upheld the right of Congress to withdraw appellate jurisdiction, thereby relieving itself of the obligation to pronounce judgment in the case.

While the Supreme Court never passed on the constitutionality of the Reconstruction Acts, it did contribute, in *Texas* v. *White,* to the discussion of the nature of the Union in that era. After the war the Lone Star State brought suit to recover certain United States bonds owned by the state before the war but disposed of by the government of Texas during the war in payment of supplies for the Confederate government. The defendants contended that Texas was no longer a state and could not bring suit in the Supreme Court. In April, 1869, the Court rejected this contention, maintaining that the fact had been clearly determined that no state could leave the Union. The Court admitted that at the close of the war the state of Texas was not in proper constitutional relations with the Union, but insisted that Texas had never left the Union. The Court concluded that the disposition of the bonds had been illegal and the state was entitled to recover them. This is as close as the Court ever came to dealing with the fundamental question of the legality of the reconstruction program.

In its principal concerns the Supreme Court seemed to reflect the mood of the times. Within a matter of months after congressional reconstruction was launched, the great issues were not the status of the former Confederates, the Southern states, or African Americans. Rather they turned on questions of property, the impact of industrialization, and the role of government in the expanding economy. Thus, during the critical period in the life of the reconstruction program, when both Congress and the President wondered anxiously whether violence would overturn the

Southern governments, the Supreme Court was deeply engrossed with currency questions. In 1870 it decided that the Civil War acts making United States notes legal tender for the payment of public and private debts were unconstitutional. In the following year, after much nationwide debate and after some changes in the personnel of the Court, this decision was reversed. In his concurring opinion Justice Bradley expressed a position comforting to those who looked to the federal government for support and protection. "It is absolutely essential to independent national existence," he said, "that government should have a firm hold on the two great sovereign instrumentalities of the sword and the purse, and the right to wield them without restriction on occasions of national peril." But the Court did not seize the opportunity to uphold the use of the sword by the government during the reconstruction period.

The Supreme Court had to face new problems that arose as state governments sought to regulate business and industry. When Louisiana enacted legislation to regulate the slaughtering of livestock in New Orleans, several butchers claimed that the statute violated the Fourteenth Amendment in depriving them of their business by granting a monopoly for slaughtering livestock to one corporation. By a vote of five to four the Court declared in 1873 that the Fourteenth Amendment was framed and adopted not to protect businessmen but to protect the former slaves. Further, the Amendment protected privileges and immunities of persons as citizens of the United States but not as citizens of states. If, as the Court argued, most civil rights were derived from state and not from federal citizenship, the Fourteenth Amendment would give little protection to individuals who might suffer from state laws that regulated their rights or deprived them of their rights altogether.

As the reconstruction period formally drew to a close, the preoccupation of the Court continued to be with matters relating to the business community. Farmers who suffered from various forms of abuse at the hands of the railroads turned to their state legislatures for relief. The states responded by enacting laws to regulate railroad rates. The railroads, in turn, challenged the legislation; and in 1875 and 1876 they asked the Court to strike down the regulatory acts that were in force in Illinois, Minnesota, Iowa, and Wisconsin. In 1877 Chief Justice Waite spoke for the Court and asserted that since railroads—and grain elevators, too—were invested with a public interest, they ceased to be *juris privati* only and were, consequently, subject to public regulation. Such regulation could, of course, be abused, but when it was, the public must resort to the polls and not to the courts.

That the polls were in fact not open to all persons, and particularly not to African Americans in the South, was a persistent contention of the supporters of congressional reconstruction. The Fifteenth Amendment, adopted in 1870, had not succeeded in making it possible for qualified blacks to exercise the franchise. Nor had the laws enacted in 1870 and 1871 to enforce the Fifteenth Amendment been effective. Nevertheless, the Amendment was bitterly assailed by those opposed to the enfranchisement of blacks, and the Enforcement Acts were under fire from the time of their passage. Persons indicted under these Acts began to challenge their constitutionality and sought a determination of the question in the federal courts.

In 1874 a federal circuit court was called on, in *United States* v. *Cruikshank,* to decide on the validity of the indictment of a group of persons held in connection with some riots in Louisiana in the preceding year. The provisions of the Act of 1870 that were under examination provided punishment for persons who should conspire "with intent to violate any provision of this act, or to injure, oppress, threaten, or intimidate any citizen with intent to prevent or hinder his free exercise and enjoyment of any right or privilege granted or secured to him by the Constitution or laws of the United States." The circuit court, through Justice Bradley, said that the power of Congress to legislate for the enforcement of the guarantees in the Fifteenth Amendment did not extend "to the passage of laws for the suppression of ordinary crimes within the states. . . . The enforcement of the guaranty does not require or authorize Congress to perform the duty which the guaranty itself supposes it to be the duty of the state to perform, and which it requires the state to perform." The case went on to the Supreme Court, where the decision of the circuit court was upheld. The highest court agreed that the indictments were improper and that the accused persons therefore should not be prosecuted.

The decision in the Cruikshank case dealt an effective blow to any effort to protect African Americans in exercising the franchise. In the same year, in *United States* v. *Reese,* the Court held unconstitutional two significant provisions of the Enforcement Act. The Court declared that the Fifteenth Amendment did not confer the suffrage on anyone. Instead, it merely sought to prevent the states or the United States from discriminating in such matters on account of race, color, or previous condition of servitude. Congress was thus empowered merely to enact legislation to prevent the discrimination that had been forbidden by the Amendment. The Act of 1870, the Court stated, went beyond the scope of the powers of Congress and was, therefore, unconstitutional. The victory of the counter-reconstructionists was made complete by this decision of the Supreme Court. With the President in no mood to enforce reconstruction, with Congress turning its attention to other matters, and with the federal judiciary finding no legal basis for crucial enforcement measures, there was no prospect for holding the line against the tireless opponents of congressional reconstruction.

All that remained by 1876 was for the nation to take cognizance of the fact that reconstruction was a shambles. In eight states there was no longer even a pretense, for the Conservatives had come to power and had begun systematically to destroy every vestige of the reconstruction program. Only South Carolina, Florida, and Louisiana had not been "redeemed." In South Carolina the "Red Shirts," inspired by the success of counter reconstruction in Mississippi, resolved to place their state in the Conservative column. By organizing Workingmen's Democratic Associations pledged to employ loyal Democrats only, and by programs of violence and intimidation, they moved toward overthrowing the reconstruction government there. In Louisiana the White League armed its members when the Democrats failed in their bid for control in 1874. The next two years were plagued by rioting and other forms of violence in which scores of black would-be voters were killed and hundreds of others intimidated. In Florida tension between the Radicals and Conservatives mounted as the number of Democratic voters increased and as the Republican organization lost both numbers and influence.

The election of 1876 marked the end of reconstruction pretensions even in South Carolina, Florida, and Louisiana, as well as on the national scene. In the summer of 1876 the riot in Hamburg, South Carolina, set the stage for the final overthrow in that state. The black militia, parading in observance of Independence Day, was ordered from the streets; and when they failed to obey, they were arrested. At their trial, armed groups of whites came into the court to see that the blacks received "justice." When they refused to apologize and surrender their arms, the whites fired on them, killing five. Others were killed as they attempted to flee. This and other disorders set the stage for the election in which Wade Hampton, supported by the Red Shirts, successfully opposed the re-election of the Republican governor, Daniel H. Chamberlain. If the Florida Conservatives incited fewer riots than their Carolina colleagues, they were no less committed to the redemption of their state at any price. When the Republicans could not agree on a candidate for governor, one group backed the incumbent, Marcellus L. Stearns, while another "reform" group backed Senator S. B. Conover. Nothing contributed to the election of Democratic candidate George F. Drew as much as did the dissension among the Republicans.

There was also much wrangling among the Republicans of Louisiana. Governor William P. Kellogg sought to secure the nomination for his friend, Stephen B. Packard but was bitterly opposed by the former governor H. C. Warmoth and the African American leader P. B. S. Pinchback, who had just been denied a seat in the United States Senate. Warmoth finally withdrew from the race in the interest of party harmony, but much damage had already been done. The Democrats, standing behind their standard-bearer, General Francis T. Nicholls, had the support of Rifle Clubs, White Leagues, and other similar groups. These groups undertook to swing doubtful parishes into line by methods that came to be known as "bulldozing." Although Nicholls denounced such methods, it can hardly be denied that they greatly benefited his candidacy.

On the national scene, the significance and implications of the coming election were almost universally recognized. The Democrats, having enjoyed no national victory for twenty years, were trying to cast off the stigma of treason under which they had labored since the war. The Republicans, weary of crusading, were seeking to establish another basis on which to make their appeal to the voters. The "redeemed" South was trying to clinch "home rule" in Florida, Louisiana, and South Carolina. And, at the same time, it must have been interested in seeing whether or not the terroristic methods that had been so successful would continue to go unchallenged. The remnants of the Radicals and their black friends, disillusioned by the bitter experiences of the past decade, eyed the future with distrust and pessimism. On the outcome of the election, then, depended the future of the political parties, the ultimate fate of the reconstruction program, the status of the freedmen, and the future course of intersectional relations.

The nomination of Rutherford B. Hayes for the presidency suggested the policy that the Republicans planned to pursue. A Civil War general with a satisfactory record as governor of Ohio, Hayes was acceptable to the politicians as well as to the reform wing of the party, although without much enthusiasm. The Democrats staked their hopes on the widely respected reform governor of New York, Samuel J. Tilden. With a distinguished record as an anti-crime crusader who had broken the Tweed Ring and exposed the Erie Canal grafters, Tilden had no taint of disloyalty or wartime Copperheadism. In the campaign the Republicans, sensing the possibility of defeat, concentrated on the old issues of war and reconstruction. "Every man that shot Union soldiers was a Democrat," cried Robert G. Ingersoll. "The man that assassinated Abraham Lincoln was a Democrat. . . . Soldiers, every scar you have got on your heroic bodies was given you by a Democrat." Meanwhile, the Democrats, supported by a considerable number of Liberal Republicans, raised the battle cry, "Tilden and Reform." They never tired of inveighing against Grantism and describing the graft and corruption of "Carpetbag-Negro" rule. If Democrats had betrayed their country during the war, Republicans had come close to destroying it during reconstruction. No holds were barred in the battle of 1876.

The early election returns on November 7 seemed to indicate a victory for the Democrats. The next morning the New York *Tribune* carried a story under the caption, "Tilden Elected." New York, New Jersey, Connecticut, and Indiana were clearly in the Democratic column, as well as all the Southern states except Florida, South Carolina, and Louisiana, which were still doubtful. Tilden had 184 electoral votes, only one short of the figure necessary for election. Surely, he would be able to pick up one along the way, his supporters thought. They had every reason to believe, therefore, that the victory celebration could begin. Republicans began to hope that the celebration was premature. They had 165 undisputed electoral votes. If they could secure *all* the disputed votes— seven from South Carolina, four from Florida, eight from Louisiana, and one from Oregon—Hayes would be elected. They launched a careful, well-laid scheme to win all the disputed votes for their candidate; and they were successful!

In each of the "unredeemed" states both sides claimed a victory. In each case, however, the state canvassing boards were in the hands of the Republicans who, after rejecting the Democratic claims, approved the Republican electors. The Democrats refused to accept these decisions, and when the Republican electors met in their state capitals on December 6 to cast their votes for Hayes, the Democrats met and cast their votes for Tilden. The Democratically controlled House appointed committees to investigate the electoral disputes in the Southern states, while the Senate, controlled by Republicans, dispatched its own committees. With both sides claiming victory, with tempers flaring up, and with many Democrats expressing a determination to inaugurate Tilden, the prospects for political peace were not bright at the beginning of the new year.

The dispute was so complicated and the need for its resolution was so pressing that Congress created a bipartisan electoral commission to settle the matter. Five members were from the Democratic House, five from the Republican Senate, and five from the Supreme Court. The commission, after examining the returns and refusing "to go behind the returns," assigned all the disputed electors to Hayes. The Tilden supporters were furious and threatened to obstruct the counting of the votes and prevent the inauguration of Hayes. Only a series of conferences and agreements between Republican leaders and influential Southern spokesmen made possible the acceptance of the decisions of the commission. On March 2, Senator T. W. Ferry announced that Rutherford B. Hayes had won by an electoral vote of 185 to 184.

The achievement of this Republican victory and the Democratic acquiescence in it is one of the most fascinating stories related to the end of reconstruction. The agreement by the Democrats to concede the election of Hayes without a bitter fight is usually credited to the "Wormley House Bargain" of February 26, 1877. On that date, several Southern congressmen and Major E. A. Burke, who represented the Democratic claimant for the governorship of Louisiana, arranged a meeting with certain influential Republicans. Among them were John Sherman, James A. Garfield, Charles Foster, and Stanley Matthews. The Republicans assured the Democrats that Hayes had no evil designs on the South. If, therefore, the Democrats would accept the election of Hayes, the new President would withdraw the few remaining troops from South Carolina and Louisiana.

The importance of the Wormley Bargain has been exaggerated, as C. Vann Woodward has argued. The provisions of the bargain were insufficient to placate the South. The withdrawal of troops alone would not have satisfied it. Only a few remained in two or three states, and Tilden was already committed to withdrawing them. The Democrats could therefore have had the presidency *and* home rule, had there been no other considerations. But there *were* other important factors leading to the South's acquiescence in the election of Hayes.

In *Reunion and Reaction* Woodward examines an elaborate scheme to secure the presidency for Hayes that was hatched the moment it appeared he had lost the election. A group of sensitive and discerning Republicans, realizing that there were responsible Democrats in the South who would not countenance the violence threatened by some Southerners to secure the presidency for Tilden, began to make overtures. They hoped to reach the Southern moderates, former Whigs, who spoke their language and were interested in causes more substantial than attacks on the "bloody shirt" Republicans. In the officials of the Western Associated Press the Republicans found ideal mediators. Murat Halstead of the Cincinnati *Commercial* and Joseph Medill of the Chicago *Tribune* were among those with good Southern contacts. These journalists made the most of the fact that many of the South's new leaders were former Whigs with latent Northern connections. They had merely to find out what the South needed and wanted, and they would have a basis for negotiation.

The Achilles' heel of the South was its economic plight, drastically worsened by the panic of 1873. If only the South could secure federal aid to bolster its economic life, it would be willing to pay dearly. The Republicans began to whisper into the ears of their new friends that they might very well support federal subsidy for the uncompleted Southern railway system if some "arrangement" could be worked out. In previous years Southerners had been unable to get outside support for federal subsidies. Even their Northern Democratic colleagues could not be counted on. By December, 1876, they were desperate. That was the point at which the Republicans intervened with their promises—and their price.

In January, 1877, while the debate on the electoral commission was in progress, L. Q. C. Lamar, who had been in close communication with the Western Associated Press officials and Northern Republicans, reported for passage the Texas and Pacific Railroad bill. In the ensuing debate the Southern Democrats received greater support from Republicans than from Northern Democrats. This show of Republican co-operation was heartwarming to the Southerners. When the Northern Democrats began to lay plans to obstruct the inauguration of Hayes after the electoral commission's decision, they found themselves deserted by their Southern colleagues. The Southern Democrats were looking instead to the Republicans for help in getting what they wanted for the South— not only support in securing federal subsidies but also a promise that a Southerner would be Postmaster General. In turn they would help the Republicans elect James A. Garfield as Speaker of the House.

On February 22, while these arrangements were being made, the *Ohio State Journal,* a paper close to Hayes, printed an editorial bitterly attacking the South. There had been no immediate provocation for this attack. It merely restated the conventional hostility to Southern racial and political practices. Coming when it did, it was especially disturbing. Southerners needed fresh assurances, which they got four days later at the celebrated meeting at Wormley House, the exclusive Washington hotel owned and operated by an African American businessman, James Wormley. The agreement coming out of that meeting was widely heralded, while the earlier and more important agreements and bargains went unnoticed. After the inauguration Hayes nominated Senator David Key of Tennessee as Postmaster General. Within a short period the President withdrew federal troops from Louisiana and South Carolina. Radical Reconstruction was no more. The Southerners did not deliver enough votes to elect Garfield the Speaker, but the Republicans did not deliver enough votes to pass the Texas and Pacific bill. The rapprochement, though short-lived, had secured the election of Hayes. The Republicans were happy, despite the fact that their reconstruction program had gone down to ignominious defeat.

12

The Aftermath of "Redemption"

The peaceful inauguration of Rutherford B. Hayes on March 4, 1877, as the nineteenth President of the United States marked the formal end of reconstruction, but not the final solution of the problems created by the war and its aftermath. At last the former Confederate states were back in the Union under conditions favorable to those who had led the secession movement and fought the Civil War. But their political position was actually no better than it had been in 1860. The South had made more permanent than ever its distinctive minority status, and its intransigence might well give it greater unity but hardly an opportunity for greater power and influence on the national scene. Meanwhile, within the states themselves, the Redeemers, the self-styled saviors of the South, in order to secure their position, resorted to ruse, conspiracy, and violations of the Fourteenth and Fifteenth Amendments. These practices further dulled whatever sense of political integrity remained.

Politically, then, the South retreated further from democracy and proceeded to institutionalize and make permanent the redemption policies by which it had overthrown reconstruction. African Americans could still vote and hold office after 1877, but it became increasingly difficult—almost impossible—for them to

discharge their responsibilities of citizenship. While their participation in politics declined sharply toward the end of reconstruction, blacks as a political issue in Southern politics tended to gain
in importance as the years passed. "Waving the bloody shirt" was
abandoned by the Republicans, but the Redeemers never tired of
warning their fellows of the dangers of a recurrence of "Negro
domination." Their consequent determination to maintain their
own powerful position led not only to incredible schemes to disfranchise blacks but also to the decline of white manhood suffrage.
Last-minute changes in polling places, long, complicated ballots,
and even literacy tests could hardly have been calculated to encourage the common white populace to exercise the franchise. Effective political power therefore remained where it had been before
the war—with an oligarchy, a small ruling clique that wielded
power far out of proportion to its numerical strength.

Nor did the end of reconstruction usher in an entirely new era
in the economic life of the South. Agriculture, having made a dramatic recovery, continued to dominate the scene not only as a way
of making a living but as a way of life. By 1880 the planting aristocracy had settled down to habits not unlike those that characterized it in 1860. Contrary to the widely held view, there was no
significant breakup of the plantation system during and after reconstruction. Day labor, renting, and sharecropping were innovations, to be sure, but those occupying such lowly positions bore
a relationship to the planter that, while it was not slavery, was
nevertheless one of due subordination in every conceivable way.
The role of the planter remained that of paternal despot, controlling the destiny of his many wards and determining the social position of all, including those having little or no connection with
agriculture.

There was more industry in the South in 1880 than there had

ever been before. This fact, however, was not so much a measure of progress as it was an indication of the South's industrial backwardness in earlier years. Most Southern states had increased their railroad mileage between 1870 and 1880, but the significant increases were just beginning. By 1880 iron furnaces were being fired in Alabama, Tennessee, and Virginia, and the patenting of the first cigarette machine in that year merely suggested the possibilities that lay in the processing of tobacco products. Already, by 1880, the Southern cotton textile industry was rapidly gaining ground, but the mills of the Carolinas and Georgia were not yet within sight of those of New England. Everywhere, however, the young, aggressive spokesmen began to speak confidently of a "New South," implying that their faces were turned resolutely toward the future with no serious desire to keep more than one foot planted in the past.

Whether the spokesmen wanted to or not, the South, even as it moved haltingly toward industrialization, did more than look over its shoulder to the past that had been. It bathed itself in glorious memories and retained much that was a part of that past. Its values continued to be those of a plantation society; and the aspirations even of some of those whose opportunities lay in the new industrialization were geared to an agrarian way of life. The most highly respected member of society in 1880, and indeed the most powerful in many ways, was still the planter. He was still the lord of the manor, setting the tone and the values of all others and occupying a position of respectability if not of affluence to which even the young industrialist aspired.

Where there was industrialization, the similarities between the Old South and the New South were striking. For one thing urbanization in the South increased only slowly in the first two decades following the war. The older towns showed almost no signs of growth, while the new ones crept painfully beyond the stage of hamlets. Unlike the bustling industrial cities of the North, the Southern communities where the cotton mills were built remained relatively small towns for decades. The general atmosphere was bucolic, and the influence of farms and plantations could everywhere be seen.

Despite Southern pride that stimulated local support for the new industries, much of the substantial capital came from the outside. By 1880 Northern capitalists were investing heavily in Southern lands. Northerners, as Paul Gates has observed, controlled the best pine and cypress lands, and they were to reap the benefit by taking most of the profits from the rising lumber industry. Likewise, the railroad boom that was well under way by 1880 was stimulated by Northern capital and directed from New York. Already, with more than $150,000,000 being invested in Southern railroads by Northern and foreign capitalists between 1879 and 1881, the foundation was being laid for the building of the great Morgan empire in the South that came with the consolidations of the 1890's. In minerals the story was essentially the same. New Englanders dominated coal mining in Alabama. When the iron industry emerged there and elsewhere, it was Northern capital that gave it the first big push. If Southerners gave greater support to the cotton textile industry, it was because mills could more easily assimilate small investments. Indeed, the multiplicity of them, scattered over the Southern countryside, captured the imagination of those prideful Southerners who could find a few dollars to invest. Before the war Thomas Kettell had complained that the enormous resources of the South were being turned into profits which only the North enjoyed, while Hinton Rowan Helper had asserted that the South was dependent on the North for almost everything except a few staples. If, by 1880, the South was producing more commodities than at any previous time, it remained a favorite place for Northern investors to reap handsome profits. Real economic independence had not yet come to the South.

And what of the human elements that had played a large part in the drama of the previous decade or so? African Americans who watched political developments began to entertain serious doubts about the Republican party. Those who had fought for effective civil rights legislation in 1874 and 1875 were not satisfied with the law that was finally passed. They were even more disturbed by how some of their friends seemed to be tiring of the fight. When Hayes withdrew the last troops from the South and toured about befriending the former Confederates, some African Americans felt that the party of Lincoln had deserted them. "The party of great moral ideas," said the editor T. Thomas Fortune, "relinquished its right to the respect and confidence of mankind when, in 1876, it abandoned all effort to enforce the provisions of the war amendments. . . . The black man, who was betrayed by his party and murdered by the opponents of his party, is absolved of all allegiance which *gratitude* may have dictated."

Perhaps few blacks were prepared to condemn the Republican party as unequivocally as Fortune did, but all of them had good reason to be unhappy about their condition at the end of the reconstruction era. Wholesale intimidation and obstructions left them without the ballot to give them a share in making the policies affecting them. Not only had the federal government done almost nothing to protect them from bodily harm, but it now entered upon a course of action committing it to do even less. The Civil Rights Act of 1875 was a dead letter from the day of its enactment, and white Southerners boasted that it was not being enforced and could not be enforced anywhere in the South. With no active political support and with no federal officials willing to enforce the constitutional amendments and the laws that protected them, blacks had reason to despair for their own future.

Their economic condition was no better than their political status. Some blacks, of course, had made significant strides during reconstruction. The great mass of them, however, remained impoverished, with only their labor to sell under conditions peculiarly disadvantageous to them. In the rural areas most remained in the employ of planters or entered into a sharecropping relationship that was hardly better. And the convict-lease system provided black labor for many whites who needed such labor. In the towns and cities they were barred from employment in the new industries that were rising. Persistent myths about their inability to handle machinery and a determination to maintain racial peace kept them in the position of unskilled, untrained menials. Capital and management in the New South placed them in that lowly position; white labor unions and inferior, segregated education would keep them there.

The African American's severe political and economic disabilities insured his continued social degradation. They had not "died out" in freedom, as some Southerners had confidently predicted in 1865. In 1860 there had been 4,441,000 blacks in the United States. By 1880 the number had increased to 6,580,000. But, if anything, population growth increased their troubles. They migrated from place to place; some moved from the country to the towns, others from one part of the South to another. Already, a small number, disgusted with their lot and pessimistic about the future, began to migrate to other sections of the country. In communities where the black population was numerically dominant, the machinery to maintain its due subordination was strengthened. This was a gradual process not perfected until the turn of the century, but it had its beginnings in the early post-reconstruction years. In every important social relationship African Americans were kept at a "safe distance." The result was that in education, religion, social welfare, and the like, they had to build institutions completely separate from those of the whites. The response to the existence of a white world to which blacks were denied entrance, these institutions contributed to the emergence of a black world with all the trappings of an entirely separate community. Suspicion and distrust were the inevitable by-products of such racial division.

As for the whites, particularly the Redeemers, they had outdone themselves. They had overthrown the reconstruction governments, and they were rapidly rising in the national councils of their party and, indeed, of the federal government. By 1880 they had attained a respectability that had all but obliterated their earlier identification with secession—their war for independence. Presidential pardons and acts of amnesty had brought them back into full citizenship, and they had made the most of it. With a determination equaled only by their energy, they had worked diligently to regain their former positions of influence. Robert E. Lee felt "honored" to pay a courtesy visit to President Grant at the White House on May 1, 1869. On slightly lower levels other former Confederates sought to establish with other parts of the country lines of contact which might prove useful in the future.

The Redeemers' move toward acceptance and respectability precluded by its very nature a move toward democracy. In the reforms they instituted upon their return to power they displayed a singular distrust of the masses, black *and* white. In North Carolina, where they feared that blacks might enjoy some power in counties where they outnumbered whites, they passed the County Government Act in 1876. Among other things this Act empowered the legislature to name the county justices of the peace who, in turn, would name the county commissioners. In some other states where conditions were different, the Redeemers were inclined to limit the power of the legislature. In Texas, for example, the constitution of 1876 severely limited the powers of the legislature and favored the greater concentration of power in the executive. The Louisiana constitution of 1879 is an eloquent expression of "no confidence" in the legislature. In a lengthy section entitled "Limitation of Legislative Powers" the constitution, among other things, enjoins the legislature from contracting any debt or issuing any bonds except to raise money to repel an invasion or suppress an insurrection.

The Redeemers made much of the alleged corruption and extravagance of the reconstruction governments and based their claims to office on their promise to deal sternly with offenders and to eliminate any such dishonest practices in the future. Once in office, they did deal sternly with offenders, although the Redeemers themselves had frequently shared the spoils with former Republican officeholders. The elimination of dishonest practices, however, was another matter. The Redeemers in power clearly proved that the Republicans had no monopoly on perfidy and that both sides had a share in the apparently universal public immorality. In 1879 several officials in Georgia, including the state treasurer, the comptroller-general, and the commissioner of agriculture, resigned under fire or were impeached for scandals and irregularities in the conduct of their offices. In 1873 the state treasurer of Virginia was indicted for embezzlement and escaped trial only on a plea of insanity. In 1883 the treasurers of Tennessee and Virginia disappeared with more than $400,000 and $200,000, respectively. Each was a Confederate veteran who had been active in the movement to restore honesty in government. There were similar defalcations in Arkansas, Kentucky, Mississippi, and Louisiana.

For all their professions and promises and for all the claims that were to be made in their behalf, the Redeemers failed to provide the South with governments free of the faults they had laid at the door of the Radicals.

Reconstruction was over. The South was back in the Union, with a leadership strikingly like that of the South which had seceded in 1860. The period had brought changes, to be sure, but most of them had taken place in the North. The section that had expressed deep feelings about slavery and human degradation and had gone to war to preserve the Union had itself been transformed. It was now an industrial colossus with new values, new leadership, and new aspirations. No longer was it interested in activities that might distract or disturb its phenomenal growth and expansion. The South, having changed much less, was more than ever attached to the values and outlook that had shaped its history. Even its once-belligerent adversary was now conciliatory. On the points most important to the white South the North was willing to yield; and on the points most important to the North the white South was willing to yield. In a sense, then, both sides were pleased with the outcome of reconstruction. In another sense, however, both sides suffered an ignoble defeat. The Union had been preserved and human slavery had been abolished; but these were achievements of the war. In the postwar years the Union had not made the achievements of the war a foundation for the healthy advancement of the political, social, and economic life of the United States.

Important Dates

1863   President Lincoln's Proclamation of Amnesty and Reconstruction, December 8

1864   Wade-Davis bill passed by Congress and vetoed by Lincoln, July 8

Manifesto of Benjamin Wade and Henry Winter Davis denouncing the President's veto published in the New York *Tribune,* August 5

1865   Establishment of Bureau of Refugees, Freedmen, and Abandoned Lands, March 3

Freedmen's Savings and Trust Company chartered, March 3

Death of Abraham Lincoln and succession of Andrew Johnson to the presidency, April 15

Order No. 77 issued, calling for military demobilization, April 28

Johnson's Proclamation of Amnesty and Reconstruction, May 29

"Negro conventions" held to protest their treatment: Newbern, May 10; Norfolk, May 11; Petersburg, June 6; Vicksburg, June 19; Alexandria, August 2; Nashville, August 7; Richmond, September 18; Raleigh, September 29; Jackson, October 7

Black codes enacted by all-white legislatures in former Confederate states, summer and fall

Thirteenth Amendment becomes a part of the Constitution, December 18

Ku Klux Klan founded in Pulaski, Tennessee, winter, 1865–66

IMPORTANT DATES

1866   Fisk University receives charter, January 9
Civil Rights bill passed over the President's veto, April 9
Riot in Memphis, Tennessee, May 1
Report of the Joint Committee on Reconstruction, June 20
Supplementary Freedmen's Bureau Act passed over the President's veto, July 16
Tennessee restored to the Union, July 24
Riot in New Orleans, July 30
National Labor Union organized, August 20

1867   Congressional investigation of Johnson begins, January 7
Blacks in District of Columbia enfranchised, January 8
First Reconstruction Act becomes law, March 2
Tenure of Office Act passed, March 2
Command of the Army Act passed, March 2
Union League begins to organize clubs in the South, spring
Second Reconstruction Act becomes law, March 23
Alaska purchased from Russia, March 30
Third Reconstruction Act becomes law, July 19
Constitutional conventions begin to meet in the former Confederate states, fall

1868   Impeachment trial of Johnson begins, March 4
Fourth Reconstruction Act becomes law, March 11
Impeachment vote fails to convict Johnson, May 16
Arkansas readmitted, June 22
Omnibus bill readmits North Carolina, South Carolina, Louisiana, Alabama, and Florida, June 25
Fourteenth Amendment becomes a part of the Constitution, July 28
Thaddeus Stevens dies, August 11
Blacks expelled from Georgia legislature, September 3

1869   Inauguration of Ulysses S. Grant as President, March 4
First transcontinental railroad completed, May 10
"Black Friday" on the New York Stock Exchange, September 24
Conservatives win control in Tennessee, October 4, and in Virginia, October 5

National Labor Convention of Colored Men, Washington, D.C., December 6

1870 Standard Oil Company organized by John D. Rockefeller, January 10
Virginia readmitted, January 26
Mississippi readmitted, February 23
First African American to be elected to United States Senate, Hiram R. Revels, takes seat, February 25
Fifteenth Amendment becomes part of the Constitution, March 30
Texas readmitted, March 30
First Act passed to enforce the Fifteenth Amendment, May 31
Georgia readmitted, July 15
Conservatives win control of North Carolina, November 3
First African American to be elected to the United States House of Representatives, Joseph H. Rainey, takes seat, December 12

1871 Second Act passed to enforce the Fifteenth Amendment, February 28
Third Act passed to enforce the Fifteenth Amendment, April 20
Treaty settling the "Alabama" claims ratified, May 24
Conservatives win control of Georgia, November 1

1872 Frederick Douglass presides over Colored National Convention, New Orleans, April 15
Grant re-elected over Horace Greeley, Liberal Republican candidate, November 5

1873 Conservatives win control in Texas, January 14
Jay Cooke and Company closes, September 1

1874 National Grange issues Declaration of Purpose, February 4
Conservatives win control in Arkansas, November 10, and in Alabama, November 14

1875 Civil Rights Act passed, March 1
Conservatives win control in Mississippi, November 3

1876   Presidential election between Rutherford B. Hayes and Samuel Tilden in dispute, November 7
Conservatives win control in South Carolina, November 12

1877   Conservatives win control in Florida and Louisiana, January 2
Electoral commission decides election in favor of Hayes, February 8
Wormley House Bargain, February 26
Troops withdrawn from South Carolina, April 10

Former Confederate States	Readmission to Union under Congressional Reconstruction	Conservative Victory End of Congressional Reconstruction
Alabama	June 25, 1868	Nov. 14, 1874
Arkansas	June 22, 1868	Nov. 10, 1874
Florida	June 25, 1868	Jan. 2, 1877
Georgia	July 15, 1870	Nov. 1, 1871
Louisiana	June 25, 1868	Jan. 2, 1877
Mississippi	Feb. 23, 1870	Nov. 3, 1875
North Carolina	June 25, 1868	Nov. 3, 1870
South Carolina	June 25, 1868	Nov. 12, 1876
Tennessee	July 24, 1866	Oct. 4, 1869
Texas	Mar. 30, 1870	Jan. 14, 1873
Virginia	Jan. 26, 1870	Oct. 5, 1869

Note: Tennessee was admitted before congressional reconstruction was launched. In Virginia the Conservatives were in power before the state was admitted.

Suggested Reading

This study of the years following the Civil War rests much more on the author's interpretation of sources already known to most students of the period than on the discovery and use of new materials. For many years historians have been calling for a new interpretation, and several have undertaken the task either by examining "established" interpretations or by rewriting the history of the period in its entirety or in part. Among those who by 1961 had given critical attention to the reconstruction period and its historians were A. A. Taylor, "Historians of the Reconstruction," *Journal of Negro History,* XXIII (January, 1938), 16–34; Francis B. Simkins, "New Viewpoints of Southern Reconstruction," *Journal of Southern History,* V (February, 1939), 49–61; Howard K. Beale, "On Rewriting Reconstruction History," *American Historical Review,* LV (July, 1940), 807–27; John Hope Franklin, "Whither Reconstruction Historiography," *Journal of Negro Education,* Fall, 1948, 446–61; and Bernard Weisberger, "The Dark and Bloody Ground of Reconstruction Historiography," *Journal of Southern History,* XXV (November, 1959), 427–47.

In the years following the first edition of this work, numerous students of the period published findings ranging from general works on Reconstruction to monographs on selected subjects to articles in learned and popular journals. In the following "Working Bibliography" the reader will find primary materials and works of an earlier period, some of which undertook to correct earlier treatments of Reconstruction. Some may be regarded as "fresh treatments" of old subjects, while others may be regarded as truly revisionist in nature. Many of them have been incorporated in this bibliography in appropriate places. Articles dealing with various aspects of Reconstruction have become so numerous while technological innovations have facilitated one's ability to consult them so that, for the most part, they do not appear in this brief bibliography. This in no way minimizes their importance.

Among the official publications of the reconstruction period, some are, of course, quite indispensable, while others add substance and color to the picture. At the federal level, the *Congressional Globe* for the years 1865–73 (after 1873, the *Congressional Record*) is basic, since it contains the day-to-day transactions of Congress for those years. Several special reports of Congress are invaluable. Among them is the *Report of the Joint Committee on Reconstruction* (1866). See also B. B. Kendrick, *Journal of the Joint Committee of Fifteen on Reconstruction* (1914). Others include *Report of the Select Committee on the New Orleans Riot* (1866); *Report of the Joint Select Committee To Inquire into the Condition of Affairs in the Late Insurrectionary States* (Ku Klux investigation), 13 vols. (1872); and *Report of the Select Committee on Condition of the South* (1875). For the student who desires to go further there are congressional reports on the New Orleans riot of 1866, the elective franchise in South Carolina in 1877, and the migrations of African Americans of 1879.

In the executive branch of the federal government the messages and papers of Lincoln, Johnson, and Grant are in James D. Richardson (ed.), *A Compilation of the Messages and Papers of the Presidents, 1789–1897*, 10 vols. (1907); special reports from the executive branch are the "Report of Benjamin C. Truman" (1866); Carl Schurz, "Condition of the South" (1866); "Report of the Secretary of War" (1865–68); and "Pardons by the President" (1868). Other invaluable reports are J. W. Alvord, *Semi-Annual Report on Schools for Freedmen* (1866–70); *Report of the Commissioner of the Bureau of Refugees, Freedmen, and Abandoned Lands* (1865–80); *Annual Report of the United States Commissioner of Education* (1870–80).

Indispensable to a serious consideration of this period are the official documents of the states, including the minutes of the constitutional conventions, the journals of the legislatures, reports of bureaus of immigration, superintendents of education, boards of health, and other state agencies. One can examine the changes in the state constitutions in Francis N. Thorpe, *Federal and State Constitutions* (1909).

A wide variety of documentary materials is provided in the *American Annual Cyclopaedia and Register of Important Events* (1866–80); Herbert Aptheker, *A Documentary History of the Negro People in the United States* (1951); Walter L. Fleming, *Documentary History of Reconstruction*, 2 vols. (1906–7); John Hope Franklin, "Reconstruction" in *Problems in American*

History, edited by R. W. Leopold and A. S. Link (1952); and Edward Mc-Pherson, *The Political History of the United States of America during the Period of Reconstruction* (1871).

Many contemporary accounts of Southern reconstruction come from unofficial observers and reporters whose impact on the current interpretation of the period has been far-reaching. Most notable are Sidney Andrews, *The South since the War: As Shown by Fourteen Weeks of Travel and Observation in Georgia and the Carolinas* (1866); Georges Clemenceau, *American Reconstruction, 1865–1870* (1928); John William DeForest, *A Union Officer in the Reconstruction,* edited by J. H. Croushore and D. M. Potter (1948); Edward King, *The Great South* (1875); Charles Nordhoff, *The Cotton States in the Spring and Summer of 1875* (1876); Whitelaw Reid, *After the War: A Southern Tour, May 1, 1865 to May 1, 1866* (1866); Robert Somers, *The Southern States since the War, 1870–1871* (1871), and John T. Trowbridge, *The South: A Tour of the Battle-Fields and Ruined Cities, a Journey through the Desolated States, and Talks with the People* (1866). One of the "classic" accounts is James S. Pike, *The Prostrate State: South Carolina under Negro Government* (1874), but Robert F. Durden's searching, critical study of Pike's life and work, *James Shepherd Pike, Republicanism and the American Negro, 1850–1882* (1957), should also be read.

Many public leaders as well as private persons have left recollections, memoirs, and the like. It is possible here merely to indicate a few as illustrations of the more important categories. These may be regarded as a starting point for the study of a whole body of post-Civil War writings: John Wallace, *Carpetbag Rule in Florida* (1885); Henry C. Warmoth, *War, Politics, and Reconstruction: Stormy Days in Louisiana* (1930); James G. Blaine, *Twenty Years in Congress,* 2 vols. (1884–86); George W. Julian, *Political Recollections, 1840–1872* (1884); John Sherman, *Recollections of Forty Years in the House, Senate, and Cabinet,* 2 vols. (1895); Carl Schurz, *Speeches, Correspondence, and Political Papers,* edited by Frederic Bancroft, 6 vols. (1913); and Benjamin F. Perry, *Reminiscences of Public Men* (1889). Another valuable contemporary source is the letters and journals left by participants and observers. Among those that have been published are J. W. Alvord, *Letters from the South Relating to the Condition of the Freedmen* (1870); Mary T. Higginson (ed.), *Letters and Journals of Thomas Wentworth Higginson, 1846–1906* (1921); and C. L. Marquette (ed.), "Letters of a Yankee Sugar Planter," *Journal of Southern History,* VI (November, 1940), 521–46.

One of the best ways to get the views and experiences of blacks during reconstruction is through the accounts of their conventions and their memoirs. They were regularly reported in the Northern press, but most of them have left full accounts of their deliberations. Among them are *Proceedings of the Convention of the Colored People of Virginia Held in the City of Alexandria, August 2, 3, 4, 5, 1865* (1865); *Proceedings of the National Convention of Colored Men of America, Held in Washington, D.C. . . . January . . . 1869* (1869); *Proceedings of the Colored National Labor Convention Held in Washington . . . December . . . 1869* (1870); and *An Address to the People of the United States, Adopted at a Conference of Colored Citizens, Held at Columbia, S.C., July 20 and 21, 1876* (1876).

Among the general histories that deal with reconstruction the works of E. P. Oberholtzer and James F. Rhodes have had great influence. William A. Dunning's *Reconstruction, Political and Economic, 1865–1877* (1906) is the definitive statement of the most influential of the early historians of the period. Walter L. Fleming's *The Sequel to Appomattox* (1919) is a brief survey in a similar vein. See also James W. Garner (ed.), *Studies in Southern History and Politics Inscribed to William Archibald Dunning* (1914). John R. Lynch's *Facts of Reconstruction* (1913) seeks to correct the claims of Dunning and his "school" regarding "Negro rule" in the Southern states. James G. Randall's *Civil War and Reconstruction* (1937) is concerned largely with the war years, and the postwar period is treated sketchily and without originality. The 1961 revision by David Donald is a significant revision of the earlier edition. Allan Nevins' *The Emergence of Modern America* (1927) emphasizes social and economic developments. Paul H. Buck's *Road to Reunion, 1865–1900* (1937) is concerned primarily with reconciliation but contains valuable data on the social and intellectual history of the postwar years.

In the first two decades of the century professors and graduate students at Columbia and Johns Hopkins universities examined reconstruction in a series of state studies. Although varying in quality as well as in scope, most of them bore the stamp of the prevailing view, usually ascribed to the influence of Dunning, that little good came out of the reconstruction experience. The leading works are James W. Garner, *Reconstruction in Mississippi* (1901); Hamilton J. Eckenrode, *The Political History of Virginia during the Reconstruction* (1904); Walter L. Fleming, *Civil War and Reconstruction in Alabama* (1905); John R. Ficklen, *History of Reconstruction in Louisiana through 1868* (1910); Charles W. Ramsdell, *Reconstruction in Texas* (1910); William W. Davis, *The Civil War and Reconstruction in Florida* (1913); J. G. de Roulhac Hamilton, *Reconstruction in North Carolina* (1914); C. Mildred Thompson, *Reconstruction in Georgia, Economic, Social, Political, 1865–1872* (1915); and Ella Lonn, *Reconstruction in Louisiana after 1868* (1918). In the next decade two other works appeared that had a similar approach: Thomas S. Staples, *Reconstruction in Arkansas, 1862–1874* (1923); and E. Merton Coulter, *Civil War and Readjustment in Kentucky* (1926).

Claude Bowers did much to popularize the reconstruction period as a "travesty on honesty and on good government" in his *The Tragic Era: The Revolution after Lincoln* (1929). In a similar vein although not as strident is George Fort Milton, *The Age of Hate* (1930). A more recent general work in the same vein is E. Merton Coulter, *The South during Reconstruction* (1947). Among the better-known popular accounts are Robert S. Henry, *The Story of Reconstruction* (1938), and Hodding Carter, *The Angry Scar: The Story of Reconstruction* (1959). James Whyte is concerned primarily with life in the nation's capital during reconstruction in his *The Uncivil War* (1958).

Among the earliest efforts to revise the story of reconstruction was W. E. B. DuBois, "Reconstruction and Its Benefits," *American Historical Review*, XV (July, 1910), 781–99. His *Black Reconstruction* (1935) is a full-length reinterpretation with a strong Marxist bias. See also James S. Allen's *Reconstruction: The Battle for Democracy, 1865–1876* (1937) for a similar interpretation. Brief general accounts that suggest a revision of the older version of the period are John Hope Franklin, *From Slavery to Freedom* (1994) and Carl N. Degler, *Out of Our Past* (1959).

New interpretations of the reconstruction in the several states began about the same time and reflected themselves in a reexamination of the role of blacks as well as of the larger social and economic implications of the revolution of 1865. Among the studies devoted to their role are the works of A. A. Taylor, *The Negro in South Carolina during Reconstruction* (1924), *The Negro in the Reconstruction of Virginia* (1926), and *The Negro in Tennessee, 1865–1880* (1938); and Horace Mann Bond, *Negro Education in Alabama: A Study in Cotton and Steel* (1939), which is much more extensive than its title suggests.

Among the studies that deal with the larger social and economic picture are Francis B. Simkins and Robert H. Woody, *South Carolina during Reconstruction* (1932), and James W. Patton, *Unionism and Reconstruction in Tennessee, 1860–1869* (1934). Two outstanding reinterpretations are Roger W. Shugg, *Origins of Class Struggle in Louisiana* . . . (1939), and Vernon Lane Wharton, *The Negro in Mississippi, 1865–1890* (1947). An important contribution to the study of the closing years of the period is George B. Tindall, *South Carolina Negroes, 1877–1900* (1952). In their focus on and reinterpretation of the first years of Reconstruction, several studies are essentially revisionist. The outstanding work for this early period is Leon

Litwack, *Been in the Storm So Long: The Aftermath of Slavery* (1979). Others are Roberta Alexander, *North Carolina Faces the Freedmen: Race Relations During Presidential Reconstruction, 1865–1867* (1985); Herman Belz, *A New Birth of Freedom: The Republican Party and Freedmen's Rights, 1861–1866* (1976); Michael Les Benedict, *A Compromise of Principle: Congressional Republicans and Reconstruction* (1974); Dan Carter, *When the War Was Over: The Failure of Self-Reconstruction in the South, 1865–1867* (1985); LaWanda Cox and John H. Cox, *Politics, Principle, and Prejudice, 1865–1866* (1963); Peter Kolchin, *First Freedom: The Responses of Alabama's Blacks to Emancipation and Reconstruction* (1972); William C. Harris, *Presidential Reconstruction in Mississippi* (1967); Michael Perman, *Reunion Without Compromise: The South and Reconstruction, 1865–1868* (1973); Willie Lee Rose, *Rehearsal for Reconstruction: The Port Royal Experiment* (1964); Michael Lanza, *Agrarianism and Reconstruction Politics: The Southern Homestead Act* (1990); Carl Moneyhon, *Republicanism in Reconstruction Politics* (1980), and *The Impact of the Civil War and Reconstruction on Arkansas: Persistence in the Midst of Ruin* (1994).

Several other writers have undertaken an extensive revision or reinterpretation of the period. An outstanding participant in Reconstruction and a pioneer revisionist was John R. Lynch, *Facts of Reconstruction* (1913). In due course others followed, including Kenneth M. Stampp, *The Era of Reconstruction, 1865–1877* (1965); Robert Cruden, *The Negro in Reconstruction* (1969); James McPherson, *The Struggle for Equality: Abolitionists and the Negro in the Civil War and Reconstruction* (1964); William R. Brock, *An American Crisis: Congress and Reconstruction, 1865–1877* (1963); and Eric Foner, *Reconstruction: America's Unfinished Revolution, 1863–1877* (1988). See also Eric Anderson and Alfred A. Moss, Jr., eds., *The Facts of Reconstruction: Essays in Honor of John Hope Franklin* (1991).

There have been numerous studies of the various reconstruction leaders. Some are biographies, others are essentially studies of the problems the leaders faced and how they coped with them. In addition to the numerous biographies of Lincoln, see Charles H. McCarthy, *Lincoln's Plan of Reconstruction* (1901), and T. Harry Williams, *Lincoln and the Radicals* (1941). The principal biographies of Johnson are Robert W. Winston, *Andrew Johnson, Plebeian and Patriot* (1928), and Lloyd P. Stryker, *Andrew Johnson: A Study in Courage* (1929). More valuable, however, is Howard K. Beale, *The Critical Year: A Study of Andrew Johnson and Reconstruction* (1930). A later and important re-examination of the same problem is Eric L. McKitrick, *Andrew Johnson and Reconstruction* (1960). Thaddeus Stevens has been severely criticized in Richard N. Current's *Old Thad Stevens: A Story of Ambition* (1942), warmly praised in Ralph Korngold's *Thaddeus Stevens, a Being Darkly Wise and Rudely Great* (1955), and praised and criticized in Fawn M. Brodie's *Thaddeus Stevens, Scourge of the South* (1959). David Herbert Donald, *Charles Sumner and the Rights of Man* (1970), sheds new light on an important figure. See also Otto H. Olsen, *Carpetbagger's Crusade: The Life of Albion Winegar Tourgee* (1965); Lillian A. Pereyra, *James Lusk Alcorn: Persistent Whig* (1966); Hans L. Trefousse, *Ben Butler* (1957), and *Benjamin Franklin Wade: Radical Republican from Ohio* (1963).

Other "lives" that add to an understanding of the problems of reconstruction are E. Merton Coulter, *William G. Brownlow, Fighting Parson of the Southern Highlands* (1937); William B. Hesseltine, *Ulysses S. Grant, Politician* (1935); Glyndon G. Van Deusen, *Horace Greeley* (1953); and Jonathan Daniels' life of M. S. Littlefield, *Prince of Carpetbaggers* (1958).

The political and legal aspects of reconstruction are the preoccupation of a wide variety of writers ranging from the bitterly critical diatribe of Hillary Herbert, *Why the Solid South? Or, Reconstruction and Its Results* (1890) to the denunciation of the white South in William H. Skaggs, *The Southern Oligarchy* (1924). In between is John W. Burgess, *Reconstruction and the Constitution, 1866–1876* (1902). In more recent years the following valuable works on the subject have appeared: Richard Abbott, *The Republican Party and the South, 1855–1877: The First Southern Strategy* (1986); Erwin S. Bradley, *The Triumph of Militant Republicanism* (1964); Richard O. Curry, *Radicalism, Racism, and Party Realignment: The Border States During Reconstruction* (1969); David Herbert Donald, *The Politics of Reconstruction, 1863–1877* (1965); Harold Hyman, *A More Perfect Union: The Impact of the Civil War and Reconstruction on the Constitution* (1973); James C. Mohr, ed., *The Radical Republicans in the North: State Politics During Reconstruction* (1976); David Montgomery, *Beyond Equality: Labor and the Radical Republicans, 1862–1872* (1967); Elizabeth Nathans, *Losing the Peace: Georgia Republicans and Reconstruction, 1863–1871* (1968); Michael Perman, *The Road to Redemption: Southern Politics, 1869–1879* (1984); Richard N. Current, *Three Carpetbag Governors (1967);* and Sarah W. Wiggins, *The Scalawag in Alabama Politics, 1865–1881* (1977). See also, Joe M. Richardson, *The Negro in the Reconstruction of Florida, 1865–1877* (1965); Richard N. Current, *Reconstruction in Retrospect: Views from the Turn of the Century* (1969); and Michael Perman, *Emancipation and Reconstruction, 1862–1879* (1987).

The manner in which the former Confederates recovered their political rights is the subject of many works. Jonathan Dorris, *Pardon and Amnesty under Lincoln and Johnson* (1953) is valuable. The special problem of oath-taking receives attention in Harold Hyman, *The Era of the Oath: Northern Loyalty Tests during the Civil War and Reconstruction* (1954). Violence and intimidation are the concern of John C. Lester in *The Ku Klux Klan: Its Origin, Growth, and Disbandment* (1905) and Stanley Horn in *The Invisible Empire: The Story of the Ku Klux Klan, 1866–1871* (1939).

The political activities of African Americans are an essential part of most reconstruction studies. Some works, however, give special attention to this question. An important general work is Paul Lewinson, *Race, Class, and Party: A History of Negro Suffrage and White Politics in the South* (1932). See also Walter L. Fleming, *Union League Documents* (1904); Samuel D. Smith, *The Negro in Congress, 1870–1901* (1940); and Luther P. Jackson, *Negro Office-Holders in Virginia, 1865–1895* (1945). The careers of individual African Americans are discussed in Howard Rabinowitz, ed., *Southern Black Leaders of the Reconstruction Era* (1982); Peggy Lamson, *The Glorious Failure: Black Congressman Robert Brown Elliott and the Reconstruction of South Carolina* (1973); Peter D. Klingman, *Josiah Walls* (1976); Loren Schweninger, *James T. Rapier and Reconstruction* (1978); Okon E. Uya, *From Slavery to Public Service: Robert Smalls, 1839–1915* (1971); Charles Vincent, *Black Legislators in Louisiana During Reconstruction* (1976); and John Hope Franklin, ed., *Reminiscences of an Active Life: The Autobiography* of John Roy Lynch (1970). An African American member of Congress has written about his colleagues in William L. Clay, *Just Permanent Interests: Black Americans in Congress, 1870–1991* (1992).

Difficulties and disillusionment came in the wake of blacks' disfranchisement, and the problem is discussed in Hampton M. Jarrel, *Wade Hampton and the Negro: The Road Not Taken* (1949); and T. Thomas Fortune, *Black and White: Land, Labor, and Politics in the South* (1884). Extremely valuable in this regard is Rayford W. Logan, *The Negro in American Life and Thought: The Nadir, 1877–1901* (1954). Some efforts to bolster the sagging reconstruction governments are treated in Otis Singletary, *Negro Militia and Reconstruction* (1957). Legal problems are discussed in Robert Kaczorowski, *The Politics of Judicial Interpretation: The Federal Courts, Department of Justice and Civil Rights, 1866–1876* (1985). For a discussion of the difficulties in establishing equality, see Roger A. Fischer, *The Segregation Struggle in Louisiana, 1862–1877* (1974).

Perhaps no aspect of reconstruction activities has been re-examined more than the Freedmen's Bureau. An early work was Paul S. Peirce, *The Freedmen's Bureau: A Chapter in the History of Reconstruction* (1904). A later one was George Bentley, *A History of the Freedmen's Bureau* (1955). Donald G. Nieman, *To Set the Law in Motion: The Freedmen's Bureau and the Legal Rights of Blacks, 1865–1868* (1979); and Claude F. Oubre, *Forty Acres and A Mule: The Freedmen's Bureau and Black Land Ownership* (1978). State studies of the Bureau include Martin Abbott, *The Freedmen's Bureau in Alabama* (1978) and Howard A. White, *The Freedmen's Bureau in Louisiana* (1970). See also, William McFeely, *Yankee Stepfather: General O. O. Howard and the Freedmen* (1968). See also, John Eaton, *Grant, Lincoln, and the Freedmen* (1907).

One of the early treatments of education during reconstruction and highly critical of the Radicals is Edgar W. Knight, *Influence of Reconstruction on Education in the South* (1913). A significant revision that goes far beyond the problems of education is Horace M. Bond, *Negro Education in Alabama: A Study in Cotton and Steel* (1939). One may also read with profit Henry Lee Swint, *The Northern Teacher in the South* (1941). Among works that reexamine educational efforts during the period are Robert C. Morris, *Reading, 'Riting, and Reconstruction: The Education of the Freedmen in the South, 1861– 1870* (1981); Ronald E. Butchart, *Northern Schools, Southern Blacks, and Reconstruction: Freedmen's Education, 1862–1875* (1980); Jacqueline Jones, *Soldiers of Light and Love: Northern Teachers and Georgia Blacks, 1865–1873* (1980); and William P. Vaughan, *Schools for All: Blacks and Public Education in the South, 1865–1877* (1974). In addition to general religious histories of the period, Hunter D. Farish's *The Circuit Rider Dismounts* (1938) and Ralph Morrow's *Northern Methodism and Reconstruction* (1956) are valuable.

Economic development, particularly in the South, was one of the first subjects of postwar writers and continues to claim their attention. One of the first works was Thomas W. Conway, *Report Read before the Chamber of Commerce of the State of New York on the Introduction of Capital and Men . . . into the Southern States . . .* (1866). Recent major studies of the subject are George R. Woolfolk, *The Cotton Regency: The Northern Merchants and Reconstruction, 1865–1880* (1958), and Robert P. Sharkey, *Money, Class, and Party* (1959). One problem related to economic recovery in the South is considered in Frank W. Klingberg, *The Southern Claims Commission* (1955).

Major economic problems besetting African Americans are treated in Walter L. Fleming, *The Freedmen's Savings Bank: A Chapter in the Economic History of the Negro Race* (1927) and a much more recent and definitive work, Carl R. Osthaus, *Freedmen, Philanthropy, and Fraud: A History of the Freedmen's Savings Bank* (1976). Other aspects of economic development are canvassed in Charles H. Wesley, *Negro Labor in the United States, 1850–*

1925 (1927); Sterling Spero and Abram Harris, *The Black Worker: The Negro and the Labor Movement* (1931); and Carter G. Woodson, *A Century of Negro Migration* (1918). More recent works include Lawrence N. Powell, *New Masters: Northern Planters During the Civil War and Reconstruction* (1980); James L. Roark, *Masters Without Slaves: Southern Planters in the Civil War and Reconstruction* (1977); Gerald D. Jaynes, *Branches without Roots: Genesis of the Black Working Class in the American South, 1862–1882* (1986); Edward Magdol, *A Right to the Land: Essays on the Freedmen's Community* (1977); Roger L. Ransom and Richard Sutch, *One Kind of Freedom: The Economic Consequences of Emancipation* (1977); Thomas Holt, *Black Over White: Negro Political Leadership in South Carolina during Reconstruction* (1977); Howard Rabinowitz, *Race Relations in the Urban South, 1865–1890* (1978); and Joel Williamson, *After Slavery: The Negro in South Carolina During Reconstruction* (1965).

Works dealing with the factors leading to the end of Reconstruction include Allen Trelease, *White Terror: The Ku Klux Klan Conspiracy and Southern Reconstruction* (1971); George C. Rable, *But There Was No Peace: The Role of Violence in the Politics of Reconstruction* (1984); James E. Sefton, *The United States Army and Reconstruction, 1865–1877* (1967); and Forrest G. Wood, *Black Scare: The Racist Response to Emancipation and Reconstruction* (1968). Two of the most important contributions to a reinterpretation of the end of reconstruction are C. Vann Woodward's *Reunion and Reaction: The Compromise of 1877 and the End of Reconstruction* (1951) and *Origins of the New South, 1877–1914* (1951).

John Hope Franklin and His *Reconstruction**

By Michael W. Fitzgerald

Reconstruction scholarship provides one of the more enduring interpretive reversals of any aspect of American history. As Eric Foner describes in the introduction to this volume, a century ago academic and popular defenders of Jim Crow dominated popular discourse of the post–Civil War era. White supremacy was the premise of the Dunning school, and with the civil rights transformation after midcentury, this established version came under withering attack. Revisionists swept the field, offering scholarly support for the demolition of segregation. Even now, half a century later, Revisionists dominate the literature with a rehabilitation of the egalitarian intent, and often the accomplishments, of Republican Reconstruction. The changes in America's racial presuppositions gave their views an almost unprecedented longevity.

Now, long after this historiographic groundswell and the circumstances that gave it traction, the time is perhaps opportune to reexamine one of its founding documents. John Hope Franklin's *Reconstruction after the Civil War*, published in 1961, is the first synthesis of the emerging viewpoint.[1] Other scholars had been critiquing the racial presuppositions of the older interpretation, but this was the first book-length study to win broad notice. Along with Kenneth Stampp's *Era of Recon-*

Note: All in-text citations include page numbers to the present volume.

struction (1965), it was among the most visible statements of the new consensus, widely distributed in inexpensive paperback editions. By this point in his career, Franklin was an established scholar with several books to his credit, the most prominent African American historian of his generation. He was also a civil rights pioneer, having personally integrated the staid sessions of the Southern Historical Association in the late 1940s. He served for months as a historical advisor to the NAACP legal defense team in the landmark *Brown* case, leading ad hoc seminars on the Fourteenth Amendment. As he recalled, "we had raised a crop of legal historians who were able to walk into the Supreme Court and discuss with great ease the developments of the Reconstruction period."[2]

The topic mattered to Franklin, and he approached writing this book with his scholarly viewpoint already formed. In 1948, he had published an ambitious review entitled "Wither Reconstruction Historiography?" Franklin criticized the work of Southern historian E. Merton Coulter, who had restated the Dunning view. Among other things, Coulter compared Radical Republican enthusiasm to the cults of Fascism and Nazism. Franklin pointedly observed that there were better historical analogies available for the racist enormities of World War II. Franklin likened Reconstruction to a "denazification process," however imperfectly it was executed. Franklin pulled no punches, emphasizing the prewar South's "annihilation of almost every vestige of free thought and free speech" and its "enthusiastic glorification of the martial spirit."[3] According to his autobiography, Franklin sent out two hundred offprints of his review, for fear scholars would overlook it in the small journal in which it appeared. This personal commitment inspired starting the Reconstruction book a decade later. As he recalled, "The need was urgent, and I undertook to meet that need. I could no longer endure the claim that Negroes were the ignorant dupes of white radicals whose sole interest was amassing wealth for themselves."[4] His work thus reflected the antiracist struggles of his time, in which he was an eager academic recruit.

Given these commitments, reading the book provides something of a revelation. In both its 1961 version, and its slightly modified second edition reprinted here, *Reconstruction after the Civil War* presents a temperate statement of what would become the prevailing interpretation. Scholars from the Left, like W. E. B. DuBois, anticipated some Revisionist formulations decades before, but Franklin deemphasized class struggle in favor of mainstream themes. As Eric Anderson and Alfred A. Moss carefully observed, he wrote "the first comprehensive response" to Dunning that "scholars were willing to hear."[5] Unlike Kenneth Stampp's *Era of Reconstruction*, published four years later, Franklin did not provide an introduction assailing the prevailing Dunning literature. Anticipating criticism from established scholars, Franklin strove for a balanced tone suited to the interracial, legally focused, integrationist northern constituency for civil rights. The relevance was obvious: everyone saw the contemporary analogy with the earlier federal intervention in the South. Simply stripping the white supremacist baggage from existing scholarship bolstered the movement. Franklin depicts the central issue as national protection for the former slaves, without making aggressive claims for the results of what was accomplished. The result is a work that wears well, at least on the topics that most mattered to him, long after the context changed.

Franklin emphasized high politics. He provides an overview of events in Washington, in the southern states, and social and intellectual developments across the nation. His chronological narrative explained the basics of what the laws meant and what actually occurred with concision. In one respect, however, this book continues the historical scholarship of a previous generation. Franklin repeatedly invokes the older "Beardsian" interpretation of the Civil War, as the moment when industrial capitalism solidified its control over the national state. The war had "spawned in the North an industrial plutocracy" that sought to keep its wartime stranglehold on government (12). He thus avoids strong identification with the Republicans, who appear simultaneously as the party of civil rights protections and expansive government on behalf of corporate interests. Franklin similarly escapes an uncritical stance towards the Radical Republican faction, sometimes even echoing the tone of the Dunning literature. He blames the "hysterical fringe" of Radicals for impeachment, the "hostile, vindictive element" who sought President Johnson's ouster (74–75). The Republicans are clearly his protagonists, but that theme is nuanced by the larger national context and also by the need to respond to the long-dominant literature.

Franklin engages readily with the motives of white southerners who opposed Reconstruction, likely because his previous book, *The Militant South* (1956), examined the proslavery mind. The returning Confederate soldier "looked upon the broken and scattered pieces of the way of life he knew and loved," hardly knowing what to do (2). In the first five chapters of the book, the fears of white southerners receive vivid consideration, perhaps even an overemphasis. A "horde of Treasury agents" moved through the South to seize Confederate government cotton, a process he termed "revolting" (40). After war's end, confiscated southern lands were "restored to the rightful owners," a moral evaluation that some might question (5). Franklin similarly demonstrates little sympathy for Radical Republican efforts to deprive ex-Confederate leaders of the ballot, even temporarily. He credits the older versions of how many ex-Confederates were disfranchised. "All whites who registered were required to take the 'ironclad oath,'" he writes, referring to a pledge of having never aided the Confederacy (80). Franklin probably misreads the legislation. The Military Reconstruction Acts of 1867 disfranchised only those who were barred from office under the pending Fourteenth Amendment, mostly prewar officeholders. Franklin's treatment of the issue reflects his desire to meet potential critics partway, and perhaps his support for widespread voting rights as well.

If Franklin sought a balanced tone, sometimes even to excess, his underlying Revisionist intent could not be clearer. Given the early 1960s context, constitutional issues and the political motivation of Federal intervention are central to his account. His chapter entitled "Reconstruction: Confederate Style" indicts the Black Codes as designed to fetter the freedpeople. The tone is factual, a simple recounting of invidious legislation, but the effect is damning. These laws "forecast, to a remarkable degree, the future attitude of former Confederates toward the place of blacks in the South and in American life" (47). Republican congressmen responded to the arrogance of southern lawmakers, whom President Andrew Johnson had allowed to act without restraint. Like most Revisionists, Franklin finds little to admire in Johnson, whose vanity left him susceptible to elite blandishments. Congress thus had no choice but to intervene; the main motivation was not vindictiveness, but simple recognition of how badly things were going in the South.

It was easier for Revisionists, then and later, to critique the racist intent of Presidential Reconstruction than to defend all parts of what Radical Reconstruction achieved. Franklin does provide an upbeat reading of several aspects of that record. He largely exonerates the northerners moving into the South from the charge of profiteering and political opportunism. When black suffrage finally came, the emphasis of Franklin's book changes, and African American leaders come into focus as political actors. He approves the Reconstruction conventions for institutionalizing baseline racial equality, describing their constitutions as competently written and democratic. He endorses the freedmen's sensible desire to expand public education for both blacks and whites too. He emphasizes the efforts of black representatives to integrate the schools, limited as the results were. In one of the few overt contemporary references in the book, he notes state provisions during Reconstruction allowing integrated schools only with unanimous consent of parents. He compares these practices directly to the 1950s "pupil placement" provisions enacted to evade the *Brown* decision (110). Clearly, his legal background inspired his interest in the topic, and his sympathetic treatment of the era's opponents of school segregation.

Franklin is vaguer on the actual workings of the Reconstruction governments, which were sometimes less edifying, and upon which the Dunning school had lavished considerable attention. Franklin does attend to the railroad programs pursued by the Reconstruction governments. He concedes that large subsidies and substantial corruption characterized several southern states, but he also emphasizes similar difficulties elsewhere. "Corruption was bisectional, bipartisan, and biracial," he concludes (147). Other troubling aspects of Republican rule receive less attention. Franklin does not dwell on the racially charged factional divisions within the southern Republicans. Nor does he emphasize the related topic of patronage politics, in this era of the spoils system. The author minimizes direct black participation in local government, essentially contending that whites held most of the offices and exercised most of the control. What he does say about black officeholders is nonetheless favorable. As his autobiography observes, it would be difficult to find anywhere "a more serious and responsible group of people so recently in bondage."[6]

Franklin's work is emphatic on the insurrectionary violence that overthrew Reconstruction, and the racial extremism that motivated it. He anticipates the field in his negative depiction of the northern retreat from Reconstruction, especially in its judicial and intellectual aspects. He is critical of President U. S. Grant, seeing him as half-hearted in his support for Reconstruction, and in his measures to repress the Ku Klux Klan. In this respect, one might even term some of Franklin's formulations as "post-Revisionist," anticipating some 1970s scholars in emphasizing the limited commitment of Reconstruction's architects. For example, he notes the near absence of any economic dimension of the Republican program, at least for the freedmen. In conjunction with this prefiguring of "post-Revisionist" scholars, Franklin's Beardsian framework works. He concludes that the dominant classes in both the North and the South were pleased with the outcome of Reconstruction. Business got control of the national government, and white southerners control of the racial politics of their region. But neither should have been pleased, because both had received an "ignoble defeat" by reinstalling racial supremacy as the South's dominant ideology. The nation thus "had not made the achievements of the war a foundation for the healthy advancement of the political, social, and economic life of the United States" (219). This recognition of the defeat of Reconstruction concludes the book, highlighting that the issue remained unresolved for his own generation.

When the work appeared, comment in the popular press was largely appreciative. In the *New York Times*, David Potter hailed the book. The existing literature was "painfully lacking," and Potter emphasized the need for a short introduction in keeping with "current ideas."[7] The scholarly reviews were also favorable, though more mixed. Several older historians, like Avery Craven, attacked its Revisionist premises, the only aspect of the newer work that mattered: "It is thus becoming quite clear that scholars sitting in Northern libraries reading the official documents are not reconstructing Reconstruction in a very realistic way."[8] Craven's "desperation" persuaded Franklin that he had "truly said something worthwhile."[9] Quite different were the criticisms of Eric McKitrick, a pioneer Revisionist himself. Franklin merely repeated formulas "that we all accepted years ago," he thought, and the diffuse book did not do justice to the era's complexity.[10] But McKitrick, the author of an exhaustive work on Andrew Johnson and Congress, misses the importance of a concise modern statement for public consumption. Several reviewers welcomed the work on precisely these grounds, praising Franklin for having bent over backward to be fair. The polarized scholarly response itself reflects the book's popular reach and political currency.

How, then, does *Reconstruction after the Civil War* appear from the vantage point of today? The work is not infallible on matters of fact, as several of the critics noted. Franklin had to rely on the older Dunning school studies of uneven quality for state-level detail. The Reconstruction acts did not require ratification of new constitutions by a majority of registered voters, as Franklin says, but only for a majority of those voting in an election in which half of those registered participated. In Alabama, Robert M. Patton was not appointed provisional governor, he was elected. Nor did that state have an election in August 1870, and the Klan's official dissolution order is a year off too. In Mississippi, Adelbert Ames was not elected governor and then to the Senate, as Franklin implies. And, as previously noted, Franklin overstates the prevalence of disfranchisement. Factual issues of this sort are precisely what one might expect in a synthetic work, which runs readers through a sea of political details. None much detract from his basic interpretation (115, 147, 162, 137).

Franklin notably foreshadows some of the formulations of the 1970s "post-Revisionists," who criticized the Republicans for not going far enough. Michael Les Benedict noted that Radical Reconstruction was "not very Radical after all," and Franklin similarly emphasizes the limitations of northern support for civil rights.[11] Franklin's sense of the era's failures, of how much Reconstruction left undone, mitigated any excessive praise for its accomplishments. Today, Franklin's political reading of the era still seems sensible in the era of Barak Obama, an impressive result given the subsequent changes in all aspects of American life. His criticism of the Dunning framework remains spot on, but he engages with the older literature more readily than does Stampp a few years later. Given Franklin's commitments, his restrained tone represents an achievement which aided the popular reach of the book.

Franklin explored many of the themes of the civil rights movement to come, but he did not emphasize the internal fissures that soon would be highlighted by the Black Power movement. African American politicians and their struggles figure prominently in Franklin's account, but he emphasizes their essential unity and their respectable social profile. These dignified men demonstrated "no bully, no swagger" as they rose to positions of leadership based on unusual education and social attributes (90). Scholars broadly agree, though some take a less favorable view of its implications, most notably Thomas Holt in *Black Over White* (1977).[12] Holt sees the freeborn, mostly light-skinned political elite in South Carolina as pursuing civil rights legislation, at the expense of the land reform and other economic measures needed by the mass of rural freedmen. Franklin's integrationist perspective and Revisionist goals inhibited exploration of these caste and class divisions, which became salient as the 1960s unfolded.

More problematic from our perspective is Franklin's attention on governmental matters, to the near exclusion of the social changes brought by emancipation. This emphasis may have been strategic, as Franklin suggests in a historiographic aside. Focusing on social and economic aspects facilitated the Dunning school's long predominance, he thought, as opposed to the pristine legal and constitutional issues where the flaws were obvious (49). African American politicians figure prominently in Franklin's accounts, but the constituency they represented is less visible. Franklin did not anticipate the subsequent generation of social historians who emphasized the African American role in emancipation. One might reference numerous examples, but Leon Litwack in his *Been in the Storm So Long* (1979) is perhaps representative.[13] He exhaustively examined the diverse social process of liberation, seeking out black perspectives on their world. African American popular agency comprised the burden of Litwack's work, and much of the more recent literature.

Franklin did not focus on the grassroots upsurge that reshaped agriculture, and the disintegration of the centralized plantation system that planters tried to restore after the war. Much was in transition in plantation agriculture after the war, and Franklin's curt assertion that sharecropping left power relationships intact needs qualification. Ira Berlin and Leslie Rowland's *Freedom: A Documentary History* (1982–) provides evidence of the social grounding of emancipation, highlighting the actions of the freedmen.[14] Several former project editors have produced works focusing on the evolution of the plantation and grassroots movements during Reconstruction. Julie Saville's study of emancipation in low-country South Carolina, Susan O'Donovan's study of labor and gender in southwest Georgia, and John Rodrigue's work on sugar in Louisiana, among others, all explore this theme.[15] The emphasis on popular movements encouraged reappraisal of the political history. In his landmark work *Reconstruction: America's Unfinished Revolution* (1988), Eric Foner integrates the labor struggle into the Revisionist framework.[16] He depicts the political struggles of Reconstruction as paralleled by the conflict over the shape of plantation agriculture. Foner encapsulates the wider evolution of the field, in fusing the Revisionist political framework with other aspects of the emancipation process.

A more recent exploration of the politics growing out of the plantations has less in common with Franklin's viewpoint. Steven Hahn's *A Nation Under Our Feet* (2003) observes that "something of a liberal integrationist framework" governs the modern work on Reconstruction. Hahn instead emphasizes the collective aspiration for land, even through confiscation, and the black nationalist implications of the agrarian struggle from Reconstruction through the Garveyites. Hahn highlights grassroots emigrationism as a countercurrent to the compromises fostered by black leaders operating in the political sphere. He speaks of early activists promoted by white Republicans who "may have reflected official, as opposed to grassroots, conceptions of leadership" early in Reconstruction.[17] Hahn's image of black politicians as bourgeois bears some resemblance to that of Franklin, in terms of their class origins. Franklin, though, viewed them more favorably as representative of community aspirations. His relevant chapters have titles like "The South's New Leaders," or "Constitution-Making in the South," clearly privileging their role over that of the agrarian movement that pushed them into prominence. At this juncture, it is unclear whether Hahn's emphasis will prevail over the more favorable depiction of Franklin, or of Foner for that matter.

A different dimension of the subsequent scholarship bears mention. Much of the writing on the social process of emancipation focuses on gender, and on family life. Franklin's coverage of such issues is notably sparse. Freedwomen don't appear in the index, nor do children save in the context of education, which does admittedly receive sustained attention. For all his attention to the courts and legislation, Franklin does not explore the legal aspects of the transition to the rule of formal law, and how legal marriage influenced relationships among the former slaves. For these social changes, one has to look elsewhere, in works like Laura Edwards's *Gendered Strife and Confusion* (1997).[18] Other aspects of Franklin's book seem dated as well. He is attentive to the intellectual developments that influenced the tale he wished to tell. Still, his assertion that "there were no really significant developments in American religion" might surprise modern scholars (185). To take one obvious example, the spectacular sexual scandal involving Henry Ward Beecher fit into the wider Gilded Age currents that undermined Reconstruction, in ways that prefigure contemporary developments surrounding celebrity.

A litany of omissions is beside the point. A work of synthesis can hardly draw upon a secondary literature that does not yet exist. Nor is it fair to criticize historians for not anticipating the subsequent evolution of scholarship. Franklin wrote the book that he wanted to write about the historical topics that then mattered; academics generally enjoy a cushion of irrelevance, but not Franklin. As America's premier black historian, he felt an obligation to speak out on the meaning of Reconstruction. Afterward, Franklin moved on to his broader role, marching with other historians at Selma, and spending decades as a public intellectual on racial issues. He had the opportunity to update the work for the second edition, appearing in 1994, but he satisfied himself with a few additions, primarily to the bibliographic essay. Franklin had spoken his peace on the subject on the topics he cared about. He was satisfied to let the work stand on its merits, and even its backward glances and equivocations offer insights into the politics of its time.

On the issues central to the book, governance in the South and in Washington, and on the central role of violence in overthrowing Reconstruction, his interpretations are still persuasive. For the political developments of the era, John Hope Franklin's *Reconstruction after the Civil War* remains in the mainstream of historical scholarship. Historians have extended the arguments in the half century since, but few reject them, and few works of history can claim this interpretive durability. One of the profession's more urgent tasks of the midcentury was debunking the rationale for Jim Crow, and Franklin undertook that enterprise as a personal mission. Given how imperative the political demands of the moment were, it is impressive that Franklin could produce lasting scholarship. The emotional nuance and compassion he brought to this book make it a milestone of enduring significance.

NOTES

1. John Hope Franklin, *Reconstruction after the Civil War*, rev. ed. (Chicago, University of Chicago Press, 1994).
2. Raymond Arsenault and John Hope Franklin, "The Sage of Freedom: An Interview with John Hope Franklin," *The Public Historian* 29, no. 2 (Spring 2007): 45.
3. John Hope Franklin, "Whither Reconstruction Historiography?" *Journal of Negro History* 17, no. 4 (Autumn 1948): 460.
4. *Mirror to America: The Autobiography of John Hope Franklin* (New York: Farrar, Straus and Giroux, 2005), 140, 195.

5. Eric Anderson and Alfred A. Moss, Jr., eds., *The Facts of Reconstruction: Essays in Honor of John Hope Franklin* (Baton Rouge, Louisiana State University Press, 1991), x.

6. *Mirror to America: The Autobiography of John Hope Franklin* (New York, Farrar, Straus and Giroux, 2005), 195.

7. David M. Potter, "Freedom Without Equality," *New York Times*, November 19, 1961, BR65.

8. Avery Craven, review of *Reconstruction*, by Franklin, *Journal of Southern History* 28, no. 2 (May 1962): 255–56.

9. *Mirror to America: The Autobiography of John Hope Franklin* (New York, Farrar, Straus and Giroux, 2005), 19.

10. Eric L. McKitrick, review of Franklin, *Reconstruction*, *Mississippi Valley Historical Review* 49, no. 1 (June 1962): 153–54.

11. Michael Les Benedict, *A Compromise of Principle: Congressional Republicans and Reconstruction, 1863–1869* (New York: Norton, 1974), 13.

12. Thomas Holt, *Black over White: Negro Political Leadership in South Carolina during Reconstruction* (Urbana: University of Illinois Press, 1977).

13. Leon Litwack, *Been in the Storm So Long: The Aftermath of Slavery* (New York: Knopf, 1979).

14. Ira Berlin, Leslie Rowland et al., eds., *Freedom: A Documentary History of Emancipation, 1861–1867* (Cambridge: Cambridge University Press, 1982–).

15. Julie Saville, *The Work of Reconstruction: From Slave to Wage Laborer in South Carolina, 1860–1870* (Cambridge: Cambridge University Press, 1994); Susan E. O'Donovan, *Becoming Free in the Cotton South* (Cambridge, MA: Harvard University Press, 2007); John C. Rodrigue, *Reconstruction in the Cane Fields: From Slavery to Free Labor in Louisiana's Sugar Parishes, 1862–1880* (Baton Rouge: Louisiana State University Press, 2001).

16. Eric Foner, *Reconstruction: America's Unfinished Revolution, 1863–1877* (New York: Harper and Row, 1988).

17. Steven Hahn, *A Nation Under Our Feet: Black Political Struggles in the Rural South from Slavery to the Great Migration* (Cambridge, MA: Harvard University Press, 2003), 3, 197.

18. Rebecca F. Edwards, *Gendered Strife and Confusion: The Political Culture of Reconstruction* (Urbana: University of Illinois Press, 1997).

Acknowledgments

Numerous persons have been responsible for shaping my thinking about the years following the Civil War. Many of them are listed in the "Suggested Reading," which itself indicates the extent of my indebtedness. There are others, however, whose names are not in the list. I am grateful to all of them. My students have provided valuable means for testing my views and interpretations, while one former student and friend, Herbert Gutman, has provided ideas as well as materials for this book. My colleagues, Hans L. Trefousse and Abraham S. Eisenstadt, have given the manuscript a thoughtful and critical reading that saved me from many errors. Daniel J. Boorstin has been not merely the efficient editor of this volume in the "Chicago History of American Civilization," but a warm and friendly critic. Since this work first appeared, numerous students, colleagues, and friends have offered valuable criticisms and suggestions for which I am deeply grateful. Margaret Fitzsimmons, my valued assistant for thirty years has been most helpful in the preparation of this edition. My wife has assisted me at every step in the writing of this book, and it is not possible for me to express my continuing obligation to her. The first course I had on the reconstruction period was taught by the late Professor Theodore S. Currier of Fisk University. The dedication of this work to him is an inadequate expression of my gratitude for having had, in my undergraduate years, the influence and stimulation of a great teacher.

Index

Adams, Charles Francis, 147
Advertiser (Montgomery, Ala.),
127
African Americans: in army of occupation, 35–36; black legislators expelled in Georgia, 106,
130–32, 222; black schools
burned, 151; condition of after
the war, 3; in Congress, 135–
36, 223; Conservatives seek
support of, 123; in constitutional conventions of Southern
states, 101–2; conventions to
protest their treatment, 56–57,
221; Democrats seek support
of, 123–24, 127; disenfranchised in the South, 168–69;
disenfranchised in South Carolina, 168; dissatisfaction with
their condition after reconstruction, 215–17; economic condition after reconstruction, 216;
economic revolution not attempted by, 92; educated black
leaders in the South, 88–90; education denied in the South,
88; education desired by,
107–8; education due to
Freedmen's Bureau, 38, 51,
107, 108; elevation in status,
183–84; emancipation leading
to increased political strength
in the South, 11–12; excluded
from voting and holding office
in Lincoln's plan for reconstruction, 16; fear of "Africanizing"
the country, 93, 94, 97; fear of
Negro rule, 94, 101, 132; first
black elected to House of Representatives, 223; first black
elected to Senate, 223; Joint
Committee of Fifteen investigation into treatment of, 58–59;
Joint Committee of Twenty-
one testimony of, 166–67; Ku
Klux Klan forces out of Radical activity, 101; labor violence
against, 182; land question,
113; Lincoln hopes blacks will
leave the country, 26; in Mem-

ugees, Freedmen, and Abandoned Lands), 36–39; educated blacks employed by, 90; education program, 38, 51, 107, 108; establishment of, 221; Johnson's opposition to, 37, 39, 60, 61, 155; Joint Committee of Fifteen investigation into necessity of, 58; Ku Klux Klan opposition, 155–56; Memphis riot investigated by, 63; Radical support for, 60, 61; reports of violence against freedmen, 150–51; Supplementary Freedmen's Bureau Act, 222; Union League work promoted by, 124; voter registration in the South, 84–85

Freedmen's Savings and Trust Company, 181, 221

Gallatin (Tenn.), 51
Galloway, A. H., 89
Gantt, E. W., 26
Garfield, James A., 164, 207, 209, 210
Garland, Ex parte, 198
Garrison, William Lloyd, 8
Gates, Paul, 214
Georgia: army of occupation, 121; Athens, 177; Atlanta, 121, 178; Augusta ring, 137; black leaders in, 89; black legislators expelled, 106, 130–32, 222; black officeholders in, 134–35; black Representatives from, 136; black suffrage in, 105; borrowing capital, 142; Bullock elected governor, 128; car-

petbagger officials, 137; Columbus, 177; Congress expels from Union, 130–31; Conservatives in legislature of, 128; Conservative victory of 1871, 223, 224; constitutional conventions, 40, 102; convict labor, 140; cotton mills, 177, 213; Democrats expelled from legislature, 132; Democrats seek black support in, 123; election of Confederate veterans, 43; Fifteenth Amendment rejected by, 132; Fourteenth Amendment ratified by, 129; Fourteenth Amendment rejected by, 67; *Georgia v. Stanton,* 73; graft, 146; Johnson's restoration proclamation for, 31; Joint Committee of Twenty-one investigation in, 167; Ku Klux Klan, 158; Macon, 131; militia formed in, 122; parts untouched by the war, 5; peach production, 176; political corruption after reconstruction, 218; poll tax, 141; Radical Reconstruction in, 191; Radical Reconstruction resisted in, 190; readmission to Union, 129, 223, 224; Reconstruction Acts challenged by, 198; Relief Act, 44; repudiation of Confederate debt, 40, 41; Savannah, 99–100, 121, 178; segregated public education, 45; slavery abolished in, 41; in South divided into military districts, 70; Turner's assistance to white

14; ordinances repealed, 41–42; scalawags' failure to support, 98

Semmes, Raphael, 33

Sentinel (Columbus, Miss.), 50

'76 Association, 153

Seward, William H., 29, 41, 66, 173

Seward's Folly, 173

Seymour, Horatio, 81, 82

Sharecropping, 175, 212, 216

Sharkey, William L., 42, 50

Shepley, George F., 23

Sheridan, Philip, 65, 78

Sherman, John, 207

Shugg, Roger, 175

Sickles, D. E., 44, 78

Simkins, Francis B., 91

Slavery: compensation for emancipation, 41, 62; education denied to slaves, 88; emancipation leading to increased political strength in the South, 11–12; fear of slave revolts, 150; Georgia abolition of, 41; Johnson as slave owner, 28; Louisiana abolition of, 24; Mississippi abolition of, 41; postwar conditions similar to, 175; in restoration constitutions, 40, 41; South Carolina abolition of, 41; Tennessee abolition of, 25; Virginia abolition of, 41

Smalls, Robert, 89, 136

Smith, James M., 191

Social welfare programs, 114, 190

South, the: aftermath of the war, 1–6; agriculture, 174–75, 212; army of occupation in, 34–36,

58, 120–21; attempts to alleviate postwar destitution, 44–45; black codes, 47–51, 140, 175, 221; black leaders in, 88–90; blacks denied education in, 88; blacks disenfranchised in, 168–69; black status raised in, 183–84; black suffrage adopted, 105–6; black suffrage urged on, 42–43; black voters and officeholders in, 83; capital investment before and during the war, 6–7; capital requirements, 174, 176–77; carpetbaggers in, 93–96, 100, 102, 103, 137; cheap labor in, 175; Congress refuses to seat representatives from, 57; as conquered but not subdued, 4; Conservative opposition to Radical Reconstruction in, 127–30; constitutional conventions under Reconstruction Acts, 79, 84, 101–2, 104–26, 222; corruption in, 144–49; development programs of reconstruction governments, 137–43; division into military districts, 70; economic life after reconstruction, 212–15; economic recovery, 174–78; economic resources of, 4–7; economic revolution not attempted by blacks, 92; fear of slave revolts, 150; former Confederates take control of reconstruction, 32–52; Fourteenth Amendment ratified by, 80; Fourteenth Amendment re-

Made in the USA
Middletown, DE
14 April 2019